E n d u r

ALSO BY F. A. WORSLEY

Shackleton's Boat Journey

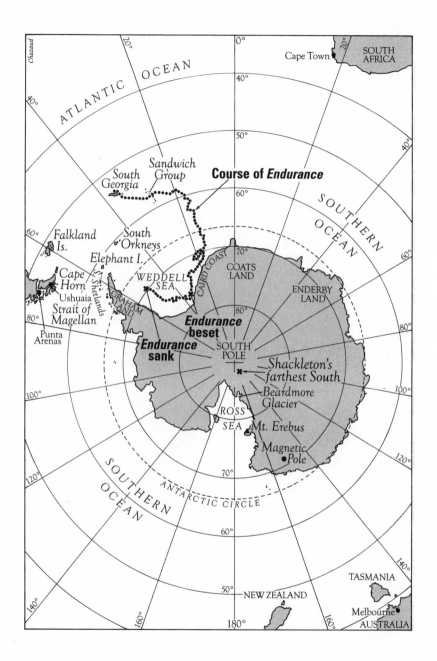

Sir Ernest Shackleton

Endurance

An Epic of Polar Adventure

By F. A. Worsley

W. W. Norton & Company

New York · London

Copyright 1931 by the Estate of F. A. Worsley
Introduction copyright © 1999 by Patrick O'Brian

First published as a Norton paperback 2000

The text of this book is composed in Goudy Old Style
with the display set in Minion and Donatello
Composition by Allentown Digital Services Division of
R.R.Donnelley & Sons Company
Manufacturing by Courier Companies
Book design by Margaret M. Wagner

Library of Congress Cataloging-in-Publication Data

Worsley, F. A. (Frank Arthur) 1872–1943.
Endurance: an epic of polar adventure / by F. A. Worsley.
    p   cm.
ISBN 0-393-04684-2
1. Shackleton, Ernest Henry, Sir, 1874–1922–Journeys.
2. Antarctica–Discovery and exploration.   3. Imperial Trans-Antarctic
Expedition, 1914–1917.   4. Explorers–Great Britain–Biography.
I. Title.
G850 1914.S53W66   1999
919.8904–dc21   98-48135
                     CIP

ISBN 0-393-31994-6 pbk.

W. W. Norton & Company, Inc., 500 Fifth Avenue, New York, N.Y. 10110
www.wwnorton.com

W. W. Norton & Company Ltd., 10 Coptic Street, London WC1A 1PU

1 2 3 4 5 6 7 8 9 0

to the memory of my friend

SIR ERNEST SHACKLETON

to his family, to our folk

and all our shipmates

Acknowledgment

IN thanking Lady Shackleton for her help and photographs I recall joyous days that I and others of Sir Ernest Shackleton's men spent at Eastbourne, and his delight at being home again with his family and able to entertain his comrades.

I thank Messrs. Heinemann for their kind permission to use four pictures from Shackleton's book *South*, and the Royal Geographical Society and the Discovery Committee for their courtesy in supplying me with prints of many of the photographs reproduced herein.

But particularly are my thanks due to the late Phyllis Lewis, to whose suggestion this book is due, for her valuable co-operation and aid in the arrangement and sequence of the book. She was the bravest soul I know.

F. A. WORSLEY
London, March 1931

Contents

Preface *xv*

Foreword *xxv*

I. We Lose the *Endurance* *3*

II. Looking Back *27*

III. On the Pack-ice *50*

IV. We Reach Elephant Island *64*

V. On Elephant Island *82*

VI. The Boat Journey Begins *101*

VII. We Reach South Georgia *123*

VIII. The Crossing of South
Georgia *145*

IX. The Rescue *163*

X. Northwards Once More *180*

XI. The Ross Sea Party *198*

XII. In Northern Waters *217*

XIII. Southwards Again *245*

XIV. Shackleton Looks Back *266*

XV. The Death of a Hero *290*

Index *303*

Illustrations

Sir Ernest Shackleton   Frontispiece

Shackleton examining a remote chance of escape   10

An effort to free the ship   11

"Squeezed out of the ice, and flung over . . ."   17

Crushed by the floes   18

'Saint'   24

Cheetham and Crean   25

Cutting out a berth   25

"The icy uplands of South Georgia"   32

"Right beneath our feet was Grytviken Harbour"   33

Grytviken Whaling Station, South Georgia   40

"At the edge of a small floe . . . stood three Emperor penguins"   41

Patience Camp   59

Ocean Camp   59

Elephant Island   80

After landing on Elephant Island   81

Preparing the James Caird   92

Launching the James Caird   92

The next sea rolled her over   98

The departure from Elephant Island   98

The glacier front   138

Illustrations

A bull sea-elephant   139

"In front of us stretched a truly magnificent view"   152

The country that we crossed   153

The rescue   175

Our arrival at Valparaiso   187

Blackborow and 'Mrs. Chippy'   188

The author   234

One of the dangers of Polar navigation   236

The Quest   246

Where Shackleton died   296

The cairn   297

Preface

BY PATRICK O'BRIAN

ERNEST SHACKLETON, an Irishman from Kilkee in the County Clare, was born in 1874 and educated at Dulwich, an English public school; he then joined the Merchant Navy, and as a lieutenant in the Royal Naval Reserve he sailed with Scott on his fatal expedition to the Antarctic. Yet before Scott began his unhappy inland march, Shackleton's health broke down, probably from over-exertion, and he was obliged to be sent home. But in January 1908 he set out again for the South Pole in *Nimrod*, heading another expedition; and when he and some other members had climbed the enormous Beardmore glacier they came within 97 miles of the Pole, travelling up from the south, of course, from the comparatively sheltered Ross Sea: but at that point they had to turn back for want of food.

When he returned to England he was knighted and was made a Commander of the Victorian Order. But he could not rest easy until he was in those grim waters again and he set about organizing yet another attempt. He was busy in his Burlington Street office, collecting funds for the Imperial Antarctic expedition designed to cross the vast Antarctic continent from the north while another ship, the *Aurora*, should sail to the other side, to the Ross Sea, to take the members of the expedition off when they had completed their traverse. He was arranging countless details and recruiting officers and seamen who came up to his very high standards when Frank Arthur Worsley, the author of this book, came in, moved by a prophetic dream. Both men had served in the Merchant Navy—Worsley had commanded several small vessels and he was now second officer in a ship bound for Canada—and they understood one another very well. It soon became apparent that Worsley longed to join the company, and presently Shackleton said "You're engaged. Join your ship until I wire for you."

On 1 August 1914, when the coming of the war was by no means apparent to the world in general, Shackleton's *Endurance* sailed for the northern shores of the Antarctic, and by 13 July 1915 she was in the middle of the Weddell Sea, 400 miles from the continent itself and a thousand from the whaling station in South Georgia. July was midwinter in those latitudes and the ship was entirely icebound: at this point neither seals nor penguins were any longer to be seen. Sea, ice and wind were extraordinarily wicked, and the creatures knew by instinct what was to come; and so, from experience of Polar seas, did Shackleton who soon told Worsley that the ship was doomed, very strongly built though she was, and with tapering sides to prevent the closing ice from crushing her. Immediately after this the first officer appeared. "The play can begin, Sir," he said to Shackleton, "whenever you are ready."

"We shall all be in the 'Ritz' " (our name for the living quarters in the hold of the ship) "in five minutes. You can go back and say so."

A preface is not a summary, God forbid, and this little

piece is quoted solely to give Worsley's general tone: he draws Shackleton with the closest attention—even devotion—and here as in many other places he shows Shackleton as a seaman superior to those under his command, picked, experienced men though most of them were. But Worsley is largely indifferent to his other shipmates. There was an artist aboard, said to have come to paint the extraordinary Polar seascapes, and above all colours; but he is mentioned only once, when he finished off the caulking of a boat with his oil paints and a little seal's blood. Much the same applies to the medical men and the naturalist, although they must have messed with him. Upon the whole, therefore, his fellow-men, apart from Shackleton and a few of the hands, did not interest him much. What he concentrated upon with the closest and most intelligent perception was the sea in all its countless forms, the snow, the ice, the currents and the truly appalling winds of those latitudes, far below the Roaring Forties of evil reputation. He is a sailor through and through, very highly skilled in his calling and often remarkably successful in describing various aspects of it: he possessed a highly developed aesthetic sense and he was deeply moved by the extraordinary beauty of Polar colour, its clarity, its prismatic brilliance in the more-than-frozen air, the unimaginable beauties of the ice, of tumbled, shattered pack-ice and of majestic bergs, large as half the county.

The *Endurance*'s sides did indeed prevent the ice from crushing her by sideways pressure, as so many whalers have been crushed, and even men-of-war; but if a steel wedge is driven between two prodigious blocks of ice and the lateral pressure mounts to some millions of tons, the wedge is likely to be squeezed out: this is what happened to *Endurance*. She rose to the surface of the ice and stood there almost upon her keel, with a heavy list to port. Blizzards and very strong winds were an everyday occurrence and presently she fell right over with a perfectly enormous crash, terrifying the huskies, the powerful northern dogs that were to pull the sledges.

With infinite toil they righted her (there were only twenty-nine of them, including Shackleton) but she settled in the water and leaked so cruelly that they had to pump for seventy-two hours without a pause. And when they had her really dry, the winds and currents of the Weddell sea converged from three directions, driving the massive pack-ice upon her. Two great floes, one on each side, held her fast; a third struck her stern, tearing off her rudder and mortally wounding her keel. The ship's timer-ends opened; water poured into her. They had time to unload some of the stores, the sledge-dogs and the boats on to the floe: then, when the pack-ice round her loosened, she went down.

It is not for an introducer to enumerate the almost incredible hardships they endured in those ice-coated boats over so immense an extent of ocean, nor to speak of the prodigious courage with which they bore them: but it may properly be said that after a great variety of disasters most of the people were landed on Elephant Island, as dismal a place as can well be imagined, while the stronger men took the remaining boat, the *James Caird*, to South Georgia, where they landed where they could and walked the rest of the way to the whaling station over country little more hospitable than the moon, except for the albatross chicks (fourteen pounds apiece) and a seven-foot sea-elephant. Yet throughout this boat-voyage, or rather these boat-voyages, Worsley was continually at Shackleton's side, and he, in this long, very highly detailed book, is the man to write about him.

Through the kindness of the Uruguayans and Chileans they did get back to England. The unfortunate seamen left on Elephant Island were, after several attempts, taken off; and all hands were pretty well received at home in April 1917.

After the necessarily abbreviated celebrations (the war was nearing its climax), Worsley was given command of a Q-boat, a vessel designed to lure, deceive and destroy submarines; and she did indeed sink the German U23, whereupon Worsley was appointed to another craft in the Mediterranean. Somewhat later he and Shackleton met in London and Shackleton asked him to go to North Russia: Shackleton's word obviously carried great weight, for Worsley was lent to the War Office. They reached Murmansk in October 1918, where Shackleton also held an important army appointment on the Murmansk front: they carried out some dashing, valuable forays in search of intelligence behind the Russian lines—interesting in themselves, but in a wholly different key from the rest of the book.

When at last the war was over, Worsley was much in Shackleton's company; but understanding that Sir Ernest would not soon be ready for another expedition, he and some friends bought a small schooner to trade with the newly-formed Baltic republics. Yet seamen are notoriously inept ashore: the bottom fell out of the freight market and they operated at a loss, struggling with costly delays, fraudulent or at least unpaying intermediaries, and with the fact that hands did not like to ship in a sailing-vessel without auxiliary power. But there is one episode in this dreary chronicle that is very well worth quoting, since it so clearly displays the prodigious seamanship of a man who considered Shackleton his superior. The schooner, homeward bound from the difficult Icelandic port of Bildurdal, ran into a hurricane. Sails blew out, all the bulwarks were destroyed, and when the rigging showed signs of parting the people begged him to run for Reykjavik. But he already knew that Shackleton was preparing for another Antarctic voyage: he temporized, and when at last the gale came fair he drove the schooner east under a press of sail.

"On the morning of the fourth day after the sou'wester had sprung up we sighted Suderoe, the southernmost of the Faroe Islands. I brought the ship up to the wind until it was abeam and we were thundering along three to four miles to windward of the island, where we could see a heavy sea breaking on its weather shore. I watched more closely than ever the weather shrouds of the foremast, and presently decided that these could not hold very much longer. Therefore immediately after breakfast I had all hands out and unshackled fifteen fathoms of the schooner's heavy chain cable, to pass it aloft to secure the mast. This was a difficult job as the ship was driving hard in the gale, most of the ratlines were carried away, and it was complicated by the fact that my knowledge of Icelandic was as meagre as the crew's knowledge of English. However, this last difficulty was compensated for somewhat by the fact that I was dealing with fine seamen. The orders they did not quite understand their seamanship led them to guess.

"We dropped the bight of the chain until it was below the keel, and then drew both parts—one on each side—along till these were abreast of the foremast. Both ends were then drawn up tight so that the ship was girdled underneath with the cable, and we made the chain temporarily fast with a long end left over on the one side. This end was then taken aloft on the starboard side and passed round the fore-lower-mast head, where it was made fast with a round turn and well secured to prevent it slipping down. There was sufficient left over to bring down on the port side, where it was shackled to the opposite end of the chain. Wires were made fast on each side to the cable, led through the hawse pipes forward, and hove taut on the windlass. We next put a frapping of stout rope round both parts of the cable and across the deck, and bowsed the two parts of the chain together till they were bar-taut."

The job took them from eight in the morning until two in the afternoon; and when Worsley had looked to see that all was well the last pair of shrouds to windward parted as he dropped on deck—certain loss of the mast and shipwreck if they had not been so brisk.

The schooner reached Kirkwall four days later and Worsley telegraphed Shackleton "Tally ho! Just arrived. Sails blown away. Ship frapped and mast held up with cable." He replied "Well done, Skipper. Join me as soon as possible."

Worsley did so; and he was not alone. At least half a dozen former shipmates who were on shore and free, including the medical men, offered their services, although it was public knowledge that the ship, the Quest, a Norwegian sealer, was pitifully small for her task, only a hundred and eleven feet long, twenty-four feet in beam, and under two hundred tons. What kind of daemon it was that drove Shackleton is very far from clear, but there is no doubt that it was a daemon much respected at sea.

Small though she was, however, the ship was very well equipped from the hydrographical point of view, with treasures of a scientific nature and a radio lent by the Admiralty, for the respect reached even into the highest places.

So Shackleton was received at the Palace, where he had always been treated very kindly, and on 18 September 1921 he sailed, dropping down the Thames to the salutes of all the craft lying along the shore. But some of the Quest's people disliked the omens: Tower Bridge very nearly failed to open, and her tall masts only just passed through the narrow gap between the rising bascules; and to be sure they had foul weather as far as Lisbon, where they had to put in for engine repairs. Foul weather again to Madeira, and the *Quest* proved so lively in a cross-sea that hardened seamen grew uneasy and others were incapacitated. On in somewhat kinder winds to the Cape Verdes, then across to St. Paul's Rocks—minute islands in the Atlantic with fascinating inhabitants, including boobies and noddies—and so to Rio de Janeiro and still more repairs. This meant a month's delay and Shackleton abandoned the idea of Tristan da Cunha and Capetown as a base, deciding to make straight for South Georgia, there to take in coal for the far south.

They sailed again on 18 December in fine weather, and Shackleton spoke "with rare eagerness" of the Antarctic soon. But this did not last, and presently he took to spending much of the day in his severe cabin, smoking and telling Worsley about his earlier days with Scott in the Antarctic and his learning how to cross snow and ice with a sledge and a team of dogs—learning the hard way.

He had had a heart-attack in Rio, bad enough to prevent him from going ashore for a party given in his honour. He soon recovered, but it was evident to those who knew him best that he was no longer what he had been (though he was not yet fifty).

He looked back into the past almost continually, and although there were brief periods of keen interest and happy anticipation the whole tone of the book is that of declining hope and strength, with Shackleton telling of the failure of his southern attempt on the Pole, stage by stage.

On Christmas Day it blew a hurricane: they had to heave to and Worsley resorted to the ancient way of taking an oil-filled bag to windward, so arranged that it would leak from a corner, the oil film having a wonderful effect on the wave-crests. But then the boiler began to give serious trouble: fortunately this did not crush Shackleton, indeed it roused him; and by the time they were close in with South Georgia he kept the deck, pointing out the cliffs and mountains he knew so well. When they reached Grytviken he went ashore to make the necessary arrangements, and returning he dined with Worsley; then they played cards and talked for a while. But Worsley was uneasy: he could not tell why, but his instinct was sound. That night after an attack of angina pectoris, Shackleton's heart stopped beating.

They buried him in South Georgia and built a cairn over his grave as the snow swept down upon them.

Foreword

BY ADMIRAL OF THE FLEET
THE RIGHT HON. EARL JELLICOE,
R.N., G.C.B., G.C.V.O., O.M.

IN writing this account of the work of Sir Ernest Shackleton and his men, Commander Worsley is not recounting the adventures of one man, or even of one man and his followers. He is telling a tale of high courage, of invincible endurance and irrepressible humour through hardship and danger.

This story of British seamanship parallels for our Merchant Navy the imperishable record of Captain Scott's in the Royal Navy.

It is a story that Shackleton's modesty naturally forbade his telling in full, for he would not speak of his sacrifices for the welfare and safety of his men.

Commander Worsley has chosen to write this book not only because he was with him, nor for the sake of friendship, but because he realises that Shackleton possessed qualities which it is right to remind our countrymen are essentially British. Worsley states frankly that Shackleton was not without faults. What man is without faults? If we as a nation have only such failings as were Shackleton's side by side with the splendid qualities he possessed, we shall not do badly.

Foreword

Shackleton is dead, but the Shackleton spirit goes on. It is the spirit which animated our seamen during the Great War; the spirit which led the officers and men of the Merchant Navy to carry on their essential work in the face of all the dangers and horrors of unrestricted submarine warfare; the spirit with which, as Commander-in-Chief of the Grand Fleet, I was familiar in respect of the officers and men of the Royal Navy. And the same can, of course, be said of our comrades in the sister-services, the Army and the Air Force.

Commander Worsley is justifiably indignant—as evidenced at the end of his book—at the attempts made to belittle the great part played by the men of the British Empire during the world war. I have no fear myself that posterity will fail to realise the magnitude of our effort and the splendid qualities of our officers and men of every service.

Shackleton embodied in himself those great qualities, and it is for that reason that Commander Worsley wishes to see valued at its true worth the memory of a man who typified so much that should continue to be beloved by his countrymen.

JELLICOE, A.F.

Endurance

We Lose the *Endurance*

Sir Ernest Shackleton, Frank Wild, his Second in Command, and I were sitting in Shackleton's cabin in the *Endurance*. The date was July 13th, 1915. The ship was fast set in the ice of the Antarctic, and while it was apparent that the difficulties of the 'Imperial Trans-Antarctic Expedition' (to give our 'show' its correct title) were becoming acute, it had never occurred to me that we should lose our ship.

The shriek of the wind interrupted our conversation, and in the lull that followed, the ice-floe ground against the side of the *Endurance*, causing her to quiver as though she were a human being.

Shackleton looked at me. "She's pretty near her end," he said. Frank Wild, the friend of both of us, gazed down at the deck. He knew how I, her skipper, would feel the loss of the ship.

"You mean that the ship will—go?" I said to Shackleton; and he replied briefly, "I do."

The gale seemed to increase every minute. The wind howled in the rigging, and I couldn't help thinking that it was making just the sort of sound that you would expect a human being to utter if he were in fear of being murdered. The snow was falling so fast that each gust would hurl a fresh sheet of it over the ship. But snow didn't matter. It was the ice that we had to fear. And the ice, thousands of miles of it, was all round us. Still I couldn't believe that the *Endurance* would have to go. I turned to Shackleton again.

"You seriously mean to tell me that the ship is doomed?"

He rose and paced the cabin. His hands were behind his back, and he had hunched his shoulders slightly, as he had a way of doing when he had a disagreeable job to perform, and his chin was thrust out. It is not a pleasant task to have to tell the captain of a ship that his vessel is doomed: Shackleton was in the position of a doctor who has to tell a man that his wife is dying. He knew far better than I, of course. He had been in the Antarctic ice-fields before. I had not. And I could not picture conditions worse than those in which we had worked these many weeks past. But Shackleton realised that we were only at the beginning of our troubles, and that he had better break the news to me at once.

"The ship can't live in this, Skipper," he said at length, pausing in his restless march up and down the tiny cabin. "You had better make up your mind that it is only a matter of time. It may be a few months, and it may be only a question of weeks, or even days. Wild and I know how you feel about the *Endurance*, but what the ice gets," and I recognised the ring of prophecy in his tone, "the ice keeps."

Wild, who had risen and come over to us, said cheerily, "Yes, but we are not going to let the ice get us. The poor little *Endurance* may have to go, but we won't."

He had said just the right thing. To an old seaman like myself the very idea of giving up a ship is something like having an arm or leg amputated; but Wild's words made me realise that in spite of the importance which the ship might have in my eyes, there were human lives at stake, fine and splendid men, and that our job was to see that the ice didn't get them—even if it got my ship.

"If the *Endurance* does have to—well, get left behind," I said, "we will manage—somehow."

I saw Shackleton's lips move, but I couldn't hear what he said because the gale was blowing up again with fresh force, and the little cabin, shut in as it was, had become as noisy as a railway station. The turmoil of sound made it seem as though ghostly trains were rushing past the ship—trains of snow, I said to myself in the stupid way in which a person talks to himself when he has received a severe and unexpected blow.

There came a lull, and Shackleton spoke again.

"We shall hang on as long as we can," he said. "It is hard enough on the men as it is. Without a ship in which to shelter from these blizzards, and in this continuous cold——"

He resumed his pacing, deep in thought.

Wild and I exchanged glances. I said to him in an undertone, "Perhaps he's wrong. He has never sailed before in a ship that had tapered sides, so that even the squeezing of the ice-packs would only make her rise and ride them. Perhaps——"

I suppose my anxiety must have been betrayed by my voice; for Wild smiled.

"My dear chap," he said, in a lighter tone, "it is no good talking as though the decision rested with him, you know."

Greenstreet, the First Officer, at that moment knocked at the cabin door, and came in.

"The play can begin, Sir," he said to Shackleton, "whenever you are ready."

"We will all be in the 'Ritz' " (our name for the living

quarters in the hold of the ship) "in five minutes. You can go back and say so."

I admired his self-control. Greenstreet could never have guessed that a few minutes earlier the great explorer had broken to me the tragic news that in his opinion the ship was doomed, and that we should be cast, homeless, upon the dreary wastes of ice from which so few returned. To him, Shackleton was the cheery, happy chief, who was leading his men in a great and successful adventure. And a few minutes later, sure enough, we were in the 'Ritz' watching one of the burlesques that our men had become adept at producing, and the three of us who had talked so solemnly were laughing heartily—especially at two of our boys who, on the improvised stage, were playing the part of ladies.

We were a queer-looking company. Most of us, except the two men who acted the parts of girls, had let our beards grow. We had done this partly to save ourselves the bother of shaving, and partly to enjoy the warmth of a beard and whiskers. The two who did shave, solely in order to be able to entertain us, must have had something of the hero about them. Most of us were fairly young men, and there was something indescribably comic in the sight of an assembly of bearded youths. We all had the appearance, at least so far as I was concerned, of being in a masquerade and of wearing false hair. It gave a certain quality of unreality to the scene.

There were twenty-eight of us—nineteen consisting of scientists, ship's officers and engineers, the rest being forecastle hands. The crew was made up of the boatswain, the cook, six A.B.'s and firemen, and a stowaway. The stowaway was only nineteen years old. He had come to us at Buenos Aires, a Briton who wanted to be among his own countrymen again, and had asked for a job. We had refused, because we considered that we had a sufficient crew, and because, also, he was too young. After we had been out a couple of days, however, one of the seamen had come to me in some concern when I was on the bridge, and had rapped out, "If you would come to the locker where the oilskins are kept, sir, I wonder whether you'd see what I think I see." I had followed the seaman and looked at the oilskins, which hung about eight inches from the deck. And what I saw against the wall was a pair of legs. I put my hand in under the oilskins, and pulled, and out came young Blackborow, the boy we had turned away. He had been there for a couple of days, with scarcely any food and nothing whatever to drink.

I took him to Shackleton and suggested that he should let the lad join us and sign on the articles, otherwise we should have had to put him ashore and let him take his chance of getting home in one of the whalers—not a very happy position for him. Shackleton, like myself, was rather drawn to the youngster, and so it was fixed up. We made him one of the crew, and I may add that we never regretted it.

The crew, of course, was always with us when any festivity was going on, and that night I remember looking at each one of the company present, and trying to imagine how he would feel had he heard Shackleton speak as I had heard him. But at that time none of them guessed. They sang and fooled and laughed—and our chief himself entered into the fun as heartily as any, for which, in my heart, I humbly praised him. Time enough to let them know the drama that he saw was being staged by man's enemy the elements, and which all too soon would put an end to such frivolous amusements as burlesque.

Up to that time the party which Shackleton had organised with the intention of reaching the South Pole had been happy enough. His journey entailed crossing the Antarctic Continent for which we had set off on board the *Endurance* on August 1st, 1914. A year had passed since then, but we had had no particularly terrible experiences, despite the latitude in which we had found ourselves during the past twelve months. Shackleton had a genius—it was neither more nor less than that—for keeping those about him in high spirits. We loved him. To me, he was as a brother. The men had felt the cold it is true; but he had inspired the kind of loyalty which prevented them from allowing themselves to get depressed over anything, and they had stood up to the hardships inseparable from Antarctic exploration without a murmur. But they had always had plenty to distract their minds, and keep them diverted. Every evening we fixed up some sort of entertainment. The ship had become to them, as to me, the centre of the Universe, and they felt, as I did, that nothing mattered much as long as we had the good *Endurance* in which to preserve some measure of warmth and comfort.

Without the ship—how would they be without the ship? How would they, how could they, withstand the grim relentless grip of ice, snow and freezing cold? How, with the best will in the world, would they keep up enough heart to find their way out of the vast desert of ice, if—which seemed very doubtful—there was a way out?

These and similar thoughts passed through my mind as, mechanically, I applauded the songs and bravoed our two very hefty and deep-voiced 'ladies,' the stars of the show of course, who 'took a curtain' and minced their way off, retorting nevertheless with extremely unladylike words to the many personal remarks flung at them.

Next morning I awoke to the usual gloomy half-dawn with a sense of oppression. For a few minutes I could not quite make out what was wrong with me, and then I recalled the conversation of the day before. And I looked with a resentful eye at the lowering heavens heaving forth their grey wrath. For weeks, on the best of days, we had never had more light than would be seen in England in the dusky sky that follows sunset. Within the ship, to counteract the depression caused by darkness, we had a particularly brilliant scheme of lighting, to which much of our cheerfulness may have been due. Among the ancient Hebrews, if I remember rightly, happy occasions were celebrated always by bright lights, and their psychology in this was sound. Thinking of this I wondered how the men would feel if they were compelled to spend months without any more illumination than was afforded by the forbidding grey skies, which, in that tempest-scourged region, are overcast or metallic-hued for the greater part of the year. At that time such dim, storm-laden daylight as we did get lasted at the most one-fourth of the twenty-four hours. For the rest of the time the darkness was complete. At times it was almost as though it were tangible and were closing round us. Sometimes we half expected to be able to touch it, as though it were a curtain that had been hung in front of us to impede our progress.

To keep up the spirits of the men Shackleton now worked as I had never seen him work before. Each day, conditions seemed to grow a little worse. Ice-floes ground against the little *Endurance* continually. Even now as I write I can feel the thuds and shocks as distant floes drove heavily against those near to us and can hear the noise made by the snapping of the floes as large pieces would break from their impact with the ship. I can hear too the dreadful grinding and scraping whenever the floe was solid all the way round and had no edges sufficiently thin for the ship to break.

Of wonderful shapes were those ice-floes, weird too, and curious. Some of them were miles wide, and more than once it seemed as though we had come upon some marvellous city of ice. Great floors of ice, piled one on top of the other, would give the appearance of houses, sometimes of a streetful of houses. And perhaps there would be a flat snowcovered space in front of these huge erections, which would

Shackleton examining a remote chance of escape
(*SCOTT POLAR RESEARCH INSITUTE*)

appear exactly like gardens with their winter canopy. In the distance we would see other floes, the tops of which towered white and gleaming, and would be almost ready to swear that these were streets, built upon and lived in by human beings. The illusion was so perfect, so striking, that I do not exaggerate when I say that many of us would not have been surprised had we been hailed by voices. And in the days that were to follow my conversation on that July evening in 1915 with Sir Ernest Shackleton we would have given much for that to happen.

The days and nights that followed our chief's declaration to me were the most trying, perhaps, that I have ever lived through, and I have been in some tight corners in my life. There was nothing that I, the ship's commander, could do to save the ship. I had to stand passively by as she drifted to

An effort to free the ship (ROYAL GEOGRAPHICAL SOCIETY)

meet her doom. Perhaps only those who have sailed the high seas can really understand what that means; but anybody who has had someone dear to him close to the brink of death can imagine it.

We were four hundred miles from the Antarctic Continent, a desolate mass of land covered by a sheet of ice one thousand feet thick, broken only by rocky peaks and a few isolated beaches. Nearly five hundred miles separated us from a hut built by Nordenskjold's Swedish Expedition. There we hoped to find a few stores which they had left twelve years before. We were also a thousand miles from the whaling stations of South Georgia. At that time it seemed to me that there was little difference between four hundred miles and a thousand. We were in the heart of the Weddell Sea and in a particularly severe season, when the currents were fiercest and the winds were piling ice up on the land, which had the effect of throwing back a certain amount of extra ice upon us, despite the distance. There was not room for it all, and the result was that it got even more closely jammed than usual, cutting off our always doubtful escape.

For months we had seen no living thing on that great ice desert, save a few seals and Emperor penguins. These birds had interested us greatly, for their life history surely is different from that of all other birds. The climate does not allow the female to leave its egg in a nest, and so it carries it in a depression on its large flat feet, a self-propelling perambulator. Over this saucer-like depression hangs a flap of skin and feathers, so that the egg is kept warm. The mother lays only one egg, and when she wants to be relieved she gives this egg to her mate, who keeps it warm in the same way. Parenthood is a passion among these birds, in fact one might almost call it a frenzy; for if a couple is deprived of its egg by some mischance, both male and female will endeavour to steal some other bird's egg, or, if it is hatched, a chick. Dreadful battles ensue between the birds that want to keep their own young and bereaved parents that want to steal or adopt a baby. The unfortunate thing is that often, in the heat of the fray, the chick, over which the fight rages, is killed. Now, however, we did not see either seal or penguin. Our craving to see some living, breathing creature, any creature at all, may be imagined when I say that we missed them as though they had been our personal friends. There was no living thing on the surface of the ice save ourselves.

During our next conference Shackleton, with characteristic foresight, began talking of the preparations that we should make against the time when the ship would be no more. He was bitterly disappointed, as sorely grieved as I was myself, and he let me get a glimpse of his mind when he said, sadly, one day: "It looks as though we shan't cross the Antarctic Continent after all." He paused, and then squaring his shoulders, added cheerfully, "It's a pity, but that cannot be helped. It is the men that we have to think about." He had schooled himself always to consider his men before his own personal wishes.

I nodded. It was the shattering of one of my most prized dreams too, for Shackleton had done me signal honour in promising me that if we reached the Continent I should be his companion in crossing it. Originally it had been arranged that if we landed we should separate, and that I should take the ship to New Zealand. Since that time our friendship had grown, and Shackleton had discovered that, as a traveller, I had as much endurance as he himself. I jumped at this offer, for he could take with him five men only.

For a while I hoped against hope that he was wrong and that we should not encounter any worse weather nor conditions any more dangerous than those which we had already met. Little by little I came to see the uselessness of such optimism. Better, I reflected, to follow Shackleton's lead and prepare. But alas, there was woefully little preparation one could make. The men seemed to know instinctively that the game was up and that it was only a matter of time before the ice became our only home. They pretended, nobly, not to suspect, but there was a change in their looks, and the entertainments and merry-making lacked the spontaneity and gaiety that had been kept up for so long.

Shackleton remarked to me one day, in a rather melancholy tone, "Perhaps it's a pity, Skipper, that you dreamed a dream, or a nightmare, or whatever it was, that sent you to New Burlington Street that morning we met."

"No," I replied, "I've never regretted it, and never shall, even if we don't get through."

"Right, right." Undemonstrative as he was, his tone was affectionate. He lighted his cigarette and wandered off. Just before he moved out of sight he looked back, and I caught the words, murmured to himself, "Good old Skipper." I wasn't meant to hear that, but I'm glad I did. I've treasured those words ever since.

But Shackleton had sent my thoughts wandering back to the day that I had joined the Expedition, joined it by accident, if one can put it that way. One night I dreamed that Burlington Street was full of ice-blocks, and that I was navigating a ship along it—an absurd dream. Sailors are superstitious, and when I woke up next morning I hurried like mad into my togs, and down Burlington Street I went. I dare say that it was only a coincidence, but as I walked along, reflecting that my dream had certainly been meaningless and uncomfortable and that it had cost me time that I could have used to better purpose, a sign on a door-post caught my eye.

It bore the words "Imperial Trans-Antarctic Expedition," and no sooner did I see it than I turned into the building with the conviction that it had some special significance for me.

Shackleton was there. He and I spent only a few minutes together, but the moment that I set eyes on him I knew that he was a man with whom I should be proud to work. He quickly divined what I wanted, and presently said to me, "You're engaged. Join your ship until I wire for you." (I was then second officer in the Canadian trade, and had been in command of small vessels.) "I'll let you know all details as soon as possible. Good morning." He wrung my hand in his hard grasp, and that was that. I was committed to my fate. Not a superfluous word had been spoken on either side, but we knew by instinct that we were to be friends from that hour, and, as a matter of fact, we were together until Shackleton died.

Remembering this in that dim cold twilight, surrounded by a world of snow and ice, I silently breathed a prayer of thankfulness that I had gone to Burlington Street that morning that seemed so long ago, for whatever befell, I was living a great adventure, working side by side with a great man.

Conditions, as Shackleton had foreseen, grew rapidly worse. The blizzards seemed unending, and the ice-floes appeared to us to be alive, fighting each other, hurtling against one another, and uniting only to use their mighty force to attack the poor little *Endurance*.

And so things went on, until one day when we were sitting at lunch there was a terrible noise, as of a thousand guns going off, and, before we could realise what had happened, the *Endurance* was lying on her side—squeezed up and out of the ice and flung over. The dishes and food were scattered everywhere, but the furniture, of course, was fixed, and so nothing particularly heavy fell against us as we slithered on to the wall of the dining saloon.

My first thought was of the fires. Heaven alone knew what effect this disaster might have on the stoves that were alight, and so, walking along the bulwarks and shouting to some of the men to follow me as best they could, I made a round of the ship, never being able to step on the decks, but crawling along the bulwarks, catching hold of anything to which I could cling. Luckily we were saved the horror of fire.

It took several days to right the *Endurance,* and she was so wonderfully built that, to our astonishment, she was scarcely damaged at all. After we had spent a few nights sleeping at extraordinary angles and working so hard all day that we hadn't time to grouse about it, her weight bore down the ice until she was again partially afloat. That didn't mean anything approaching safety, for she was being jammed and battered constantly by the pack-ice. But she did not leak much as yet. We did not worry. What was the good? We were destined to go through unexpected ordeals before we were finished, and it was as well for our peace of mind that we did not have much time to speculate upon the future.

Our sledge-dogs were Canadian huskies, and of the original hundred, sixty still remained. These poor beasts were badly frightened, and since we could not afford to lose them and knew from experience that when they were alarmed they were apt to blame each other for it and fight, some of the men had their work cut out looking after them.

Soon after the *Endurance* had taken to the water again she was subjected to such terrific pressure from thousands, indeed millions of tons of ice that despite her wonderful resistance she began to leak badly. I was forced to admit that my ship's defences were being battered in. Inevitably the time came when we all had to pump continuously over a period of seventy-two hours without sleep, with the main engine running also, in an effort to get her dry. Nevertheless, the water gained on us. We then built a wall across her hold, known to seamen as a 'coffer-dam,' which was designed to confine the water to the stern. This manœuvre was successful. Then a new complication arose.

Through the terrible heaving, the coal, we found, was getting down and blocking the pumps, in addition to which these had become frozen up. Then began a desperate struggle to clear them. We passed red hot irons into them, and the cook poured pot after pot of boiling water down them; but it soon became obvious that this was not enough, and I saw that I should have to go down into the hold to shift the coal and clear the bottom of the pumps from ice. Green-

"Squeezed out of the ice, and flung over..."
(ROYAL GEOGRAPHICAL SOCIETY)

Crushed by the floes
(*ROYAL GEOGRAPHICAL SOCIETY*)

street, the First Officer, and Hudson, the Navigating Officer, volunteered to come with me.

I think that this was the most eerie and nerve-racking job that I had undertaken up to that time. The beams of the ship, cruelly overstrained, cracked loudly and suddenly at irregular intervals, so that we continually expected the ship was going to collapse on top of us and bury us alive. Then as fast as we shovelled the coal away, the ship hurled more and more down upon us and round us. We were bitterly cold, for the icy water swirled round our legs as we worked. The temperature was twenty-five degrees below freezing point. After hours that seemed endless we succeeded in making everything secure, and went on deck. I thought that we were all right for the time being.

Soon after this there occurred a most uncanny incident which produced a startling effect upon us.

As some of us stood gazing at the heavily grinding ice, we heard a funeral dirge, measured and deliberate in its dolefulness, apparently coming from nowhere in particular. For a moment we looked at each other, and although none of us was particularly given to belief in the supernatural, I'll swear that we each had the idea that this eerie lament came from some wandering ghost. It was with an effort that we pulled ourselves together and, half-frozen though I was from standing there only a few moments listening, my brow was wet as I forced myself to try to find an explanation.

Happily I found it. I have remarked on the fact that for months previously we had not seen the Emperor penguins. But now there were eight of these birds intently regarding the ship, and although as a rule they utter only a peculiar sound that is something like a low whistle, they began, as I approached, to make the funeral chant which had so startled us.

The strange thing about this occurrence is the fact that these birds had always been supposed never to utter any sound other than the whistle I have described. And I myself must confess that I have never, either before or since, heard them make any sound similar to the sinister wailings they moaned that day. I cannot explain the incident. But I don't mind admitting that it was one of the queerest, and also one of the most disquieting, things that had hitherto happened to me.

It was on the morning of October 24th that Greenstreet, Hudson, and I had gone down into the hold of the ship. The weather had been comparatively calm. When we returned to the deck a blizzard was raging again some distance away, driving the ice forward in grinding confusion. And three nights later, by the irony of Fate, the first night that the *Endurance* had been pumped really dry for some time, she got the whole force of the pack-ice driven by the winds and currents of the Weddell Sea, converging from three different directions on to one point.

That point unhappily was her stern. Two massive floes, miles of ice, jammed her sides and held her fast, while the third floe tore across her stern, ripping off the rudder as though it had been made of matchwood. She quivered and groaned as rudder and stern-post were torn off, and part of her keel was driven upwards by the ice. To me the sound was so terribly human that I felt like groaning in sympathy, and Shackleton felt the same way.

The shock of the impact was indescribable. To us it was as though the whole world were in the throes of an earthquake. At the beginning the sides of the ship had buckled in and out as though she had been a concertina—which indeed is how some of the men described it. It gave me the horrible impression that the ship was gasping for breath. Never before had I witnessed such a scene, and I sincerely hope I never may again.

Shackleton and Wild stood beside me. Everybody had been ordered on deck. Shackleton said:

"This is the end of the poor old ship. She's done for. We shall have to abandon her, as I warned you."

I made no answer but looked at her timber ends, which had opened out and were letting the water pour, like a cataract, into the ship.

We stepped on to the surrounding ice and walked round to her stern. Our inspection took but a few minutes, and our worst fears were confirmed.

As soon as we came back Shackleton ordered the dogs, which had now become all-important to us, to be transferred to the ice, and the last boat to be lowered. The lowering of the boat was not difficult, but the handling of the dogs was distinctly so. They are savage creatures, weighing about a hundred pounds, and difficult to control at any time. Now we had to look after a large pack, somewhere and somehow on the ice. Eventually we stretched a canvas sheet from the ship's side and let each dog slide down to where some of the men were waiting for it.

I have explained that the gale which was affecting us was some distance away. Thus, save for the slow but irresistible movement of the ice, the scene was one of apparent calm and peace. We resented Nature mocking at us—although of course she was as indifferent to us as though we had been insects. This delusive serenity was but a sorry jest of the Antarctic. The calm all around us was maddening. Actuated by an invisible force countless miles away, the rigging tautened and sang like harp strings, then snapped under the strain as the ship was twisted and wrung by the giant hands of ice that grasped her. The men worked almost in silence. To talk was impossible. Each man knew that it was the end of the ship. We had lost our home in that universe of ice. We had been cast out into a white wilderness that might well prove to be our tomb.

As soon as the dogs were safely tethered, shivering and whining with fear and cold, we had to attend at once to the stores and sledges. Great spikes of ice were now forcing their way through the ship's sides. By degrees her head was getting more deeply buried. We knew that she could not sink immediately, for the ice was holding her, but many of our stores were irretrievable, and that made us anxious. A shortage of food was not a pleasant prospect.

It was a heart-breaking sight to see the brave little ship, that had been our home for so long, broken up by the remorseless onward sweep of a thousand miles of pack-ice. To see her crushed, and know that we could do nothing whatever to help her, was as bad as watching a chum go out.

At last, moving about drearily and draggingly as though at a funeral, we realised that we had done all that we could do, and that it remained to us only to leave the *Endurance*. Even as we stepped over the ice we could hear her beams snapping, broken as easily as match sticks by the irresistible strength of the ice. We were now on the only solid ground that we were fated to see for many a long day—an ice-floe. There we stood, the whole twenty-eight of us, awaiting our leader's commands.

Shackleton made a characteristic speech to hearten our party, the sort of speech that only he could make. Simply and in brief sentences he told the men not to be alarmed at the loss of the vessel, and assured them that by hard effort, clean work and loyal co-operation, they could make their way to land. This speech had an immediate effect: our spirits rose, and we were inclined to take a more cheerful view of a situation that, actually, had not one element in it to warrant the alteration. We had food only for four weeks. We had nothing to keep out the biting cold save linen tents, linen so thin that when there chanced to be a moon we could easily see it through the material. And we had to sleep on the ice, on a covering that was not water-proof, so that such warmth as there was in our bodies would melt the ice and cause us to lie in pools of water. We knew that we had to face all this. But there was no point in admitting it even to ourselves, let alone to one another. And therefore we bucked up.

I remember one of the crew, with typical Cockney humour, remarking to the man next to him: "Damn, we'll have to pack our portmantles!" and I can still hear the laugh that went up.

We all caught the spirit. We began to laugh, to joke, to buck each other up. Only we resolutely turned our backs upon the little *Endurance*, trying our best to shut out the thought that a hundred yards from us, lying out there in her icy grave, was the ship that to us had been 'Home.' Every man among us had unbounded faith in Shackleton. We knew that if mortal man could lead us to safety, Shackleton was that man.

But there was an 'if.' In that universe of dreary ice it was questionable whether even a super-man could save us. I know that Shackleton thought this himself, and although he was the most modest of men at heart (albeit he could put on a bit of swagger when it was for the good of the party) he never regarded himself as a super-man. That he was to prove himself so he did not foresee.

The work of that day had been tremendous, and we were worn out by the time that we had put up our tents and had something to eat. Our cheeriness might have worn thin had we not turned in to get some sleep as quickly as possible. And as we lay there we heard the terrible grinding and battling of the driving packs and floes as we had never heard it before; for now we were resting on the ice, whereas previously the *Endurance* had always stood between the ice and ourselves. This served to remind us that our altered position was very grave indeed, for there was no protection to be had from the angry world of snows and winds and shattering blizzards to which we should now be exposed. But if any of us had the secret thought that this was probably the end of the great adventure he was mistaken. It was only the beginning.

As I dropped off to sleep that night I remember asking

'Saint'
(*ROYAL GEOGRAPHICAL SOCIETY*)

OPPOSITE.

Cheetham and Crean
(*ROYAL GEOGRAPHICAL SOCIETY*)

Cutting out a berth
(*SCOTT POLAR RESEARCH INSTITUTE*)

myself why people had always pictured Hell as a place that was hot. I felt certain that if there were any such place it would be cold—cold as the Weddell Sea, cold as the ice which seemed likely to become our grave.

Three times that night our floe cracked dangerously under the tents. Three times we had to move. This meant taking down our tents, hauling them to a place of safety, and setting them up again. We had also to carry our floor canvas and sleeping-bags. It was a dreary enough business with all of us dog-tired, and it added to our depression to hear, in the dead of night, over and above the grinding and tearing of the floes, the beams of the *Endurance* still snapping. Each time that we pillowed our heads on the ice we could feel tremors and vibrations running through the floe, which told us that the ship had sunk a little deeper.

There was one circumstance, small in itself, that struck me as ironic. In the *Endurance* we had an electric light by which to read the meteorological instruments. This was run off a small battery, and all night long, while the ship we had thought unconquerable was being crushed—actually while she was demonstrating our impotence in the face of primæval forces—that little electric light, triumph of modern civilisation, burned steadily!

Then, just before dawn, with the snapping of the last beam of the *Endurance*, there was a reverberating crash, the light flickered, and went out.

The Polar Ice had won.

CHAPTER 11

Looking Back

At dawn the next morning Shackleton and Wild, like good Samaritans, made hot tea for all hands. This they took along to the inmates of the various tents. It was passed into the first tent, where it was received without comment. The same thing occurred in the second. And then Wild, getting annoyed at the lack of appreciation, put his head into the entrance of a third and said:

"If any of you gentlemen would like your boots blacked, would you kindly leave them outside the hotel door?"

That made us laugh at a time when we really didn't think that we could smile.

Shackleton now determined to cut down every ounce of superfluous weight, in the hope that we could sledge to Graham Land, the most northerly part of the Antarctic Continent. He himself set the example, throwing away, with a spectacular gesture, a gold watch, a gold cigarette case and several golden sovereigns. Naturally, after witnessing this action, which brought home to me at any rate the shifting values in life and the knowledge that there are times when gold can be a liability instead of an asset, we all discarded everything save the barest necessaries. The order was that every man's personal gear was not to exceed two pounds in weight. This did not include sleeping-bags, of course.

The last work done by our cinematographer, Frank Hurley, before his valuable camera was also thrown away, was to film the masts of the *Endurance* as these were slowly twisted from her by the overpowering ice-floes. It took extreme care and patience and wonderful judgment to enable him to film the masts as they came crashing down. So fine did he cut his distance that they swept within a few feet of where he was standing. His professional instincts were so strong, however, that he was too interested in having secured a unique picture to give a thought to the fact that he had come within an ace of disaster. But Hurley was always a brave man.

Next day we started a march to the westward. The dogs dragged the stores on the seven smaller sledges, and I took charge of sixteen men, dragging our three boats placed on the larger sledges. It took only half a mile of this work, however, to prove to us that the sledges were not nearly strong enough to carry the boats across the heavily broken-up surface of the ice. Shackleton, accordingly, pitched camp on the thickest floe in the neighborhood. He then decided to revise his plans and to make stronger sledges by getting material from the wreck.

We realised that we had little time to lose if we wanted to retrieve any of our stores, for the ship was being held up only by the great spikes of ice that had pierced her sides. These might loosen at any moment, and let her sink. We knew, of course, that this might happen while we were actually on board salvaging food and gear, but that risk had to be taken. Therefore we took crowbars and axes and burst open her decks, plunging into the icy water that filled her smashed-up hold to get such materials as we could find.

A few days after we had been aboard her for the last time, there was much movement and loosening of the pack. At five in the afternoon Shackleton saw her funnel moving downwards and hailed me in my tent. I did not hear what he said, but intuition told me, and I rushed out. We dashed on to the look-out platform that we had erected, and from there we watched the death of the ship that had carried us so far and so well, and that had put up as brave a fight as ever ship had fought. A small gap remained in the ice for a few moments after she had sunk, but this soon closed up, and then there was no sign that beneath the dreary expanse of white lay the splendid little *Endurance*.

Shackleton said quietly to the men, "She's gone, boys."

That night he and I walked a little way off from the rest of the party to have a talk. He said:

"I am going to hoist the King's Flag to-morrow. I think it will be a fine thing to have the flag flying here, especially as the King himself presented it to us. It'll buck the men up."

I agreed. "Nice to see the old flag flying again," I remarked, and added, "I don't suppose the King would recognise you now. You must have looked rather different, I fancy, when you had an audience at Buckingham Palace."

"You mean the King wouldn't want to know me now?" chuckled Shackleton, as he looked at my uncouth rig and appearance, and realised that his own was no better: "I don't suppose the King thought when we were talking, any more than I did myself, that I should ever find myself in this pickle."

"How do you propose to get out of it?" I enquired, and he fell to talking of the immediate arrangements to be made.

Shackleton carried out his intention of hoisting the Union Jack the next day, and the very sight of it heartened us. It seemed a splendid gesture of defiance to the ice to see the flag flying proudly, even though it were only over a floating, freezing, wilderness.

That night Shackleton and I talked again, as we tramped round the floes on which the camp was situated.

"I wonder, Skipper," said Shackleton, "whether you fellows would not have been safer in a man-of-war after all?"

He was referring to the fact that before we had sailed at the beginning of August 1914 we had volunteered in a body to go to the War. The Admiralty, however, had not approved of our abandoning the Antarctic Expedition, and had telegraphed its opinion in one terse word of command—"Proceed." Thus we had no choice. But now that we were marooned in this desert of snow and ice, Shackleton felt acutely the fact that we were in danger. Hence his rather ironic question.

"Don't worry. We shall probably get back in time to see a spot of war anyhow," I replied, lightly. "Things may look pretty bad at this moment," I went on, "but we are bound to come through all right. Anyway, if we never do get home, the experience alone will have been worth while."

"I'm glad you think so. Nevertheless, I wish that the Admiralty had let us go to the War before we undertook this thing. For one thing, I am certain that there are a lot of people who will never understand why it was that we came to the other end of the world when a war was going on."

Shackleton was rather sensitive to criticism, as I knew. Therefore I went over the facts with him, once again, carefully.

"I don't think that anybody could fail to realise your position," I said. "You led us in volunteering. It was you that sent the telegram to the Admiralty offering our services. You were prepared, in spite of the fact that everything was ready, and that you had put all that you had got into this Expedition, to give it up to go on active service. The Admiralty has always considered that exploration was a vital thing, with which nothing, even a war, should be permitted to interfere."

"There's something in what you say," he conceded; "but the majority of people don't know that."

"I'm sure you're wrong there," I said. "The majority of people are behind the Admiralty's policy, and always have been. And that policy has been consistent. You have the precedent of Captain Cook, Flinders, and others. They were ordered to proceed, as you were in 1914, although England was at war as usual." (In 1776 the naval officers of the United States, France and Spain were instructed by their respective Governments not only to refrain from interfering with Captain Cook but to treat him with every respect as though he were a neutral subject. In 1801 Flinders had a passport, or safe-conduct, from France with whom we were at war, and in the previous year the British Government had similarly granted a passport to the French explorer Nicolas Baudin.)

"Yes, and the French arrested Flinders at Mauritius," replied Shackleton with a laugh; but it was easy to see that he was relieved.

Actually, there was later some criticism, as he had feared; but this came mainly from irresponsible people who did not realise the relations between Shackleton and the Admiralty. The Admiralty considered that the Expedition was of such importance that it would allow nothing to delay it. To be misunderstood was part of Shackleton's burden, and it could not be helped. That he immediately took an active part in war work on his return, worn out and exhausted as he must have been, and depleted of energy, was sufficient to

"The icy uplands of South Georgia"
(ROYAL GEOGRAPHICAL SOCIETY)

inform any thinking person as to his real feelings. I should like some of his critics, however, to receive a command such as we received from the Admiralty and see how they would deal with it!

Shackleton's conversation had set my memory in action,

"Right beneath our feet was Grytviken Harbour"
(ROYAL GEOGRAPHICAL SOCIETY)

and as I lay in my bag that night I could not get to sleep. I was thinking of all that had led up to our present position.

The trip had begun to be really interesting when we had reached South Georgia, where we saw towering above us the snow-clad mountains and icy uplands of that remarkable island. We had reached it three months after leaving England—nearly a year before we had lost our ship.

South Georgia, an island in the South Atlantic a thousand miles east of Cape Horn, is an anomaly. Geographically speaking, it is ninety miles by twenty of wild and barren land covered by hurricane-swept ice, savage and unfriendly to man. Socially, we had found it quite delightful. Electric light was laid on everywhere at the whaling stations—even in the pig-styes and hen-coops. There were telephones, and hot baths for us. We had received a deal of hospitality, the more striking because it was so ill-matched with the surroundings. The pivot around which South Georgia revolves is whaling. This trade is in the hands of the Norwegians, who in their ways are very like Englishmen, which made us feel at home.

I thought with longing of the decorous Church service that we had attended there, a ceremony as prim and well-ordered as in an English village. The sermon, as a compliment to us, had been preached in English, and the Lutheran pastor had very kindly asked a blessing on the Expedition. A choir sang splendidly. I wondered whether I should ever see South Georgia again—little dreaming of the circumstances in which I was destined to set foot once more on the island.

I remembered a climb that Hurley, Greenstreet and I had made. We had clambered up Ducie Fell. I had taken my aneroid up and made the height one thousand six hundred and eleven feet. Right beneath our feet as it seemed was Grytviken Harbour, with the *Endurance* at anchor, and two whalers towing in twelve carcases. All round us was a magnificent panorama, a wilderness of jagged, snow-clad peaks dominated by three imposing mountains, Snow-Top, Paget, and Allardyce, the last continuing in a fine snow-covered range to the south-east. We could see two lakes and five glaciers. Nordenskjold, the finest, appeared to offer a pathway to Mount Paget, but I heard that nobody had ever crossed the island. I remember wondering at the time what would happen to the explorer that ventured to do so. As I was ruminating there, on Ducie Fell, I heard eight avalanches, and saw two sweeping down the mountain side, which made me think that the person who tried to pioneer his way across South Georgia would probably never reach his goal.

I quickly discovered, through my compass, that the rocks were magnetic. When I put the compass on the rock, I could not get the bearings, but when I put it on a little stick, two feet above, it was all right. Hurley, our cinematographer, succeeded in taking pictures, having persuaded us to haul his camera up the almost perpendicular slope.

Clark, our biologist, was in his element in South Georgia, studying the whales and getting data on the animal life; and Wordie, our geologist, was equally busy.

I remembered that one night when Shackleton and I were playing cards in the cabin that we shared, we had suddenly been disturbed by the most terrible stench. I went on the deck of the *Endurance*, and in the gloom and thick driving snow of an easterly gale saw a huge bloated object rising up from the sea, almost level with my face. It was a Finner whale that had been killed a few days previously and had broken adrift. Rickinson, our engineer, came to my help. We jumped into our little motor boat, and after a good deal of hard exertion—for the thing weighed fifty tons—towed it about a quarter of a mile away to leeward of us. I returned triumphantly to Shackleton saying that I had disposed of the carcase, and we resumed our game. About two hours later, to Shackleton's amusement, the same thing happened again. The tide had drifted that wretched carcase back to the self-same spot as before. This time, when we got it clear, we made no mistake about it. But to have a game of cards interrupted by a whale when one is in South Georgia is regarded as all in the day's work, whether the whale is alive or dead.

After a month in South Georgia we had sailed to carry out in earnest Shackleton's intention of going through the Weddell Sea to the Antarctic Continent. This land he intended to cross. Three days after we sailed we encountered pack-ice. In this part there was a variety of birds—Cape pigeons, prions, which are a pretty blue-grey species, snow-petrels, stormy petrels, fulmars, which are not unlike gulls, Antarctic petrels, which are barred with brown and white on the back of the wings, penguins and albatross. These birds feed on little shrimps which abound, small fish, jelly-fish and any scraps that may be floating about on the surface. The wandering albatross is perhaps the most interesting of these creatures. Its wingspread, the greatest of any bird in the world, often exceeds twelve feet from tip to tip, and it circles round and round all day without ever, apparently, flapping its wings. The oldest birds are practically white all over, and the younger ones dark brown.

We passed between the snow-mantled islands of Saunders and Candlemas. These belong to the mountain chain of islands of the South Sandwich group, two of which possess active volcanoes. One island, Zavodovski, is dangerous to land upon, owing to the sulphur fumes which pour out through the cracks and crevices. C. A. Larsen, the celebrated Norwegian explorer, very nearly lost his life there through having inhaled the poisonous fumes, and was ill for months afterwards.

In this neighbourhood there were also a number of humpback and Finner whales. I saw what I took to be a mother with two young ones alongside, cruising quite happily at the edge of the pack-ice.

The heavy pack-ice, into which we were now ploughing, surrounds the Antarctic Continent and forms a great natural defence against man. It has a radius of a thousand miles and a front of ten thousand. Even in summer there is a cool two million or more square miles of pack-ice floating about.

As we were sailing between the islands with a south-west gale abeam we got into great danger through running into a deep gulf in the pack-ice that promised an opening to the south. Suddenly a long tongue of heavy old pack and small bergs swung right across our stern and cut off our retreat. The gale was freshening, and the heavy swell dashed great masses of ice against each other with tremendous thuds. Our only way of escape lay in working through the heavy masses of snow-capped ice out into the open again. For some time it was doubtful whether it could be done. Luckily it was. Shackleton pointed out to me the place he wished to break through, where the floes had been most smashed up, and we steered for it. Great blocks of ice, fantastic shapes of blue, green and white, rose and fell with amazing swiftness and violence on all sides of us. It seemed impossible that our deeply laden ship could live through it. Shackleton, however, was confident of the ship's great strength.

At last, by dint of careful manœuvring, we cut through, having received only two or three heavy blows. Leaving the smoking volcanoes of the Sandwich group astern, we coasted the pack for four hundred miles to the south-east. Then, finding that the edge ran to the north-east, Shackleton boldly entered the pack-ice to force a way through.

South of us was the ice-blink, and behind us to the north lay the dark water-sky of the open sea. The 'ice-blink' is a white glare, or reflection, on the underside of the clouds, indicating that in that direction lie many miles of close pack-ice. A 'water-sky' is the reverse. A blackness that appears almost inky in contrast to the general whiteness indicates that there are many miles of fine clear open water beneath. Where the ice-blink is seamed and crossed with dark lines, this indicates that there are lanes and leads through the pack-ice which can possibly be negotiated by a ship. And so, on a cloudy day, the conditions of both sea and ice are faithfully charted in the sky, for a distance up to sixty or seventy miles ahead. Fog kills this, and a clear blue sky, too, prevents one from seeing anything overhead, although, in the latter case, a faint glare that can sometimes be discerned on the horizon indicates the presence of pack-ice.

By these signs we now chose our course every day, and for three thousand miles, which included our turns and twistings, we fought our way through floes of every size from a few yards across to great fields of two hundred square miles.

Ramming the floes was exciting work. One never quite knew what would happen. The weakest floe that barred our way was always attacked. Great discrimination and experience were needed, for judgment was all-important, since a thin floe might be composed of hard clear ice, and as it was summer-time a thick one might be honeycombed and rotten. The floe, sometimes three feet thick, selected for attack would be approached at our full speed of eight knots. Just before striking the ice the engines were stopped, to save jarring them badly, and with the helm amidships the ship's steel-shod cut-water would be made to crash into the ice, cutting out a large V. Then, with engines reversed, she would back astern for a hundred yards. A man on the platform slung over the stern closely watched the propeller in the water, to warn the officer in charge if it came near hard masses of ice that would snap its blades off should it strike them when revolving. Again the ship would be put full speed ahead, and stopped a second before her bows entered the V previously made. The V would thus be enlarged to a length of twenty or thirty feet, and the third time, charging full speed into this, and using her bows as a wedge, the ship could usually split the floe ahead for two or three hundred yards.

As the thin, black, wavy crack ran out ahead of the ship, she would be driven full speed into it, wedging and broadening it out and turning up large slabs of the floe from either bow. Sometimes the pressure of floes on both sides of the one that we had thus cracked would prevent its opening out, and the ship would be slowed and stopped in spite of the driving engines. She would then be put astern again, and once more driven full speed ahead along the crack, without any stoppage until she shot free on the other side. We would then find ourselves crossing a lake and following down a long lead (or lane) winding like a peaceful river between miniature cliffs of snow-capped blue ice, faithfully mirrored in the opaline sea.

Once, I remembered, two great blue whales, about one hundred feet long and weighing possibly a hundred and twenty tons each, shouldered up to the surface with hissing sighs, sending up white vaporous columns twenty feet high. In the distance also white spouts appeared, standing up like sailing ships end-on, and then fading out gradually. At the edge of a small floe, in amusing contrast, stood three Emperor penguins conversing and apparently admiring the reflections of their snowy, gleaming breasts. The whales on their southward course paid no attention to us, neither did the penguins.

These and many other things passed through my mind as I lay there in my tent awake. I remembered, too, a thousand details of the ship we had lost—all those details so dear to a seafaring man. I recalled the months of careful treatment that we had given our rudder and propeller—and now both were gone! I recollected that in my log-book on January 1st, 1915, I had written: "As the success of the whole expedition depends on the rudder and propeller, we can take no risks, and so we must stop until the gale eases up." How useless it all seemed now—with no ship! Othello's occupation was indeed gone!

Then what a thrill there had been, when, at five A.M. on January 11th, 1915, we had sighted land to the southward—

and knew that it was the Antarctic Continent! The land that we saw was an evenly-sloping, gentle hill, or gradual rise to about a thousand feet, covered with soft, deep snow. It was a frozen world that we looked upon. There was no trace of life on it, so far as we could see. Birds rarely flew over it and sea beasts never got closer to it than to shelter at the foot of the ice-cliffs. Shackleton had no intention of landing there, for it was too distant from the South Pole and he did not want to undertake the long, and perhaps impossible, trek of over four hundred miles which would be entailed if we began our journey there instead of at the south point of the Weddell Sea.

But the sighting of this land was nothing compared with

Grytviken Whaling Station, South Georgia (SCOTT POLAR RESEARCH INSTITUTE)

the magnificent moment when Shackleton discovered new land, a hundred miles further south. This new land he named 'Caird Coast,' after Sir James Caird, his principal supporter.

Caird Coast connects Coats' Land, discovered in 1902 by Bruce, with Luitpold Land, discovered by Filchner in 1912. The northern part is similar in character to Coats' Land. It is roughly, though not technically speaking, an undulating barrier, the van of a mighty ice-sheet that is being forced outward from the Antarctic Continent by the pressure of the masses of ice in the interior, and sweeping over hills, plains and shallow seas in the same manner as the great ice-sheet swept over north-west Europe thousands of years ago.

"At the edge of a small floe . . . stood three Emperor penguins"
(SCOTT POLAR RESEARCH INSTITUTE)

The barrier surface from the sea was of a very faint golden brown colour, probably caused by atmospheric dust settling on it. It ended in cliffs varying in height from ten to two hundred feet. But in a very few places it swept down almost level with the sea. These cliffs form a superb contrast to each other, being either pure white or, in shadow, a deep blue.

As the eye roamed inland, higher slopes could be seen, appearing like dim blue or fleecy golden clouds. As the coast was followed to the south-west these slopes gradually increased in clearness and nearness, and also in height, while the barrier cliffs were higher and bolder and looked more like ice and less like névé.[1] Wave beyond wave, these slopes of the great ice-sheet rose, till finally, near the southern extremity of Caird Coast, the ice-sheet burst over a steep slope into the sea in a series of mighty glaciers, bristling with ridges and spikes of ice, and seamed by thousands of crevasses. In the whole length of the Caird Coast no bare land, rock or nunatak[2] was seen. The only proof of land below, indeed, was that inland the ice-sheet rose to a height of about five thousand feet.

The face of the ice was interesting, and where it came over a precipice it broke up into ridges, terraces and criss-cross crevasses that often gave the appearance of a city on a distant hill-side.

I remembered how Shackleton had longed to land, but had curbed his desire in order that he might stick to his objective, which was to land further south. He was determined to press on with all possible speed, despite the allure of this new land, which his eye had been the first to see and which

---

[1] Névé is consolidated snow in process of becoming ice.
[2] Land that breaks upwards through the ice like an island in the sea.

I knew exerted over him, in fact over all of us, a strange fascination.

All this time I was sounding and taking bearings along the coast, and the resulting charts I handed later, on behalf of Shackleton, to the Admiralty. We had the satisfaction of knowing that these charts would be invaluable to succeeding explorers, and that none need ever venture again along that savage coast without a great deal more knowledge than we had possessed.

At one point on the Caird Coast a great square peninsula, fifty miles each way, stood out from the general line of the shore and forced us so much to seaward. From my soundings (one thousand three hundred fathoms at the seaward side and two hundred fathoms at the landward side) it seemed certain that this mass was partly afloat and that it was breaking off from the main body. If this should occur, obviously it would form one of the mightiest ice-bergs ever seen. The fact that we saw a 'water-sky' at the back of this area confirmed this opinion. It is of interest to record here that about thirteen years later the Discovery and several whalers sighted an enormous tabular berg, of, roughly, the same dimensions as this mass, and there is a strong probability that they were identical. The berg had a greater area than the whole of South Georgia.

At this point we were held up for two days by heavy pack-ice, and then we resumed our coasting to the south-west. As we went along we saw numerous packs of from twenty to sixty crab-eating seals. Many of them were creamy white, with beautiful coats. Large numbers of these seals appeared on the floes, and others on low parts of the barrier, where there was an easy slope to the sea. We also saw hundreds swimming from the barrier to the ice-pack in search of euphasia, which swim under the edges of the floes and, in their turn, feed on microscopic diatoms, which are in such abundance as to colour the water a deep olive-green and stain the undersides of the floes yellow-brown. We noticed that several large schools of seal were apparently migrating to the north. Hurley got a splendid 'movie' of them as they came alongside, frothing, blowing and turning somersaults, and eyeing us with mild curiosity. Some of these seals were eating fish of a species unknown to us; they were a beautiful silver colour and Clark called them *alepidosauroidea*, but I have never looked up this word in the encyclopedia and am still sceptical as to whether it exists. I think he must have been pulling our leg.

Next day we steamed across the front of a large glacier or outflow of the continental ice-sheet. It was more than seventeen miles across, and showed huge crevasses and high-pressure ridges. There were some bays of sea-ice running into it. This bay-ice was smooth and showed hardly any signs of pressure, and was dotted all over with innumerable seals and penguins. One of these sheets of bay-ice appeared to slope upwards and merge imperceptibly through the glacier into the inland ice, and looked as though it would afford an ideal track to the interior of the Continent. Shackleton afterwards regretted that he had not landed here instead of endeavouring to go a hundred miles further south. He mentioned this to me next day, but it is easy to be wise after the event.

Twenty miles farther we came to another huge glacier over-fall of the ice-sheet. The glacier-face was nearly three hundred feet high, and the ice-surface a mile inland appeared to be about fifteen hundred feet. The front showed a tide-mark of about ten feet, proving that it was not afloat. We steamed forty miles along the face of this glacier out-flow when we were stopped by solid pack-ice that was held up by a large number of bergs 'roosting' on a hundred-fathom bank. Under the lee of one of these we sheltered. In the afternoon the wind increased to a gale, and the floes drifted past at about two knots. The gale, however, cleared the pack-ice away from us, so that next day we were able to proceed.

As we steamed along the coast we counted forty young Emperor penguins with their pretty, fluffy, pearl-grey overcoats. These birds had dark heads, and we were greatly excited because we thought that we had discovered a new species. Actually, it was only that we happened to see them at a stage of their development which had never been observed before. We captured eleven of them, for use both as food and as specimens for Clark, the biologist. We judged them to be about eight or nine months old. On liberating three or four of these, the departing birds turned round, gave us a little bow and then hopped over the rail on to the ice, where they again bowed and walked off. It was so extraordinarily human as to be almost uncanny.

When we had followed the Caird Coast for twenty miles further south we got imprisoned by the pack-ice. Then followed a series of strong north-easterly winds that drove all the ice in that part of the Weddell Sea down to us, and packed it solidly around the ship. In this manner we drifted off the coast during the remainder of January.

In February the temperature fell to fifty degrees below zero Centigrade. This was, of course, the height of summer in these regions. It froze and consolidated the pack-ice into a solid body round us, so that we were never able to free the ship sufficiently to navigate her again. The easterly winds gradually forced the pack, in which we were helplessly lying, farther and farther away from the shore, so that even had there been no open water between us and the land, it would have been too hazardous now to send a party to try to reach the continent. It would have spelt disaster had a gale sprung up when we were separated, since the ship could so easily have been carried out of sight. Shackleton was always opposed to splitting the party, and he very wisely refused to consider such a move even then, although the temptation to explore, when we had been so near, was almost overwhelming.

Shackleton really felt that his hopes of crossing the Antarctic Continent were doomed when he found that the ship was firmly beset and that there was no chance of extricating her from the drifting pack-ice that year. We all shared his disappointment. But he did not permit himself to display the regret that he felt nor to admit defeat, and talked continually of making another attempt during the following year, if the War were over. Indeed, he laughed and joked as though he had not a care in the world, and only those who understood him well could gauge the depth of his real feelings.

It might be thought that our surroundings were monotonous to the eye since all that we could see was snow and ice; but this was not so. There was a continual rainbow-like variety of colour. Outside the Arctic and Antarctic regions, of course, one is surrounded by coloured objects; and while there was nothing of this where we found ourselves beset, nevertheless we experienced colour in a way unknown outside the far North or South. It was as though our snowy surroundings were being painted upon continually by a master-hand, or the most superb lime-lights were being played upon us. When the sun was out there were nearly always striking parhelia, or mock-suns red or gold or prismatic, and always magnificent. These were great circles round the real sun, and bright straight lines of colour intersecting these circles, with a mock sun at each intersection. The weirdness of the effect is indescribable. When you gazed upon this strange and awe-inspiring sky you felt as though you had stepped into a world where the laws of Nature, as you had known them, were suspended and overruled by some vaster Power, which was thus making itself known to you. The ice also was tinged with ephemeral colour, very faint, very delicate, iridescent.

Most interesting, too, were the mirages. I see that in my log-book, I wrote: "When the sun comes out there is much refraction and mirage. Everything on the horizon appears drawn up and distorted. The tops of some of the bergs seem to boil up and rise and fall and spread themselves outwards in long overhanging streaks in the quaintest way. All round the horizon we see what appear to be barrier cliffs thrown up in the air, where we know all is deep sea. Bergs and pack-ice are thrown up and distorted into fantastic shapes, where they climb, trembling, upwards and spread out into long lines at different levels, then contract and fall down, leaving nothing but a small wavering smudge that comes and goes, and presently takes shape till there is a perfect inverted reflection of a berg, the shadow hovering over the substance.

"More smudges appear, spreading out till they meet, forming long and beautiful snow-cliffs, washed at their bases by the waters of illusion, in which they appear to be faithfully reflected. Inshore appears a beautiful, dazzling city of cathedral spires, domes and minarets, while to the south rises a line of low land or barrier that must be a hundred miles distant."

As we drifted farther away from the land, the Continent itself assumed a more and more unreal appearance. The effect of clouds was generally to throw either a mottled shadow on the ice-clad earth that made it look like a low mackerel sky, or else to darken it so completely that it seemed to be a bank of black cloud in which the crevasses and ice-cliffs appeared as shadows and rifts.

The weather was getting colder in February, and when, under the influence of wind and current, the pack-ice would split up into long lanes of open water, we could trace the course of these even at a distance by the dense masses of vapour that rose from the sea which was, naturally, forty or fifty degrees less cold than the air. Against the white surroundings this vapour appeared almost black. This is called 'frost-smoke' and it was impossible to see through it. It would rise continuously for about an hour, when it would be terminated by a sheet of ice on the water. The effect was very curious, for it was as though a heavy dark wall had been erected by invisible hands, cutting off everything beyond it from our vision.

I remembered at what pains we had been to get a sufficient water supply, although we were hemmed in by millions of tons of ice. The ice from any berg, melted down, yields fresh water; but pack-ice, being formed from seawater, is naturally impregnated with salt. The *Endurance* was surrounded by pack-ice. We overcame this difficulty by selecting ice from the high parts of the pressure ridges or hummocks, as there were no bergs close enough to be of use to us. We chose only those which had been reared high out of the water for some months, so as to be sure that the salt would have drained out of it. It is a peculiarity of sea-ice that, under these conditions, salt drains completely out of it—a fortunate provision of Nature so far as we were concerned.

Our work at this time consisted in quarrying and sledging-in the necessary ice to the ship, exercising the dogs, improving and keeping our quarters clean and warm, cutting holes through the thick floes to take soundings of the depths of the ocean (this was my particular job) and to dredge up biological specimens from the bottom for Clark. Our free time we spent playing hockey and football on the ice.

Amongst the hauls that we got were numbers of bright little prawns, a few geological boulders, and hundredweights of glacial mud dropped from ice-bergs. This blue mud, which froze into a solid mass on coming into contact with the air, is of the same nature as the blue mud underlying London, which probably was deposited in a similar manner. And one day the dredge came up full of silicious sponges. These sponges bristle with long, glass-like spicules which are very thin and splintery, many of them being nearly a foot in length. They were very unpleasant to handle, as the spicules were liable to break off and stick in one's hands.

I felt sorry for Clark, as I lay there that night and realised that he had been obliged to leave on the *Endurance* the whole of the valuable collection that he had been at such pains to classify and study.

CHAPTER III

On the Pack-ice

WHEN dawn came I thrust out of my mind all the memories that had been crowding into it. During the winter we had drifted a thousand miles from where my thoughts had dwelt that night, and now there was plenty of work to do.

Our dogs were now reduced to fifty in number, for Shackleton, wishing to economise in food, had found it necessary to have ten animals destroyed. The youngest pups that had been born on board were shot, and so was 'Mrs. Chippy' the carpenter's cat. Macklin, the doctor, and Tom Crean, who had cared for the pups, felt this badly, and the carpenter 'shed a bitter tear.' As a matter of fact the cat could have come along with us in splendid style had it not been that the dogs, now that she lacked the protection of the ship, would have eaten her.

The dogs, I may say, were huskies, from the North-West Province of Canada. They were bred with wolves, and many of our dogs were pure wolf. Our heaviest animal weighed a hundred and fourteen pounds. We had to be careful how we showed any affection for them, for if one of us patted or took too much notice of any particular dog, his neighbours, in a frenzy of jealous rage, would attack him as soon as we had walked away. One dog called Steamer amusingly enough would reverse this procedure. He was so over-joyed if he were patted that he would immediately attack the dogs nearest him. While we were on the ice, when the night was moonlit, these dogs, like their forebears, would suddenly set up in unison the mournful wolf-pack howl, creating a great volume of sound that would reverberate for miles with a most melancholy effect.

We once had a remarkable display of this wolf nature that they had inherited, and I remember the terrible struggle that we had to save 'Satan,' the leader of the team and a dog older and more experienced than the rest, from their ravening jaws.

The way in which a leader is selected is interesting. Occasionally he is chosen by his human master on account of his exceptional sagacity in finding a way through the ice, but more often the selection is made by the pack itself. A candidate for the position of leader asserts himself by going among the pack, his fangs bared, his hair bristling, a growl emanating from his great throat, challenging any and every dog that cares to respond. Invariably the bravest becomes his first opponent. Usually this means a fight to the death, although occasionally the weaker one will virtually cry 'kamerad' by lying on his back and moaning. The victor then goes among the pack again, and yet again—as many times as may be necessary to down all opponents. Once the leader has established his rule, his powers are great. He watches his team with the eye of a Vice-Admiral, and the dog that fails to pull his weight is mercilessly punished by him, which goes far towards saving man the trouble of enforcing discipline.

But like the wolves from which they are bred, the huskies are always ready to turn upon a leader who is weakening or growing old. Consequently, when our pack suspected that Satan was no longer the fighting fiend that he had been, they massed together and attacked him, intending, no doubt, to elect a new leader from among their number.

They chose the first opportunity to attack him, which occurred one day when we had released them on the ice for exercise. In a moment they were a seething, struggling, snarling mass. The snow was soon splashed with blood. We had to rush in among them, taking our chance of being bitten, and hit them over the head with the heaviest bits of wood we could lay hands on, hitting hard enough to lay them out. Although old Satan probably recognised that his leadership was drawing to a close, his indomitable spirit was unbroken. Howling and struggling to get at his enemies, he was led back to his kennel, ready to fight on to the last.

Although these dogs were friendly to us, it must be borne in mind that they were fierce and dangerous brutes which had to be thrashed into obedience at the first sign of insubordination; or it might easily have become a question of a man's life against theirs. Canadians warn drivers of dog-teams not to fall to the ground in front of a team, for in a moment the dogs might revert to type, especially if driven by hunger, and tear a man literally limb from limb. Nevertheless, we had our dogs so well disciplined that in the old happy days in the *Endurance* we used to hold Dog Derbies on the ice, at which we recklessly betted our week's ration of chocolates and cigarettes. On one occasion, I remember, Wild's team won the race at the great speed of eleven miles an hour. But there were no such relaxations for us now. Life had become too much of a problem.

For eight weeks, apart from the few sealing parties that we

organised and the work involved in the rearrangement of our plans and slight improvements to our gear and sledging equipment, so that we should be ready to trek as soon as the ice carried us nearer the land, time hung heavily on our hands. When there are twenty-eight men herded together in partially enforced inactivity, with nothing but snow and ice to look upon, life is bound to become irksome. The irritation of trying to drift north and knowing ourselves powerless to combat the inexorable laws of Nature, or to hurry the process of drifting by so much as a second, was bound to result in a certain fraying of nerves and consequent ebullitions of temper. Little cliques and factions grew up, but Shackleton's tact and diplomacy soon destroyed that spirit. He would redistribute the occupants of the tents on some pretext far removed from the real one, and would remind each man that strength lay in unity. Of loyalty towards his leadership there was never any question.

Shackleton had a wonderful and rare understanding of the men's attitude towards one another and towards the expedition as a whole. He appreciated how deeply one man, or small group of men, could affect the psychology of the others. Therefore he almost insisted upon cheeriness and optimism; in fact his attitude was, "You've damn well got to be optimistic."

It was his knowledge of men, quite as much as his executive ability, that made him such a wonderful leader. It was characteristic of him that when he ordered all superfluous weight to be cast away, he delighted the heart of Hussey, the meteorologist, by allowing him to keep his banjo. And many a weary evening was enlivened by Hussey's songs, in which we would all join, and the cheerful twang of his banjo. Hussey was a brilliant wit, and his keen repartee was one of the few joys left to us. Often we would combine to provoke

him just for the pleasure of hearing his clever retorts, and invariably he would emerge the victor, no matter how many of
us tried to best him. On an ice-floe any little diversion is
more welcome than people living in civilised conditions perhaps can imagine; for when you are drifting on Polar pack-
ice, if you are not in momentary danger nor working very
hard, monotony is your greatest enemy. I think that we
came to dread monotony far more than we did any actual
danger.

When the carpenter had completed, with material taken
from the wreck of the *Endurance*, the sledges on which we
were to transport the heavy boats, we waited eagerly for
Shackleton to give us the word "Go." We had built high
hopes on this journey; for we believed that the sledges
would be our salvation by taking us to Paulet Island, where
a small hut had been erected twelve years before by Nordenskjold. And when at last we started, none of us could
foresee the bitter disappointment that awaited us, nor guess
that we were condemned to spend months on a floe only a
few miles distant from the one we now rejoiced so heartily
at leaving.

The stores taken from the *Endurance* had become of paramount importance to us, more especially as it would be difficult to organise any sealing parties while we were travelling.
Before that I had been constantly on the watch for seal, and
in order that I might keep a good look-out for them we had
erected a platform alongside the King's Flag, and from here,
several times a day, I would search the ice-fields with my
binoculars, ostensibly only for seal but actually hoping always that we had drifted to within sight of some new land.
Shackleton used to chaff me on my passion for seal meat.
Nevertheless, he encouraged our hunting, for he recognised
that not only did we need large quantities to feed the men

and dogs, but that it was vital for keeping off scurvy. Scurvy has always been the foe of Polar explorers, and Shackleton, owing to his scientific methods and commonsense, was practically the first to make long journeys without any of his men falling victims to it—which, to my mind, is an even greater achievement than his important geographical discoveries.

During winter in this latitude the sun never rises for ten weeks. Now summer was approaching, so that for ten weeks the sun would never set. Although this would ensure us a respite from the blizzards of winter, it had its drawbacks, as we were soon to learn. The snow softened to such an extent that men trying to get through it sank waist deep and got wet to the skin, and since there was a shortage of waterproof ground-sheets, when they slept the warmth of their bodies would melt the snow and they would wake up in little pools.

Two days before Christmas we made our start. Before leaving, and in the belief that we should never see the camp again, I deposited there a tightly corked bottle in which Shackleton had placed a piece of paper on which he had written "*Endurance* crushed and abandoned in 69° 5′ S. and 51° 35′ W. All hands to-morrow proceeding to the westward. All well. December 23rd, 1915. E. H. Shackleton." This I placed in the stern of our third boat, the *Stancomb Wills*, which we were forced to leave behind as we could not manage more than two.

Once more we repeated the process of letting the dogs take the stores on the small sledges, while sixteen of us dragged the two boats, the *James Caird* and the *Dudley Docker*. Shackleton and Wild pioneered the road, cutting down some of the pressure ridges of ice in our path, chopping away the sharpest and highest parts of them with pickaxes. As we came along we cut these down still further, making at times a small cañon, until we had a possible track for the boats. Negotiating these pressure ridges was always a ticklish business, for if the sledges should overturn, a boat might have been hopelessly damaged, and we had no means of making proper repairs.

Each boat with its sledge weighed about a ton. It was impossible to drag two boats at the same time, so we had to take them in relays, thereby covering three miles for every mile of headway. After the first day's experience of this heavy going Shackleton reversed the routine, and we slept by day and travelled by night, when the sun was lowest and the snow consequently hardest.

During the days that followed I had grave doubts whether we could continue our journey in this way. On the seventh day it was my job to tell Shackleton exactly how much, or rather how little, progress we had made. I worked it out by observations, and found that in seven days of back-breaking work we had advanced ten miles! We were still one thousand miles from the whaling stations of South Georgia, and three hundred miles from Graham's Land. Shackleton had known, of course, that our progress had been extraordinarily poor; nevertheless, to have his own misgivings confirmed by such striking figures was a disappointment to him.

"At this rate," he said, "it would take us about two hundred days to get to Graham's Land. And we haven't got food enough to last us that time. In fact, we have only enough grub for about a month."

"It would help us a bit," I replied, "if the ice opened up, as it ought to be doing pretty soon, considering the time of year; then we could take to the boats. That would certainly let us make more rapid headway."

"I agree," said Shackleton; "we'll go on a bit longer and then if we can't make quicker progress, we shall have to abandon this march."

That night when sledging was resumed we came upon rotten ice, and the heavily laden sledges kept breaking through. Shackleton, knowing the danger of damage to the boats, which indeed would be fatal to our hope of escape, wisely abandoned his plan of sledging to Graham's Land. He and Hurley had prospected to the south, McIlroy and I to the north, hoping to find a good surface by which we could outflank the rotten ice ahead. But Fate was against us. All we found was chaotic ice through which it would have been folly to attempt to take the boats.

The order to retrace our steps was received with acute disappointment by our men. They knew that it doomed them to the deadly monotony from which they had been so glad to escape, and that once more day would succeed day without any respite from the inactivity. However hard and thankless the work had been, it had represented to them at least an effort to save themselves, and had held out that which was prized by all of them—a chance of meeting with high adventure.

When we had retreated half a mile we settled on the biggest floe in the vicinity, naming our quarters 'Patience Camp.' We decided to get all the seal meat that we could, both so that we should have fresh food and also that we might have a sufficient store when the time should come for our next journey, though how we were to make that journey we had then no idea. Shackleton had come to the conclusion that the best thing to do would be to mark time and trust to the northward drift of the ice.

A few days later we had our first adventure with a sea-leopard. Lees, our motor expert, had wandered from the camp on skis. I must explain that while the floes were mostly jammed solidly together, occasionally they were separated by narrow lanes of water containing small masses of ice and brash (broken ice) over which it was possible for a reckless man to go on skis. In this way Lees had got about three floes away from us, a distance of, roughly, a quarter of a mile. All of a sudden Wild saw him coming in hell-for-leather, with a sea-leopard in hot pursuit. This species of seal is a fierce, handsome brute, about thirteen feet long, with a fawn coat spotted all over with brown markings. A sea-leopard will attack any creature it meets with on the pack-ice, and owing to the fact that it moves with a snake-like, undulating movement over snow into which a man on foot would sink to his waist, its speed is much greater than a human being's. In spite of the rough surface, however, Lees, realising his danger, just managed to keep ahead of the animal. Once it dived into a lead (or lane of water) and, swimming under the floe, came up ahead of him. Fortunately he had sufficient presence of mind to make off at right angles, whereupon the sea-leopard again repeated its diving manœuvre. By this time Wild, who had seized his rifle, rushed to Lees' help, cursing him loudly the while for his foolhardiness. The sea-leopard, recognising a new factor in the situation, then turned its attention to Wild, and made a dash at him, open-mouthed. He coolly allowed it to approach within a few yards, and then brought it down with a shot through the brain.

We all hurried to drag the seal into camp and cut it up for food. It was twelve feet long, of slender and graceful build, with a cruel, thin-lipped muzzle and formidable fangs in the front of the jaws; a curiously prehistoric looking beast, despite its beautiful coat. That it was a dangerous animal was proved by the fact that we found in its stomach large balls of hair, three inches in diameter—the remains of crab-eating seals that it had devoured. As these balls were of hair and not fur, it was evident that the sea-leopard's victims were not mere babies. I can well imagine that such a beast would give rise to sea-serpent stories, for, seen from a little distance,

ABOVE. *Patience Camp* (ROYAL GEOGRAPHICAL SOCIETY)

BELOW. *Ocean Camp* (ROYAL GEOGRAPHICAL SOCIETY)

rearing two or three feet out of the water, shooting forward and retracting its head (a characteristic movement) it would resemble a serpent rather than a mammal.

We had no means of curing the sea-leopard's hide, but we scraped it as clean as possible, and then laid it, with some crab-eater skins, under our floor-cloth in the hope of preventing the water soaking through into our sleeping-bags.

While on the subject of sea-leopards I notice that in my diary a few days later the following entry occurs: "Seven Adelies (penguins) came up on the floe, and, after drilling for half an hour, one of their number gave a short address, after which a sentry was posted on a hummock and the others went to sleep for the night." I remember reflecting at the time that undoubtedly the 'address' was on the danger of sea-leopards, against whom, no doubt, the sentry had been warned to keep a sharp look-out! This may seem far-fetched, but penguins are extraordinarily human in their ways. The Emperor penguin, for example, nearly always bows on approaching you. Their manners really seem to be of a studied politeness. And all penguins seem to have a well-thought-out system of communal life, as evidenced by the fact that one is often left to guard against danger while the others sleep.

We had been living for some weeks principally on seals and penguins, when the situation changed for the worse, for suddenly we got no more. Evidently they had migrated to other latitudes. A serious shortage was the result, and we were reduced for weeks to fourteen ounces of food a day. This weakened us considerably, for it deprived us of the means of fighting the cold, and whereas at the beginning of our drift on the ice eight men had been able to haul one of the boats on the sledge, at the end it took the whole party of twenty-eight to do so.

It was when we were in this enfeebled state that we were

awakened one night by a tremendous commotion, a medley of unfamiliar and weird sounds that, for the moment, were mystifying. Going out of our tents we saw that thousands of Adelie penguins, in the course of migration, had come up round the camp. For miles, in every direction, the snow was covered with them. The effect was most odd. It looked as though the snow were covered with hundreds of little men in evening dress, a costume which the black and white markings of these birds always suggest. The sight was almost uncanny, but, as we quickly realised, a very welcome one, for it meant fresh food and provisions in store. We bagged three hundred in one day. This gave us a fresh lease of life, and soon after we got this extra food our strength came back.

I had been repeatedly urging on Shackleton the importance of getting back the third boat, which we had left at our former camp, and finally one day, when the weather was unusually fine, a party of us went over and brought her back with us. I was very glad to get her, for I now felt that we had sufficient boats in which to ship the twenty-eight men when we reached open water again.

This was the last important piece of work at which the dogs could assist us. Then came the sad day when all, save one team, had to be destroyed, to save food.

At this period the monotony had become terrible. Fortunately before the *Endurance* sank I had retrieved three packs of cards. One of these was Shackleton's own, but this did not prevent me presenting it to him with lordly generosity, for which he thanked me very much. Another I gave to the men, and the third I kept for my own tent. These cards proved a godsend. I once worked it out that they were worth two pounds a card to us.

When we did not play, or were not mending our clothes, we usually spent the evening in interminable arguments, mostly about nothing in particular. The following incident indicates the frame of mind of some of the sailors, who got so excited one night over a discussion on currency (of all things!) that the matter was looked up in one of the few volumes of the *Encyclopaedia Britannica* that we had saved, since they contained information that was valuable to us. When both sides were proved to be wrong, they united in declaring that "the—book was no good."

Gradually the rate of our drift was increased to the northward and an occasional killer-whale was now seen. These brutes have a habit of poking their noses over the edge of the floes, their malignant little eyes glancing across in their endeavour to spot seal. If there are seals on a not-too-heavy floe they will tip it up, capsizing it and throwing the seals into the water. One of these killers was once harpooned and cut open; inside were found the remains of twelve seals and fourteen porpoises, so there was no question that they would devour a man if they got the chance. Indeed that has since happened in the South Orkneys, about four hundred miles north of where we were then.

On the last day of March a party of us was bringing in seventy-five Adelies that we had killed, when the floes opened out and eighteen of us got cut off from the camp. Cheetham, the third mate, and I ferried a block of ice across the lead to where Shackleton had brought us a rope, one end of which he held round a hummock. Taking the other end with us, we ferried the block back again, and then, selecting a larger floe, marshalled the rest of the party on to it, with the sledge and the Adelies. At this moment we heard a killer whale blowing in a pool not fifty yards away.

As we hauled strenuously on the rope we could not help feeling the danger of our situation. At any moment the killer might tip up one side of our floe, throwing us all into the freezing water, after which it would devour those nearest to it. But our danger was too imminent to allow us to be frightened: it is curious, but in an emergency one is rarely scared; it is afterwards that one feels the reaction. At the time one's every nerve is responding to the need for quick action. The killer blew again—a little nearer this time; and the floe redoubled its speed.

When we were still about nine feet from the bank on which we wanted to land, our progress came to a full stop because of the loose ice between that bank and ourselves. But this space was quickly bridged by the sledge, over which we all leapt to safety. We may not have had much affection normally for an ice-floe; but at that moment the one we were on seemed to us the perfect home—solid and safe. We saw the killer once or twice again before it sheered off in search of other prey. It looked to us a regular monster, about thirty feet long and weighing, I should imagine, several tons.

This incident made Shackleton still more anxious about any of us who left the camp in search of game.

We Reach
Elephant Island

O N the 23rd March, 1916, after five months' drifting, five months' endless monotony, and five months' suspense, there was wild rejoicing in the camp. We had sighted the Antarctic Continent! Excitement reigned. Should we make it? Would our leader give orders to start sledging straight away? What should we find there? How long would the journey take? These and other questions were flung to and fro.

Shackleton was the first to see the snow-covered land, which, actually, was Joinville Island, at the northernmost point of the Antarctic Continent. We saw it through the gaps between a large number of stranded bergs, and according to my diary it appeared thus: "A large rocky mountain with snow patches in the hollows . . . two or three peaks, a cliff to the north and a long slope to the south. The summits pierce the clouds which hide their bases."

Shackleton and I went up on a hummock together to get a better look at it through the binoculars, and I asked the question that I knew was burning in every man's mind: "Will you try to make for it now?"

He did not reply at once, and I could see by his expression that he disliked having to say the word that would disappoint all of us.

At length he said shortly: "No."

I said, "Of course you are right. Look at the work that Nordenskjold's men had, twelve years ago. Their ship was crushed and sank in this neighbourhood, and they had only twenty-five miles to go. We should have sixty. It would be a terrible thing if anything happened to the Expedition now, after you've brought us nearly two thousand miles north in safety since the ship was first beset. That means that we have come two thousand miles through the pack-ice."

Shackleton nodded and said:

"I can't risk the danger of crossing ice that will be opening and closing rapidly under the influence of the tides and currents between us and the land. The boats might get crushed. We might get separated. Many things could happen. But if we keep on as we are for another hundred miles or so, we are bound to drift to open water, and then we will make for the nearest whaling station."

He could not foresee, of course, that his plans were to be set at naught through abnormal currents, and that in the end we should be forced to face danger greater, perhaps, than that which lay in crossing the sixty miles that separated us from Joinville Island.

The news of Shackleton's decision was received with silent disappointment by the men. Any struggle, however desperate, seemed preferable to inactivity, and the glimpse of land had raised their hopes high. Only their loyalty to Shackleton and their absolute conviction that whatever he did was for the best made them control their feelings. Although they did not complain it was easy to see by their faces that life had lost its zest. Some of them looked almost dazed, as though they felt that they were condemned to wander for evermore in this wilderness of ice, fighting always that intangible enemy the cold. Indeed, for most of us, I think our former lives had receded to that dim and shadowy vagueness usually associated with dreams, and, speaking for myself, I can say truthfully that I had forgotten much of the outside world. My sense of values had so readjusted itself that for the time being I was unable to picture an existence in which a desert of ice and snow, battles with sea-leopards, the dread of killer-whales, and a regard for penguins as almost personal friends did not play a part.

Perhaps this is not surprising, for the conditions, as described in my diary, show the hourly struggle that we had just to keep alive. "It is difficult," I wrote, "to keep warm in our tents, the temperature, with everything closed and six of us smoking, ranging from twenty to thirty degrees of frost. Our food gets cold in our pots before we have eaten half of it, and the water we have brought in to drink becomes instantaneously covered with ice. The afternoon we spent reading in our sleeping-bags, as we were afraid of getting too good an appetite if we took enough exercise to keep warm."

I must explain that we had to use a fine discrimination in exercising, since if we did not exercise before turning in we were cold all night, so that we could get hardly any sleep. If on the other hand we took enough exercise to warm us, the ravenous hunger engendered had almost the same effect. We had to learn how to control our exercise so that it would be just sufficient to prevent us from feeling frozen without producing sufficient appetite to keep us awake. Eventually we managed to reduce this to a science, achieving a nicely balanced adjustment between hunger and cold.

At this time we were getting short of rations again. Some of the penguins and seal-meat that we had saved had been lost through the floe cracking and the part of it on which they were stored overturning before we could recover them. We were therefore very glad of a sea-leopard which had swallowed thirty fish (apparently a new species, nine or ten inches long, and perfectly fresh) just before Wild shot the beast as it came up out of the sea on to the floe. These fish we extracted, cooked and ate. Curiously enough two of the fish had been partly digested and had to be thrown away, leaving us with just twenty-eight—the number of our party; so that each man had a splendid meal of one whole fried fish.

The brief summer was over, and the nights were becoming very dark. We were now counting the hours until we should reach the open sea, and on the last day of March, to our great joy, we felt a faint swell beneath the ice, showing that at last we were drawing near to open water. For fourteen months we had not felt the swell of the ocean. We were suddenly galvanised into life. We realised that our present existence was only a phase, and, with a chance of getting back to civilisation, we began to remember our home interests, to think of family and friends, of theatres, of dinners eaten at leisure in clean—and above all—dry surroundings, of beds and eiderdowns and fresh linen. These thoughts flashed through our minds, but were gone almost immediately; for we knew that we had a gigantic task to perform before we could reach land.

My own particular problem naturally was that of navigating. Because of the uncertainty of Antarctic conditions I had no idea which of the several plans that I had formed would be feasible, and I knew well, too, that some emergency might cause me to abandon the lot and force me to have recourse to something entirely different. That is one of the maddening features of an ice-drift. You plan carefully,

persistently, because for months you have so little to occupy your mind that you are thankful to concentrate upon
anything definite, and yet at the back of your thoughts is always the knowledge that your efforts will probably have to
give way before some upheaval of Nature, sudden and in-
conceivable, something that you cannot provide for before-
hand.

Take the following as an illustration of how swiftly unavoidable danger can arise. Two bergs had been moving towards us in the night. Suddenly, at sunrise, these accelerated
their speed and came charging towards us, ploughing
through the great masses of pack-ice as though this had been
tissue paper. Bergs of this size weigh over a million tons
apiece, so that nothing stands any chance against them.
Imagine each to represent the weight of forty battleships:
our floe was being charged by the equivalent of a fleet of
eighty men-of-war. Huge floes were lifted and flung aside by
the cliff-like fronts of these monsters, while others were
ground to fragments. For miles behind them there was a
wake of chaos, floe piled on floe and crashing in all directions. Our camp was straight in their path and it seemed as
though destruction was inevitable. Shackleton, clinging to
what then seemed a forlorn hope, had ordered all preparations to be made to try to move out of their track, although
this would necessitate leaving all our supplies, since it would
have been an impossibility to transport them in the time.
Nearer and nearer the mountains of ice approached. We
stood together watching them, Shackleton waiting to give
the word which would send us scrambling over the heaving
ice-floes—on which we should have had small chance of escaping starvation. He was quite cool, and smoking a cigarette.

Suddenly, some freak or eddy of the current—or was it

some greater Power?—swept the bergs off on to a new line. The danger was over. But fresh ones followed swiftly.

As we were getting near open water Shackleton now divided the party into two watches, so that half of us were always on the look-out, and at last, on Sunday, April 9th, 1916, the pack-ice, which had been getting looser and looser for the last three days, opened up alongside of us. Everything had long been in readiness for this great moment, and we launched the boats at 1 P.M. to make for land (at which particular spot we were not quite sure).

Now began the difficult task of rowing the three small open boats in and out through the opening leads among the charging, heaving floes. An hour after we had embarked we were nearly caught by the converging rush of two great lines of pack-ice driving together as fast as we could row. Shackleton's boat led, mine followed, then came that of the navigating officer, Hudson. Every man was straining his back to the uttermost in the effort to drive the heavily laden boats through the water before the ice closed in upon us. Up to then I had been towing one of the sledges behind the *Dudley Docker*, and another sledge was balanced across the bows of Shackleton's boat. Now, of course, the sledge that was being towed had to be cut adrift. We just managed to get clear, the last boat escaping by a matter of yards. We were still in the loose pack-ice, not yet having struck the open sea, which we judged was about twenty miles away, and when darkness fell that night we had to haul the boats up on a floe, as it was too dangerous to go on. We were obliged to unload them before we could drag them up on to the floe, which was heavy work.

The floe on which we camped was a long one, lying at right angles to the then heavy swell rolling in from the north-west. While we slept for half an hour the floe swung round until it was end-on to the swell, which, rolling underneath and lifting it in the middle, cracked it right across. We heard a sudden shout, and, rushing out, saw that the men's tent was tearing in halves, one on each side of the crack, with the sea in between. Shackleton's unerring instinct caused him to look down into the water instead of concerning himself with the tent, and there he saw a man in his sleeping-bag. He leaned down, seized the bag, and, before anyone could come to his help, with a terrific effort swung the man clear on to the floe. A second later the two halves of the floe, immediately where the man had been, came together with a terrific thud.

Having saved the man from a dreadful death by only a barest fraction of time, Shackleton turned his attention to the rest of the party. The rescued man began to rummage in his sleeping-bag, and presently was heard to mutter, "Lost my b—y tin of tobacco." Said one of the others to him, "You might have thanked Sir Ernest for saving your life." "Yes," replied the dripping sailor; "but thanking him won't bring back my tobacco."

The crack, meanwhile, was widening and dividing the whole camp, so, as fast as we could in the darkness and cold, we rushed the *James Caird* over the opening and brought back Shackleton's tent. During these operations, Shackleton, who was steadying the *James Caird* by the painter, got marooned on the piece of the floe that was leaving us. We were obliged to launch the *Stancomb Wills* as quickly as possible to bring him back. The few minutes that it took us to get Shackleton were among the most anxious that I have ever known. Knowing the force of the currents and their capriciousness I appreciated the terrible position in which he would have found himself had that floe been swept away from us and lost in the darkness. His danger was rendered more acute too by the fact that killer-whales were blowing all round us, and we knew how easily a small floe could be tipped up by them. One of the brutes, although we could not see it, was blowing quite close to us as we were launching the boat to bring Shackleton back. I don't mind confessing that the sound gave me an unpleasant feeling in my spine.

The events of that evening put an end to any thought of sleep, for they had shown Shackleton that the floe might crack again at any moment, and he wanted everybody awake and on the alert.

At dawn we tried to proceed, but the pack had closed, and we had to wait some time before we could launch the boats. When we got our first glimpse of open water an easterly gale was blowing and the seas were too heavy for us to risk taking the boats ahead in their heavily laden condition. We were obliged to return, therefore, to the pack-ice. Accordingly we hauled the boats on to a small berg, and Shackleton, Wild and I took fresh stock of the situation. We came to the disquieting conclusion that before we could face the gale again we should have to jettison some of our precious food. This dampened our spirits considerably. In the hours that followed we got the only sleep, except for brief dozes, that we were to have for six weary days and nights.

I have already mentioned that the Antarctic winter was setting in. Only those that have explored these regions can understand the full significance of this; for it means an unending series of blizzards, gales and blinding snowstorms, of pitiless winds that never give one a moment's respite, of seas that, save for brief intervals, grow continuously heavier and angrier, smashing the edges of the pack-ice to fragments and splitting great bergs as though these were of glass. The sky is a shroud of dark and gloomy grey, pall-like in its melancholy colouring. Noon itself is like a chill and cheerless evening.

We awoke to find dawn misty and threatening. A north-easter was blowing, and during the night the pack-ice had again closed round us, imprisoning us on the berg. Even so, we were all awed at the majestic spectacle before us. We beheld white hills of ice-clad sea, rolling through the mists towards us. At intervals they opened out, and a long line of water would appear, showing black between the ice-rollers. This appearance was caused by the floes, which had been smashed into pieces, none of them exceeding fifty yards across, riding the great ocean swell that was rolling towards us from Cape Horn. Magnificent as the sight was it was an alarming one to us; for our berg was being undercut and pieces of it were falling into the sea, and we feared that within an hour or two the top would be cut off and we should be thrown into the water. Thousands of seals were riding serenely on the broken pieces of floe: every now and then one would dive off and emerge on the next floe. We watched them enviously: what was play to them might soon be death to us.

Nevertheless, it was impossible to leave. To launch our party in the boats would have been suicidal. Shackleton, Wild and I went frequently up to the top of the berg and scanned the horizon to the north for open water. None was to be seen. Hour after hour our anxiety continued, and it was not until afternoon that a thin black line showed us what we had been waiting for. Gradually we drifted towards it, until at last a long arm of the sea reached us, and an opening showed right alongside. We slithered the boats down a six-foot wall of ice into the sea; but it was impossible to launch the boats with the stores in them; so we were obliged to load up after they were in the water. It was an anxious business, for each moment counted, and every man worked his hardest, realising that delay might lose us our chance. Putting their backs into it the men bent to the oars, and we escaped at last from the pack which had so long imprisoned us.

Our spirits rose as we set off. We believed that our difficulties were almost over, that we were, if not quite safe, at least well on the way to security, and, so to speak, homeward bound. As I look back I cannot help wondering how we should have felt had we known the ordeals that awaited us, the dangers and disappointments we were destined to experience. At that time, when we had been living in a world of ice for so long, we could not imagine that there were situations still worse than those which we had already faced.

When we had sailed a few miles, Shackleton, in the *James Caird*, and I, in the *Dudley Docker*, were drawing well ahead of the third boat, the *Stancomb Wills*. As my boat was travelling faster than his, Shackleton sent me back to assist the *Stancomb Wills*, which was in danger of being smashed on what I may call the 'lee shore' of the pack-ice. I made their painter fast to our stern, and both boats getting out their oars, we gradually managed to draw clear of the ice; but this manœuvre cost us two hours of precious daylight. When darkness came we tried tying up to a floe-berg, but were forced away by masses of ice sweeping round it, and we spent the night in dodging about under the lee of small patches of pack-ice. I wrote in my diary:

"A cold, wet, rotten night. All hands wet by snow and sleet showers. Only one oilskin in the *Docker*. No sleep and not enough pulling to keep us warm."

Conditions were changing so continually that we had not yet finally decided upon our destination. Since we had started in the boats it had been impossible to get a 'sight' of the sun; but on the third day luckily I succeeded in doing so. Just before that Shackleton had asked me what distance, according to my dead reckoning, we had made towards Elephant Island, which he contemplated as a landing place. I had answered, "About thirty miles." When, however, I worked out my observations, I found to my horror that instead of having approached Elephant Island by thirty miles we were thirty miles farther away than when we had started! This was due to a tremendously strong east-running current pouring out of the Bransfield Straits and setting us back.

Shackleton ran his boat alongside mine and asked me what I made the position. When I told him he did not repeat it to the men, but merely said that we had not done so well as we had expected.

The whole responsibility of an expedition rests, of course, on its leader; but in spite of that postulate the next three days were the most terribly anxious ones of the whole enterprise for me; for my 'sight' had been taken in extraordinarily difficult conditions, being merely glimpses of the sun between the icebergs on a misty day; and had my calculations been wrong in any way, it would have meant that twenty-eight men would have missed the land and would have sailed out to practically certain death.

Owing to the news that I had given him Shackleton decided to make for the northern point of the Antarctic continent. We sailed on this course for some hours, and then found ourselves barred by lines of heavy pack-ice with the sea freezing all round us. The *Dudley Docker* towed the other two boats all night to prevent their bumping against one another. At daylight we saw that we had no alternative to resuming our course for Elephant Island. Meanwhile the wind and sea were rising; again there was no sleep that night—the third that we had been deprived of rest.

About two hours before dawn we were all shivering so badly that we huddled against each other for warmth, with the flimsy covering of the tent drawn over us to keep off as much of the chill blast of the wind as we could. We lay on the stores at the bottom of the boat, bunched together into a chaotic mass, and if one unfortunate bedfellow on the outer edge moved a little, thus allowing the bitterly cold wind to get under the canvas, his immediate neighbours would wither him with the most scorching language I have ever heard. After a little time, however, I felt that I had had enough of the discomfort of it, so I crawled out and, standing in the stern of the boat, lit a cigarette and surveyed the scene. Shortly afterwards Greenstreet followed me, and as we looked at the writhing tent and the extraordinary objects bumping about beneath it we burst into yells of uncontrollable laughter.

Shackleton and I held frequent conferences that day, shouting against the wind to make ourselves heard from our respective boats. He gave the order that, as nothing could be cooked, we were to eat as much as we wanted, to compensate for lack of sleep, warmth, and shelter. In my diary I wrote:

"Some are unable to take much advantage of this, owing to sea-sickness. I am sorry for these poor beggars, as it is bad enough to be stuck out here, jammed, crowded and huddled up in deep-laden boats, half-frozen and frost-bitten . . . without having sea-sickness added to it. However, our amusement is roused by the dismay of one man, who is fond of accumulating food, and now gazes impotently at us ravening wolves."

Our progress was slowed down considerably by the blocks of ice that came from all directions and which we had to pole off with the oars. In spite of all our care the *James Caird* got a hole in the bows, which the men patched up as best they could with sealskin. The intense cold seemed to have caught certain small fishes unprepared, for myriads were lying about on the surface of the sea encased in ice. (When sea-ice first freezes, its consistency almost approaches that of barley sugar in the making, so that these fishes must have stuck in it as it froze.)

On the 14th April there was a magnificent sunset, which, however, did not compensate us for being short of ice for drinking water. On this boat journey the floes were too broken up and washed over by the breaking seas for us to obtain fresh water from them.

Before dark we were terribly thirsty—so much so that we were unable to eat. We resorted to chewing some raw seal meat for the sake of the blood. This assuaged our thirst for the time being, but afterwards it became more acute than ever. To be unable to take our food was a serious matter, for the cold was intense. We were enormously cheered, however, by sighting Elephant and Clarence Islands. I recorded proudly in my diary: "They are both exactly on the bearings I had said they would be, and Shackleton congratulates me on the accuracy of my navigation under circumstances of difficulty and after two days of dead reckoning while working in and out amongst pack-ice with no accurate means of taking compass courses and also lying-to for two nights at the mercy of the winds and currents."

We sailed and pulled as hard as we could, choosing Elephant Island rather than Clarence, because the latter had a coastline that is even more unapproachable than that of the other island; and for a short time we thought that we should make our destination that night. But the wind hauled ahead and gradually strengthened into a gale. All that day I had towed alternately the *Stancomb Wills* and the *James Caird,* but as the weight of the wind increased, the *Caird,* being the larger boat, drew ahead of us. Shackleton, therefore, took the *Stancomb Wills* in tow.

We soon realised that we were not going to touch land that night after all. Driving snow-squalls and treacherous, lumpy seas—far more dangerous to our small deep-laden open boats than a big 'true' sea, with large regular swells which they could ride—bombarded us all night from various directions, one following the other, so that the boats could never settle down, and to steer became a work of art. The gale blew so hard that in spite of all our efforts the boats were separated. The last we saw of the other two was shortly after midnight, when Shackleton shone his compass light on the *James Caird's* sail, to which I replied by lighting our compass candle.

This was our fourth night without sleep; we suffered more cruelly than ever from thirst, and the cold pierced us in a way we had not experienced before, since our inability to eat, owing to parched mouths and swollen tongues, had lowered our vitality. We were so exhausted that every bone ached. Our discomforts were intensified by the boat's mad leaps and jerks. Frost-bite had added to our wretchedness. Nevertheless, the men bore up splendidly and did their best to appear cheerful, especially when I told them to get their pipes ready as soon as Greenstreet lit the candle. Before that we had not been able to smoke as we did not want to waste a match. Matches, of course, had always been valuable, and when we lost the *Endurance* they had to become communal property.

On this particular night Cheetham the third mate let his pipe go out in the height of the gale, and persuaded me to give him a match to himself. The others were so indignant at this that later, when misfortune had again overtaken his pipe and he tried to cadge another, I refused. Seeing how crestfallen he was, however, I had not the heart to keep one from him, and said, "Look here, I'll sell you one." "Right, sir," said Cheetham; "what price?" "A bottle of champagne," I replied, laughing in spite of myself. "Done, sir," he retorted; "as soon as I get back to Hull and open my little pub the champagne's yours." Unfortunately the debt was never paid, as poor Cheetham was killed in battle in the North Sea towards the end of the War.

All night long we struggled against the gale, too concerned with our own danger to worry much about the other boats. In the darkness we ran through a tide-rip which nearly wrecked us. Water poured into the boat from all directions, and we were kept hard at work bailing.

I had been steering unrelieved for eighteen hours, and the air was so thick with snow and spindrift that although we were close to the land we could see nothing of it. Added to this, continuous peering to windward, to avoid the seas that threatened to swamp us, had given me a cold in the eyes. I could no longer see properly, and was constantly falling momentarily asleep at the tiller. For some time Greenstreet had been urging me to let him relieve me, but I had refused until three in the morning. When I tried to get down among the men I was so cramped from my constrained position on top of the stores and from the seas breaking continually over me, that I could not move myself. I had to be straightened out before I could lie down. As the men were rubbing me to restore circulation I fell asleep. They then placed me under the meagre shelter of the tent, and I remained unconscious of anything until land was again sighted an hour later. Greenstreet then, wishing to know which way to steer, told the others to waken me, but their most strenuous efforts to do this failed. Finally one of them asked Doctor Macklin whether I were dead. After examining me he said that I was alive, and McLeod, an old salt, declared that he could wake me up, and succeeded in doing so by dealing two hearty kicks on the back of the head. I never knew how I had been awakened until Macklin told me three years later (1919), when we were in the Army together in North Russia, where we were serving with Shackleton, who had got us 'lent' to him by the Admiralty.

Our first glimpse of the coastline of Elephant Island showed us its utter lack of shelter and obvious inaccessibility—a sharp disappointment to us. We were now beset by a fresh danger. As we ran before the towering seas to get to the other side of the Island, where we hoped there would be shelter, each sea threatened to poop us. Added to this, there was the ever-present risk of capsizing, should the sail gybe in our efforts to keep clear of the cliffs.

At last we rounded a point and ran into comparatively smooth water. Passing the glacier-ends, we ran among lumps of fresh-water ice. The men leaned over the side and caught bits, and chipping off the salt with their knives, sucked joyously. I remember my own gratitude to Greenstreet, who scraped a block clean and handed it to me at the tiller, and the wonderful sensation of feeling the moisture oozing down my burning throat.

The sun came out, the water sparkled, and for a time the scene was one of peace. We felt that on Elephant Island we should find comfort and a measure of ease, and all were excited and happy. It is a fact, strange though it may seem, that the night had been so filled with the violence of our struggle that I had been unable to think about the other boats. I had fought against the elements until I had fallen into a sleep that was, virtually, a stupor; then on awakening the sight of land, the idea of relaxation, be it only for a brief spell, had caused a reaction to set in, and I was feeling a sensation of gaiety such as I had not experienced since the happy days back in the old *Endurance*. But at the height of

Elephant Island

my rejoicing at our safety the thought of the other boats came back to me, and once again I was a prey to misgiving. I knew that had the *Stancomb Wills* been caught in a tide-rip similar to the one we had come through, she would stand a smaller chance of coming through safely, for she was slightly shorter than the *Dudley Docker*.

*After landing on Elephant Island (*ROYAL GEOGRAPHICAL SOCIETY*)*

I kept an anxious look-out to seaward, but saw no sign of Shackleton's party. Meanwhile our own position was none too easy, for we were still exhausted and we had to skirt fourteen miles of coast to find a landing place. At ten in the morning, however, I sighted a low, rocky beach which promised a landing.

As we made towards it I saw to my amazement two small masts. The two other boats had arrived twenty minutes before us! We were so overjoyed that in spite of our exhaustion we managed three cheers.

Soon after we were hauling ashore the scant amount that was left of our stores, and dragging our boats on to what appeared to us a Promised Land. We did not know Elephant Island then—that it was nothing more than a gigantic mass of rock, carrying on its back a vast sheet of ice.

Of our adventures there, and of the undertaking that I was to share with Shackleton at no very distant date, I shall now tell.

On Elephant Island

"THANK God I haven't killed one of my men!" These were the words that Shackleton uttered as he led me aside for our first confidential talk on Elephant Island. Without waiting for me to answer, he went on, "And now, I need have no immediate anxiety about them."

His tone was one of relief, but there was a touch of grimness in it as he continued,

"I knew that one more night of exposure would do for some of them. And I was never more thankful in my life than when I saw you coming round the point."

As I looked at him I realised, with something of a shock, all that the ordeal had meant to him. His forehead was scarred with lines, his face was haggard, and his shoulders, so often hunched for battle, were now bowed as those of an old man. At that moment, in fact, he was an old man—aged by the suspense he had undergone, worn down by responsibility. Later, indeed within a few days, he threw off all these signs of mental stress, but at that moment, to one who knew him well, it was evident that anxiety for his party rather than physical strain had exhausted him. And as we scrutinised each other in silence for a moment I realised as I think I had never done before what a great man he was. He was not only the leader of a great expedition but a true brother and shipmate to each one of us, thinking of us always before himself.

"How did you get along last night after we separated?" I asked.

"Pretty rotten. The most anxious time, of course, was when you disappeared in the snow squall. When I flashed the little compass light to you and got no reply I thought you must have capsized."

"We showed a light," I told him; "but being to windward of you our sail must have been at the wrong angle to reflect it."

"If I had known that, it would have saved me a lot of anxiety," he commented.

Shackleton had always insisted that the ultimate responsibility for anything that befell us was his and his only. But until then I had not understood the painful seriousness with which he viewed his relation to us. My view was that we were all grown men, going of our own free wills on this expedition, and that it was up to us to bear whatever was coming to us. Not so Shackleton. His idea was that we had trusted him, that we had placed ourselves in his hands, and that should anything happen to any one of us, he was morally responsible. His attitude was almost patriarchal. True, this may have accounted in some measure for the men's unquestioning devotion to him, and it always seemed to me that they bore toward him the love of sons for a singularly noble father; but as we two stood talking on that bleak bit of rock that was Elephant Island, I found it difficult to bring myself to look at all this objectively. I could see only the harm that it had done to Shackleton by giving him a burden heavier than any man should be called upon to bear.

"What do you think of this place, Skipper?" he asked me at length.

"Any solid land is a godsend when we are so badly in need of rest and food," I answered. "But I've looked round a bit and—well, it's not much like the Riviera."

I was unwilling to talk seriously just then, for obviously Shackleton needed ease of mind and sleep before he began to plan again. Fortunately some penguin and seal were in sight. I pointed these out to him, remarking, "Plenty of grub, anyway." He laughed for the first time in many days, evidently (according to my shipmates) because I was displaying true form: my appetite had been a stock joke for months past.

"Grub on your mind again, Skipper?" he retorted with a chuckle, and I knew by the lightness of his tone that I had succeeded in concealing from him certain doubts concerning Elephant Island that were already troubling me.

As we walked slowly towards the beach I felt that I ought to tell him how we all appreciated his leadership and how grateful we were to him.

"Whatever happens," I muttered, "we all know that you have worked superhumanly to look after us."

"My job is to get my men through all right," he retorted, rather gruffly. "Superhuman effort isn't worth a damn unless it achieves results."

"Well, you've achieved something," I said, and pointing to the men on the beach, I remarked, "There doesn't seem to be much wrong with them."

As a matter of fact our shipmates, all of whom were elated at being on land again, presented a strange and somewhat weird spectacle. Some of them appeared to be dancing, but they were so weak that every now and then they fell, then picked themselves up with the exaggerated carefulness which one usually associates with intoxication. Perhaps they were intoxicated with sheer relief. Others were shying stones or trying to juggle with them. After six months in a desert of ice it was natural enough. But to me there was something unspeakably grim in the sight of grown men playing on a beach rather like children on the sands at an English seaside town, and I had a feeling that there would be a rude awakening. I suppose that my expression conveyed something of this to Shackleton, for he said suddenly:

"You look a bit doubtful about it all, Skipper. Don't you—" he paused for a moment before firing his question at me—"Don't you think it's going to be all right? Don't you think that we shall be able to stay here?"

I replied slowly: "Better here than on the pack-ice, anyway. At least we are somewhere, though it may be a devil of a place."

We did not continue the conversation. Instead, he looked at the black sea-battered cliffs and at the sheet of ice that towered above, and walked away, his jaw thrust forward and his shoulders hunched—a sure sign he realised that he would soon be battling once more against the elements that were so unfriendly to us.

A few moments later we were all at the exhausting task— exhausting because we were so enfeebled—of making camp. I will not go into details but will merely assert that owing to our condition it was a painful experience. We sheltered beneath a cliff one thousand feet high.

By the time we turned in that night Shackleton, Wild and I already knew for certain that we were in grave danger; and the danger was this. We were in a latitude that was gale-ridden, perhaps the most tempestuous area in the world. We were only just above the level of high-water mark. It was obvious that the seas of every on-shore gale would sweep that beach. With a thousand-foot cliff at our back there could be no escape landward. The probability was that we should be swept away without being able to launch a boat.

Two days later we took to the boats again and landed seven miles further west at the only spot we could find which looked safer. Even here we found that to sleep in tents was out of the question. One night was sufficient to prove that; for one of the gales which batter this island rose after we had turned in, and my tent was ripped in two. In fact my tent mates and I slept with the snow-covered canvas on top of us, which was only a shade better than having no covering at all.

We decided that the only thing to do was to try the experiment of living under an up-turned boat. But an up-turned boat does not offer much comfort, though at least it gave us a roof over our heads. This meant a good deal in a spot where the wind blew practically continuously, often with terrific force, bringing down blinding clouds of snow, and chunks of ice, knocking down those who were so unfortunate as to be caught by its full force, and hurling away whatever they held in their hands—cooking-pots or anything else that they happened to be carrying.

It is impossible to describe accurately the violence of the atmosphere of Elephant Island, the screech of the wind and the driving storms, the cannon-like reports of the glaciers 'calving' masses of ice as big as the dome of St. Paul's. Nor is it any easier to convey how nerve-racking was the sense of being pounded and struck at ceaselessly by forces which one could not grapple with, how maddening it was at times, even to weather-beaten men like ourselves.

We had other discomforts too. The cold seemed to penetrate to one's bones, and when the mercury rose above freezing-point the snow that covered everything would melt, soaking the men through and making everything they touched soppy, thus adding greatly to their difficulties.

The boat under which we lived was the *Dudley Docker*. She would have been blown away but for the precaution we took of weighting her down and building her in with rocks and blocks of ice, and filling in spaces with snow so that the wind could not blow under nor lift her. At one side an entrance was formed by a piece of canvas, rather like the flap of a tent, and this too was held in position by rocks and heavy pieces of ice. We had about five foot ten head-room in the centre, and from here it sloped down on either side. We drew lots for 'berths' and a few fortunate men secured the thwarts as resting places. These lucky ones collected the oars and some pieces of board and rested their sleeping-bags on them, and for ever after referred to them as their 'feathers.' These men, who were regarded as the aristocrats, were rather more comfortable than the proletariat, who slept on the frozen rocks and earth that formed the floor.

Our sole illumination was a dim and foul-smelling blubber lamp, which really only served to make the darkness visible. Since daylight in these regions in winter time is a cheerless grey twilight, this continuous lack of brightness affected us more than we were willing to admit.

The cooking was done over a blubber stove which our cinematographer, Hurley, had made from a five-gallon oil-drum. Over this there would be a pot containing seal or penguin meat, and as the cook, Green, attended to his job, great volumes of black, greasy smoke would pour out and almost stifle the poor wretch. Every two or three minutes he would rush from his 'galley,' which consisted of a small sail spread from the rocks to some packing-cases, coughing and gasping and wiping the tears from his eyes. Long before the meal would be ready he would resemble a very shiny darkie. Wonderful to relate, the grin never left his face. All of us were grateful to him, for under the most trying conditions he would always manage to scrape together some sort of a hot meal. Clark, the biologist, helped him to add variety to the menu by finding limpets. These Green stewed with sea-weed—a small russet-red species resembling dulse—which proved a splendid tonic and later was badly needed.

We had a curious sense of isolation at this time, for we knew that no living person would dream that we were stranded on Elephant Island. They would imagine rather that we were in the south of the Weddell Sea. Thus there was no hope of rescue. We were in a world of our own, we had only ourselves to look to, and the world was as completely cut off from us as though we had come from another planet. I have experienced a good many strange things in my time, but this sensation of detachment from the living world was one of the most memorable.

During the time we were drifting on the Polar ice I had worked out routes and distances to the various points to which we might have to make boat journeys for help. Naturally Shackleton and I had discussed these during our seemingly endless weeks of drifting. Once we had landed, however, it had been an understood thing that for the first few days at any rate we would not discuss the subject. There were several reasons for this. One was that although it would be for a brief spell only, we wanted to restore the spirits of the men by allowing them to believe that we were going to spend the winter in comparative safety. Another reason was that there were so many urgent matters to be attended to. All work was difficult to us since we had been so exhausted when we made land, and although work was unavoidable we wished to conserve our energies, and certainly we were not anxious to deal with any problem that could be postponed.

But the day dawned when Shackleton had to face the fact that he would not be able to feed his men through the winter. I remember that day. He asked me to walk with him to our usual look-out promontory, and there he confided to me his ever-growing anxiety.

"Skipper," he said, "we shall have to make that boat journey, however risky it is. I'm not going to let the men starve."

Knowing what his presence meant to the others I hoped that he would remain in temporary but comparative safety on land and allow me to go in his stead. So I said, "Would you let me take the boat?"

"No," he replied, sharply, "that's my job."

I told him that, after all, I had considerable experience in boating, surf landings and so on, and that in this respect I was really better equipped for the journey than he; but he stopped me by clapping me on the shoulder and saying, "Don't worry, Skipper, you'll be with me, anyway." It was useless to attempt to persuade him to change his mind, for it was an integral part of his character to refrain from delegating responsibility.

As we retraced our steps towards the camp, Shackleton turned to me suddenly. "It's hateful to have to tell the men that we've got to leave them," he said. He was obviously upset.

"It's their only chance," I muttered.

He paid no attention to me but went on:

"If things went wrong, it might be said that I had abandoned them."

"Nobody who knew you would ever say, or think, that," I declared. But he was not to be reassured.

When Shackleton assembled the men they saw at once by his grave looks that he had made an important decision. Each man had noticed and been alarmed by the impending shortage of food. Some had not kept their thoughts to themselves, but all such talk until then had been sternly repressed by Shackleton. Now he had come to the point when it was necessary to let them know everything. Gravely he explained the situation, and told them that he had determined to make a boat journey for help.

"I'm afraid it's a forlorn hope," he said, "and I don't ask anyone to come who has not thoroughly weighed the chances."

The moment he ceased speaking every man volunteered.

It was a dramatic scene and one that I am not likely to forget. On the island there was still safety for some weeks. The boat journey promised even worse hardships than those through which we had but recently passed. Yet so strong was the men's affection for Shackleton, so great was their loyalty to him, that they responded as though they had not undergone any of the experiences that so often destroy those sentiments. They were as eager to accompany him as they had been on the first of August, 1914, the day upon which we had sailed nearly two years before.

It must have been a great moment for Shackleton. There was a long and pregnant pause before he replied, and then he said only three words: "Thank you, men." I remember thinking that this was one of the finest and most impressive utterances I had ever heard.

Five of us were chosen: Tom Crean, Timothy McCarthy A.B., McNeish the carpenter, Vincent the boatswain, and myself.

At once we began to prepare the biggest boat, the *James Caird*, so far as was humanly possible. We knew that it would be the hardest thing we had ever undertaken, for the Antarctic winter had now set in, and we were about to cross one of the worst seas in the world. But in spite of our experience, in spite of our knowledge of the Southern Ocean, we little dreamed of the trials and dangers that were to confront us. I think that those who were to be left behind felt it more than we did, but they were ungrudging in their kindliness, and hid their emotions, encouraging us to the best of their ability.

The boat, which was twenty-two feet six inches long, with a six-foot beam, had had her gunwale raised ten inches by the carpenter while we had been drifting on the pack-ice. He had managed this feat by collecting bits of wood some months before from the wreck of the *Endurance*. Similarly a flimsy covering had been built over the forward half of the boat. This had been made from pieces of board, lids of boxes, sledge-runners and other oddments. We could not get enough, however, to cover the whole boat; we therefore sewed together pieces of old canvas and nailed it over this 'decking.' Before we could sew the canvas, which had frozen hard, we were obliged to put it into the blubber fire and thaw it, piece by piece. Greenstreet, the First Officer, distinguished himself at this job, which was an awful one. Despite frost-bitten and bleeding fingers, and breaking needles, his cheerful profanity never ceased, and the job was well done.

The *James Caird* was double-ended and carvel-built (she had been built to my orders). She was more lightly constructed than was required by the Board of Trade, and this made her springy and buoyant. To make room for the men and stores we took out the metal tanks that had been fitted into her when she was a lifeboat aboard the *Endurance*, and in order to make her as water-tight as possible, we caulked

Preparing the James Caird (*ROYAL GEOGRAPHICAL SOCIETY*)

Launching the James Caird (*ROYAL GEOGRAPHICAL SOCIETY*)

her seams with cotton lamp-wick. Usually one completes such a job with 'putty,' but of this, of course, we had none. Therefore Marston, the artist who had accompanied us largely in order that he might paint the snowy scenes of the Antarctic, used his oil colours, finishing off by smearing on some seals' blood! This worked out not too badly, and was probably the first time in history that an artist's colours were used for 'paying' a boat's seams.

The carpenter took the mast out of the *Stancomb Wills*, which was a smaller boat, and secured it the best way he could along the keel of the *James Caird* inside, so that in heavy seas she should not break her back. The *Stancomb Wills'* sail was cut down to form a mizzen for the larger boat. If we had had enough canvas I should have preferred to have had a bigger mainsail and have done away with the mizzen mast, which caused the boat to gripe to windward considerably, and, being a third sail, was a third source of misery to us when it got iced up and had to be stowed away.

We ballasted the boat with over a ton of shingle to prevent her capsizing in the big toppling seas. I must here relate an incident that illustrates Shackleton's broadness of mind. He and I were not in agreement about the amount of ballast. I wanted him to use only little more than half of the amount upon which he had decided, because the men and the stores would add nearly a ton; but, filled with a dread of being under-ballasted, he insisted upon having more than a ton. The result of this was that we were lower in the water than I liked to be. Later on Shackleton said to me: "Skipper, you were right. I made a mistake about the ballast. Had I listened to you, I think the journey would have been shorter, the boat wouldn't have been so stiff or so jumpy in her movements, and we should have shipped very few heavy seas. I'm sorry." Not every leader, after he had brought his men safely through, would have conceded that he had made even a small mistake.

As much as remained of our old blankets we sewed into bags, into which we put the shingle. The remaining ballast consisted of loose stones of various sizes, taken from the beach. The time was to come when we knew every corner of those accursed stones, for they cut and bruised us mercilessly as we crawled about on them. (Most of them we actually knew by special names—not geological!)

We took enough food to last us, we estimated, for thirty days. Melting glacier ice over the blubber stove we filled the boat's two breakers. In addition to this we put large blocks of glacier ice into both ends of the boat, for drinking water.

For six months we hadn't had a bath or a change of clothing. Despite this I think we might be said to have remained clean bodily, but our hands and faces would have disgraced any self-respecting tramp. Each wore a suit of heavy Jaeger underwear, an ordinary pair of cloth trousers (mine belonged to an old dress suit), a heavy Jaeger sweater, two pairs of woollen socks, Norwegian reindeer boots reaching nearly up to the knee, a pair of Shetland wool mittens on the hands, covered by heavy dogskin mittens, and on the head a woollen Balaclava helmet. Over and above all this was worn a suit of loose Burberry overalls, and a Burberry helmet. (Sea-boots and oilskins had gone long before.) These, although windproof, were unfortunately not waterproof. We took a little extra underwear with us in the boat from the very scanty store that was left, so that in a crisis, if it became necessary, we could get some additional warmth. This, together with some fuel and matches, the Primus stove, our six sleeping-bags, and Shackleton's rifle, completed our equipment, save for my navigating instruments and books. No, it did not quite complete it, for I had an idea that I was eager to try out. In the piercing Antarctic cold, with freezing waves breaking over us hour after hour, fats, of course, were essential to us. (In England I rarely eat fat, but out there I longed for it.) Therefore I persuaded Shackleton to let me take with us a couple of gallons of blubber oil, on the excuse that we might want to pour some on the sea. As a matter of fact we did try pouring it on the sea in a blizzard, but the cold prevented it from spreading, so that I was given my chance to suggest that it should be used in the way I really wanted—as food. It was an unappetising-looking mess I must confess, but when we were almost freezing it was a life-saver. I induced Shackleton himself to take some, although the black and greasy appearance of it revolted him, and afterwards in emergencies he took small quantities and doled it out to the men as a genuine treat, as long as it lasted.

We spent our last evening on shore under the up-turned boat. Conversation was carried on a bit longer than usual that night, for each one was secretly loth to part from his own particular chums. We all crowded together, making a great show of lightheartedness which we did not feel. We were practically in the dark, and the atmosphere was hazy, for we all smoked hard. Everybody was doing his best to laugh and joke, and I remember the guffaw that went up when one of the company remarked, "The boat's sure to be safe if the Skipper's in it. He wasn't born to be drowned." I must confess that it took some time before I realised the inference that I was born to be hanged!

Wild, I remember, seconded most ably by Greenstreet, exhorted me in touching tones to bring back lots of beer; while Macklin, the doctor, and my especial pal, swore fondly at me, just for the sake of making conversation. They tell me that I seemed cheery enough that night, and I am glad I appeared so, for I certainly did not feel it. I was haunted by a series of pictures which flashed across my mind, pictures of what would become of these men should our attempt fail. I looked on their faces, and although to other eyes, I daresay, those faces, grimy and bearded, would not have seemed handsome or lovable, I felt as though I could not get my fill of gazing at them; for there was a pretty big chance that I should never see them again. As Shackleton had already told them, ours was "only a forlorn hope." It is a dreadful thing to face your shipmates, men who have been through thick and thin with you, and to realise that in all probability it is for the last time; nor does it add to your serenity of mind to know that if you fail to come back they will starve to death. However, no one showed that these thoughts were at the back of his head—in fact most of the evening we discussed the things that we should do when we returned in a month's time.

In the morning our mood had changed. Everybody was solemn and quiet, and even Wild's usual admonition, "Lash up and stow," which, translated, means "Lash up your sleeping-bags in case you have to shift in a hurry, and come to breakfast," lacked its habitually cheery ring.

Shackleton was worried over young Blackborow, our stowaway, whose toes had been so badly frost-bitten during the escape from the pack-ice that there was danger of gangrene setting in. The two doctors, Macklin and McIlroy, had asked him to take their patient in the boat, in the hope that when we landed he would receive prompt medical attention, but Shackleton very wisely decided against this—thereby saving the boy's life without a shadow of doubt. A very sick man aboard our boat would have added considerably to our danger and to his own sufferings. All the same to leave him went sorely against the grain with Shackleton, and not even Blackborow's assurances that he understood the situation and had no desire to increase our difficulties or his own risk by coming with us consoled him.

As the work proceeded, some movement of the pack-ice outside must have taken place, for the swell suddenly increased. Big waves were beating against the rocky shore, and there was a dismal moan in the westerly wind that reminded me of another wind—the wind that had howled so ominously on the night when Shackleton had first told me that he believed we should lose the *Endurance* and find ourselves stranded on the Antarctic ice-field. I shivered at that sinister memory and, with a touch of the superstition that very often affects people far from civilisation, wondered whether it was a bad omen.

As we launched the *James Caird* she fell over in the surf, and threw McNeish and Vincent overboard. McCarthy and I stretched out oars and held them up, pushing them towards the men on shore, who pulled them to safety. Some of the shore party generously changed clothes with the drenched men so that the latter might start in a dry condition. Only those who have visited the Polar regions can appreciate the fineness of this action, for to get into dripping clothes in such circumstances is almost a martyrdom. Moreover, the men who put on those wet garments knew that it would be many a day before they were dry again. Actually, it was a fortnight.

The mishap in itself did not perturb me very much, but I was sorry that it should have been witnessed by those who were to be left on shore, for I knew that the psychological effect on them would be painful, and that it would increase their anxiety about us; also, it would add to their depression during our absence, more especially if the going proved slow and their wait in consequence a long one.

Perhaps the most trying thing for them would be the fact

The next sea rolled her over (ROYAL GEOGRAPHICAL SOCIETY)

The departure from Elephant Island (ROYAL GEOGRAPHICAL SOCIETY)

that they would be unable to get any news of us, and would not know for some time to come whether we had foundered or reached land safely, and for this reason alone I should have liked everything to go smoothly at the outset. Evidently this same thought struck Shackleton, for he had said to us, almost as soon as we got away, "I'm sorry they saw that stroke of bad luck. I hope they don't take it as an omen."

It was fortunate that they did not know of a second mishap which occurred immediately after the two men had been thrown from the boat. A point of rock that had struck her had driven the plug of the boat inwards, so that she was a third full of water. I got down and searched for the plug in the darkness under the canvas, but failed to find it; so I took a treasured possession—almost the last thing remaining to remind me that I had once been a civilised man: a handkerchief, now black with soot and grime—and jammed it in the hole with a marline-spike. We then bailed the boat dry, and, having made everything secure again, anchored her to receive the stores and ballast ferried out to us by the *Stancomb Wills*.

In hauling the water-breakers off, one of them bumped against a rock, and sea-water got mixed with the drinking water. We did not know this at the time, but it was an accident that later was going to cost us dear.

Shackleton had saved two cigarettes for a last smoke with Wild, and from the boat I watched him give Wild one, while reciting his final instructions. Shackleton and I had talked the situation over often enough during the past few days for me to guess that he was telling Wild what to do in case we never returned. I had managed to avoid saying a real 'good-bye' to the shipmates we were leaving. Shackleton couldn't. I watched him shake hands all round. It was the sort of thing that affected him more than actual danger or physical suffering, and must have been a painful experience. At last he clambered aboard the *Stancomb Wills*, shouted a final "Good-bye, boys!" and the crew rowed him out to us.

As soon as he was aboard the *James Caird* we cast off the painter, hoisted the jib and were off with all possible speed. The *Stancomb Wills* hung alongside for a couple of minutes, her crew wishing us luck and chaffing us, yelling to me to see that my chum Tom Crean behaved himself when he got ashore, openly pitying the "Boss" for having to stick to us; in short very gallantly pretending high spirits. Then we parted company. It was noon on April 24th, 1916.

The men ashore formed a pathetic group, waving to us and cheering Shackleton. We all cheered in reply, and as long as they thought that we could see them they kept up a wonderful appearance of optimism and heartiness. As we drew away from them the forlornness of their appearance as they stood out against the overhanging glacier front flanked with jagged crags of massive black rock was pathetically striking, and I felt that whatever hardships we might be called upon to face, we were the fortunate ones. Inactivity and uncertainty would come harder to men of the type of my shipmates than the unknown adventure that was before us. We had in fact started on the greatest adventure of our career.

The Boat Journey
Begins

OUR first problem was to find a way of breaking through the encircling line of pack-ice to the north of the island. For days I had been watching it from the promontory north of the camp, and I knew that a gap lay to the north-east. The boat ran a considerable risk of being smashed, for the sea was crowded with big lumps of ice that were being pitched about in all directions by the heavy seas; but by lowering the sails and using the oars to dodge in between we managed gradually to work our way to the open water beyond.

By that time darkness was falling. It was blowing strongly from the west, and sea after sea swept over the boat, running through the canvas and drenching us. In its way this was a disaster, for it meant that we should remain wet for the rest of the journey. Shackleton sent everyone other than myself 'below,' which meant into their sleeping-bags in the bows of the boat; and while they were getting what rest they could we steered throughout the night, talking in low tones. We sat huddled up together, Shackleton with an arm thrown round my shoulder as I steered, snuggling against each other for warmth and mutual shelter from the seas, talking as we had never talked before. Again and again we discussed the best point to make for, Shackleton emphasising once more that he wanted to get to the north as quickly as possible, even though the route might be lengthened, so as to avoid all danger of ice and to relieve us from the almost overwhelming cold.

"What do you think about Cape Horn?" he asked, adding, "it's the nearest."

"Yes," I replied, "but we can never reach it. The westerly gales would blow us away. With luck, though, we might fetch the Falkland Islands."

"I am afraid that, although it is the longest run," he re-marked, "we shall have to make for South Georgia, as you originally suggested. The gales will drive us to leeward." (South Georgia was the island, a thousand miles east of Cape Horn, that we had visited in the *Endurance* on our way south.)

At midnight Shackleton boiled some water and added milk powder to it, and as we sipped the scalding drink he fell into a reminiscent mood.

"We've had some great adventures together, Skipper," he said suddenly: "but this is the greatest of all. This time it really is do or die, as they say in the story-books."

I said, "Well, if you can't pull through, I don't know who can."

That cheered him up considerably, for he was like a boy in his enjoyment of a little praise. "You're right," he ex-claimed jubilantly, "of course we'll do it. Look how we have got through everything else." He paused, and then added, "I wish I had been able to explore further South, though. Still, we've got two hundred miles of new land to our credit, but when we get back, if the war's over, we'll have another go at it together, and try to get across the whole Antarctic Conti-nent. What do you say?"

I nodded and we devoted ourselves to the milk for a few moments, after which he broke the silence with, "Remember those thousands of seals that we saw migrating to the north? They knew better than we did, didn't they?"

"I've never met a seal with quite the pioneer spirit of a Shackleton," I replied, and he chuckled.

"Do you think there could be gold on the Antarctic Continent?" he demanded then.

I must add that Shackleton was as romantic as a schoolboy on the subject of treasure, and always believed that he was going to find untold wealth on his expeditions. Why, I don't know. There were never any signs of it. I think it made him feel happier to imagine that he was treading on mines of gold. I reminded him that years before I had found a pearl lagoon in the Pacific, and I said, "When we come out of this, let's make for it."

"Right!" he said inconsistently. "No more shivering on ice-floes for us. Palm trees and coral islands for us after this."

But immediately he reverted to the Antarctic Continent, which indeed seemed to have cast an almost uncanny spell over him.

"I wonder what we should have seen if we had been able to go a few miles deeper inland," he mused. "Perhaps the highest mountain in the world or a chain of volcanoes; or who knows what else?"

"A beastly lot of snow and a damnable lot of ice is probably all you would find," I retorted.

"After all, I did find coal at the Beardmore glacier," he remarked, reproachfully, and I was forced to concede that there might be something at the back of Shackleton's boy-like dream of riches.

"Well, Skipper," he said, coming back to the urgencies of our immediate situation, "you're right about making to the north for Cape Horn or the Falkland Islands first, because anyway that will take us clear of the pack-ice and out of this awful cold. Where we land eventually must depend on the winds that we get. We can't come to any further decision at present than to make north, and at all events we have got South Georgia on our lee to run to, if we fail to make the nearer points."

A few minutes later he said, "I wonder how the boys are feeling on the Island. Thank God they've got a good man like Wild to look after them."

I saw that he was beginning to get anxious again about the men from whom he was separated, so I said, "With a little luck, we may be getting them off in three weeks or so."

"As you know," he said, "I've always been dead against dividing the party; but now I've been forced to it. I don't like it; but since it had to be, it's something to know they're in good hands." He paused, and then spoke anxiously. "You know, half of those men are children and want more looking after than children would. Remember how you had to play nurse to Lees?"

This referred to one of our party who was so venturesome that Shackleton occasionally directed me to dry-nurse him, for fear he should get into danger. I could not help chuckling at the recollection.

"It's nothing to laugh at;" declared Shackleton. "Foolhardiness is the most serious thing in the world. That's one reason I've always liked to keep the men under my own eye."

"One of poor Wild's troubles will be to find sufficient occupation for them to keep them from being bored," he continued. "Suspense is bound to get on their nerves, and when that happens, they'll be difficult to handle."

"I reckon Wild can manage all right," I insisted; "and

anyway, we have enough of a job on our hands here without worrying about them. Besides, we'll probably have them off within a month."

I did not really think that we should make it as soon as all that, but on the other hand I certainly did not imagine that it would be more than four months before we should see our friends again. As we talked, Shackleton rolled cigarettes, a job at which I was unhandy, and we smoked and continued to yarn all night.

As dawn broke I became drowsy, and nodded as I steered. This annoyed Shackleton who, seemingly, could always go on yarning for twenty-four hours at a stretch, and he said in a disappointed tone, "You'd better go and get a sleep," and roused one of the others to take my place.

We had passed the quietest night that we were fated to spend on that eventful and truly dreadful journey, and as I dropped off to sleep I little dreamt of the sufferings that even then were close upon us.

At this time we were living on rations devised by Shackleton in conjunction with Sir William Beveridge, the Army Food expert. The principal item of our diet was a mixture that looked like a dark brown brick, which consisted of beef-protein, lard, oatmeal, sugar and salt. This was cooked over the Primus to a thick mixture resembling pea-soup. Every four hours in the daytime we had a meal of this, which we took scaldingly hot. Sometimes after this 'hoosh,' as Shackleton called it, we would have a half-pound block of Streimer's Nut Food, a food of the nougat type, extremely sweet, which however never cloyed our appetites down there. In between meals, if Shackleton thought that we needed gingering up in any way, he would suddenly issue a block of this or half a dozen lumps of sugar and a biscuit of an especially nourishing kind that he had had prepared for his sledging trips. It was a matter of principle with him to feed everybody to the greatest possible extent, so as to give them reserves with which to overcome the cold and wet.

At night, each fourth hour, Shackleton would see to it that we got a drink of hot milk. We trained our mouths and throats to drink it scalding hot, so that in addition to the nourishment we obtained we should benefit by the warmth thus engendered inside us.

It was due solely to Shackleton's care of the men in preparing these hot meals and drinks every four hours day and night, and his general watchfulness in everything concerning the men's comfort, that no one died during the journey. Two of the party at least were very close to death. Indeed, it might be said that he kept a finger on each man's pulse. Whenever he noticed that a man seemed extra cold and shivered, he would immediately order another hot drink of milk to be prepared and served to all. He never let the man know that it was on his account, lest he became nervous about himself, and while we all participated, it was the coldest, naturally, who got the greatest advantage.

Shackleton's popularity among those he led was due to the fact that he was not the sort of man who could do only big and spectacular things. When occasion demanded he would attend personally to the smallest details, and he had unending patience and persistence which he would apply to all matters concerning the well-being of his men. Sometimes it would appear to the thoughtless that his care amounted almost to fussiness, and it was only afterwards that we understood the supreme importance of his ceaseless watchfulness over things that, at the time, we had expected as a matter of course to be all right.

Soon after that night spent in talking to Shackleton a northerly gale sprang up and very nearly drove us back on to the pack-ice, which would have amounted, virtually, to a death sentence, not only upon ourselves but upon the waiting men marooned on Elephant Island. It was the thought of these waiting men, with nothing to do save wonder what would become of them and whether they were to leave their bones on that dreary rock that added to the painfulness of each of our adventures. We knew that a disaster to us would in all likelihood be fatal to them. One night, between the drunken lurches of the boat, Shackleton said to me: "Skipper, if anything happens to me while those fellows are waiting for me, I shall feel like a murderer!" I shared that feeling.

Before the northerly gale had struck us there had been a south-west gale, so that we had a heavy swell and a dangerous cross sea, which means two swells from different directions, running through or across each other. This found out our weak spots nicely, and the water came pouring through the canvas covering, down our necks and backs. We got wetter and wetter, and colder and colder, and gradually began to gauge the magnitude of the task that lay before us.

The least soaked portion of the boat was in the bows, and there we placed our sleeping-bags. This sleeping place was indescribably uncomfortable, for it was only seven feet long and five feet broad, tapering to nothing at the bows, and in this three of us had to pack ourselves on top of cases of food, sharp angular boulders and bags of shingle. On account of the stores beneath and the canvas cover above there was scarcely any room. In addition we had to crawl under the thwart to reach this wretched place, and it was an ordeal in our heavy, wet clothes; for we would often get stuck half way and lie there temporarily giving up the struggle, until the next man's head or shoulders bumping behind would remind one that two other poor devils wanted to get into their bags and snatch a little sleep. Although it may sound a small thing, it became such a horror to us that Shackleton himself arranged the order of the queue in which we crawled in and out of our sleeping-bags. I might mention that by the time that darkness had fallen on the second night, everyone save McCarthy and myself had been seasick, and even we felt squeamish from the extraordinary switchback leaps of the boat. Within the bows of the boat our unfortunate bodies were swung up and banged down on mountainous seas as we rushed up hills and plunged down valleys, shivering as we were slung from side to side of the boat; while to our imagination she seemed to wag like a dog's tail or flap like a flag in a gale of wind.

By the second night we had set watches, Shackleton taking one, and I taking the other, so at midnight I retired to my sleeping-bag. These bags consisted of reindeer skin with the skin outside and the hair within. They were a little bit longer than a man, about two feet broad at the head, and eighteen inches broad at the foot. There was a long slit down the front, covered by a flap of skin fastened by three toggles. When we turned in we undressed—that is to say we took off our boots. We slid half way down the frozen bag, kicked our feet together until we got some warmth into them, and then slid down a little further. Finally we would shoot right inside, in which position we were completely covered, once we had thrown the flap over and fastened it. Sometimes it would take a long time and considerable kicking to get up sufficient warmth to fall asleep, regardless of the fact that we were dog-tired.

When we had slept for an hour or so we would wake up half-smothered. More than once when I woke suddenly I was unable to collect my thoughts or realise where I was, and had the ghastly fear that I was buried alive. The sensation is one that can never be forgotten, for although the illusion is momentary one suffers indescribable horrors. There is one instant of sheer and terrible panic, when the nerves tingle and the hair stands on end. In the mental confusion that would occur before I was sufficiently awake to pull myself together I would recall every tale of premature burial that I had ever heard, even as far back as my childhood. I know that some of the others experienced similar sensations, for once I heard muffled groans and found that McCarthy in the next sleeping-bag was bumping about against me. I leaned over and freed his head from the bag, and he gasped his thanks to me for "saving his life."

The divided watches gave us three men each, all three taking turns at steering. As the journey progressed, our ideas of the size of the boat increased in an amusing but curious fashion, so that we even spoke of "taking a trick at the wheel," although actually we were steering by yoke-lines. We also spoke, without any consciousness of absurdity, of "going below" and "going for'ard" and "aft."

While one man steered for an hour the other two pumped the boat, which was always shipping and making water to a degree that occasionally became dangerous, and the rest of the time was spent in attending to the trim of the sails and in an endeavour to patch and make small improvements in our miserable and worn-out apparel.

Whenever possible I wrote a few rough notes in my navigation books. My fingers were so cold in making these notes that afterwards I found it almost impossible to read them. My most important duties were those of navigation. Each day at noon I set the course. I would calculate the progress we had made during the last twenty-four hours, but for the first two or three days I was very wide of the mark. This was only natural though, on account of the erratic course of the boat during the night and because I had

only two candles, one of which I was saving for the dangerous time of making the land at South Georgia. In the night,
therefore, we steered by the feel of the wind, and by observing the angle at which the little pennant at our masthead
blew. Another disturbance to the compass was due to the
fact that the iron plunger of the pump was repeatedly working up and down within a few inches of it.

After a few days of this particular type of navigation,
however, I became so adept at it that I got some surprisingly
correct results. On the rare occasions when I got an observation of the sun I had to kneel on the thwart to use my sextant, with two seamen holding me up, one on each side,
gripping me tightly to prevent the violent motion of the boat
heaving me bodily overboard, sextant and all. As I made the
observation Shackleton, beneath the canvas covering of the
boat, would take the time by the chronometer. This
chronometer, by the way, was the sole survivor in working
order of twenty-four with which the *Endurance* had left England two years previously. It was a valuable one, and a few
months after the boat journey, when I was boastfully showing it to friends, Shackleton said jokingly,

"You're very proud of the old chronometer, Skipper.
Would you like to have it?"

"Rather," I answered, and with typical generosity he said,
"Very well. It's yours."

The pumping, which we were often obliged to carry on
day and night, was a hateful job. We had made the pump
from parts of the compass of the *Endurance*. One man with
bare hands had to hold the brass tube hard down to the bottom of the boat, while the other man had the less detestable
task of working the handle up and down. A third man
caught in our cooking-pot the water thus pumped, and emp-
tied it overboard. The man who had to hold the tube with-

out mittens invariably became chilled to the bone by the stream of icy-cold water which came up through the pump, some of which also ran down over his hands. To make it a little less difficult, the operators would change places every five or six minutes. Towards the end of the watch one man would light the Primus stove, and fill the bowl with ice, melting it down in readiness for Crean to cook the 'hoosh.'

There is a tiny hole in the nipple of a Primus stove which must be kept clear or else the flame will not burn. To ensure this a thin wire pricker has to be pushed down the hole—a very difficult operation in a small boat jumping about in a seaway. There was so much dirt and stuff in the boat that the hole frequently got clogged up, and so became a source of great trouble. Crean and I were the cooks, or rather Crean was the 'chef' and I was the scullion. We each put our backs against our respective sides of the boat and extended our feet, with the Primus jammed between them in the middle. We chose this position because it saved the pot from being dislodged when the boat threatened to stand on her head, as she frequently tried to do.

On the Primus I held the hoosh pot, into which Crean broke up lumps of ice. When these melted Crean added the hoosh, which he stirred until it was boiling. Meanwhile I held the pot, and in response to the wilder leaps of the boat, carefully lifted it up and then set it back with great caution, so that none of the precious contents was spilt. Although this normally would have been a tedious job, all hands took the keenest interest in it—an interest almost painful to see; for all our thoughts centred constantly on the next hot meal. The moment that Crean would yell "Ready" a ring of aluminum mugs was formed round the hoosh pot, into which Crean distributed the food, taking care that everybody had an equal amount. The hands of all of us were scarred with frost-bite, but Crean's and mine, in addition, were marked with burns from the Primus.

All this time the seas were very big, augmented by the intensity of the gales. Under the cheerless grey sky the water assumed a leaden hue. Not a speck of colour anywhere broke the monotony: sea and sky were a monochrome, the only relief to the sombre scene being the breaking seas. Every swell that rushed towards us hid the horizon astern and towered, an over-arching wall, above us. As the sea broke all round us the boat was lifted dizzily upwards, and we would heel over to the force of the gale. At these moments we could see for miles in all directions—but we saw nothing but grey, grey, grey—an unending series of grey hills and grey valleys. The dominant noises were the whistle of the wind through the sails and the shrouds, and the roar of the crashing seas.

To all intents and purposes we were getting soaked on an average every three or four minutes. The action of the sea is too irregular always for any statement to be true of it all the time, but with few exceptions each hour saw us get about fifteen wettings. The gales which blew continuously in that fearsome climate were responsible for it, and the procedure was something like this. A great sea would break over us, pouring water in streams over everything and making us feel for a moment or so that we were under a water-fall. Then, before the next wave would break, we would get several minor seas that would just manage to cover the boat and wet us again. This went on day and night. The cold was intense. The dry icy chill that we had experienced on the pack-ice and on that dreary rock Elephant Island was nothing in comparison. That had seemed to us dreadful, but it could be fought. Now we experienced a penetrating cold, a cold that seemed to freeze our insides and against which we could put up practically no resistance.

Gradually the constant soaking caused our legs and feet to swell, turn white, and lose all surface sensibility. I devised a system which brought us some small relief, however, when I found this condition almost unendurable. I would take off my Finneskoe boots and the two pairs of socks beneath and rinse these in the sea, wring them out, and with them rub off as much moisture as possible. Then, while the socks were still damp, but not dripping, I would put them on again. Often this brought comparative warmth that would last an hour. Soon all of us were doing it, and despite the unpleasantness of exposure to the biting air, and of dipping one's hands into the water and then having to go through the performance of putting on one's things with stiff, chilled fingers, everyone of us was so anxious to get relief at any cost that nobody hesitated to follow my lead. Shackleton described the numbness of our legs and feet as 'superficial frost-bite,' and assured us that soon after landing they would get better; actually I have reason to believe that our condition was something similar to 'trench feet.' He was very wise, in my opinion, to reassure the men against the ever-present fear that they might lose the use of their limbs, or even the limbs themselves, through frost-bite.

So deadened were our nerves by the cold that one day, I remember, while one of the men was wringing out his socks as I have just described, one of the others, apparently as a bit of horse-play, stuck a Primus pricker into his big toe. The man, who was looking over the side and gripping his socks tightly as they swirled in the water—there was, of course, some risk of their being carried away, and we all guarded carefully against this—was quite unconsious of the fact that his skin had been pierced. The joker made two or three more jabs, and the victim still felt nothing. It was not until the pricker touched him close beneath the knee that he protested.

At this time we were about a hundred and fifty miles from Elephant Island, and that day we made a fine run of eighty-three miles. In the afternoon, Shackleton, yarning with me, said,

"Do you think she'll do it all right now?"

I replied, "She's a grand little sea-boat, and I'm sure she'll do it."

That heartened him, and he asked me how many miles I reckoned we had still to cover.

"About six hundred," I said, "and, with luck, we ought to do that in about eight days."

"Luck!" he exclaimed; "Skipper, you're right. A lot depends on luck."

I happened to glance at the sky to windward and saw a heavy, dark squall bearing down upon us, and I did not feel quite so sure of our luck. I felt that more depended upon our determination even than upon our luck—determination and prudence, of course, and I was thankful at that moment that Shackleton was (paradoxically enough) an exceedingly cautious man. It may sound fantastic to call an Antarctic explorer of his calibre cautious, but I claim that it was true of him. He was brave, the bravest man I have seen, but he was never foolhardy. When necessary he would undertake the most dangerous things, and do so fearlessly; but always he would approach them in a thoughtful manner and perform them in the safest way. He was proud of his reputation for carefulness, and therefore, that afternoon, I chaffed him by addressing him by the nickname that he had won on his first expedition, that of 'Cautious Jack,' which tickled him immensely.

"I wish there were some means of keeping the men warm," he remarked.

"Oh, you're a good daddy to us," I said, "except that you don't air the sheets or see that we get hot baths!"

"I'm not worrying about hot baths," retorted Shackleton in a less jocular fashion than I had anticipated. "My problem is hot drinks. I only hope that the cooking fuel lasts out to South Georgia. What our life would be on this boat without hot drinks I dare not imagine."

The morning after this conversation the wind came clear from the south, and we could tell from its intense cold that it was blowing straight off pack-ice not very far away. All that day we ran north before it, increasing our distance from our old enemy the pack-ice. It had been a constant anxiety to Shackleton and myself that a northerly gale might have lasted long enough to blow us back on to the ice.

Before dark the seas increased so tremendously that, urged by Shackleton's caution, I got the sea-anchor ready, and we hove-to for the night. This averted the danger of running before such a sea in the darkness; but although we recognised that this measure was necessary, we realized, too, that it involved a serious loss of time. Our state of mind was always one of perturbation, for we had to maintain a constant balance between cautious seamanship on the one hand, and, on the other, the ever-impelling urge for haste, both for the sake of the men on Elephant Island and on our own account.

As we lay hove-to with our sea-anchor out, the heaviest of the seas broke over us, despite the fact that the sea-anchor enabled us to a certain extent to ride the waves. The cold became so bitter that some of the water froze as it struck the canvas covering of our over-weighted boat. At that moment we did not realise that the zero temperature might bring with it dangers other than those of intense suffering. Nevertheless, as we rode the sea a casing of ice was forming on top of the boat. Wave after wave broke over us, at first pouring through the slightly turtle-backed canvas and rushing down our necks and backs as usual. We were so accustomed to it that we paid little attention: indeed we had come to regard these drenchings as part of our daily existence and had got rather beyond feeling irritation at discomfort; but after we had been there for an hour or two we noticed that there was a decrease in the violence of the cascades of water pouring in from the top. Soon we were getting only little drops—a change that was perhaps the most agreeable thing (so we thought then) that had happened to us since that fateful morning when we had set out from Elephant Island. At first we could hardly believe that anything so wonderful had happened. Actually we were sitting there and not getting drenched.

Our relief may be imagined when I explain that ever since we had got into the *James Caird* we had been forced to sit in the most uncomfortable and cramped positions, because there was literally no room in which to sit upright, let alone stand. So bowed were we that we had all experienced difficulty in taking our food, since our stomachs were compressed, and although we leaned first to one side and then to the other as we ate, we got little ease. More uncomfortable, however, than the cramping of limbs and compression of digestive organs was the effect of moving after a wetting. A little air would then get between our bodies and our sodden clothes, and the latter would flap with icy wetness against our skins, making us even colder. Directly a wave had hit us we would huddle for a few seconds, and the clothing would take the warmth of our bodies. But nobody can sit absolutely still for long, and in any case we had so much work to do that we were on the go most of the time, and at each movement we would get the full effect of the cold wetness of our garments.

Naturally when the waves ceased to come through the canvas we were free from this unpleasant inconvenience, and the relief was great. We then grasped the fact that ice must have formed on the covering and were in high spirits at the thought that for a time at least we should have respite from the misery of the Antarctic waves washing their way every two or three minutes to our chilled, half-frozen skins. True, we guessed that as soon as we struck a warmer latitude, which would be, we hoped, within a couple of days, the ice would melt and we should once more be subjected to soakings in the old style; but our circumstances were so bad that we had learned to live entirely in the present. A few hours' relief in such conditions as we were struggling against was like the promise of ten years' happiness to men living in the civilised world. The prospect of even one night free from those terrible wettings appeared to us almost as a glimpse of paradise.

Shackleton, delighted, cried, "No watch to-night, boys. There's nothing to watch—no bergs, no ships and nothing to trouble us. So we'll all go to sleep while we are hove-to; nothing can happen to us." He looked at us all, and appreciating how tired and worn out we were, said in his fatherly way, "I want you all to get a good sleep."

It must have been about nine o'clock when Shackleton said this, and by ten or thereabouts we were all sound asleep; but towards three o'clock in the morning we awoke. I don't know who woke first, but I do remember that within a few minutes we all seemed to be stirring and that a feeling of uneasiness seemed to have communicated itself to every man aboard. Not a word was spoken as we turned out of our sleeping-bags and put on our boots, but every one of us had a strange conviction that something was wrong.

The movement of the boat seemed unfamiliar. Her movements were laboured as she climbed the rollers. She seemed to lack buoyancy. Usually there was a good deal of water washing about amongst the ballast. Now, because the seas had not been pouring into her from above, there was much less. Yet despite this she seemed to us heavier. To our experienced senses there was a palpable and sinister difference in this dragging movement. To free her of water we pumped her dry, which took us only ten minutes. Still she did not respond. We knew then that our first feeling as we awoke had been correct, and that there was something very wrong with the boat.

As I finished pumping aft Shackleton crawled out and came and stood next to me in the gap of the decking. (By 'decking' I mean the canvas covering.) With the icy wind stinging our eyes we peered forward into the darkness, and saw that the hull of the boat was enveloped in a heavy sheet of ice.

"We must get rid of that sharp," said Shackleton emphatically. "It's sinking her."

And in fact with this ice accumulating upon her she was getting not only top-heavy but lower and lower in the water, so that she was in equal danger of filling and foundering, and capsizing.

Then began the ordeal—it was nothing less—of freeing her from the ice. While one man, standing in the gap of the decking, picked with a knife at the ice breast-high in front of him, another man undertook the hazardous task of cutting a hand-hold and a foot-hold in the ice on top, and then, with nothing more to depend upon than these slight indentations, crawled up on the slippery mass and, with the boat bucking about all the time, chopped away at the encumbrance. No one could stand it for more than four minutes at a stretch since the contact with the ice practically paralysed one. But as each man fumbled his way back into the boat another took his place.

The object of this book is to describe the human side of our adventure. The point therefore deserves labouring. The reader may imagine for himself the difficulty and the peril of that climb in the darkness up that fragile slippery bit of decking, and the descent back into the boat. Had one of the men lost his grip—a not unlikely thing, considering that our hands became frost-bitten within a minute or two as we worked—he would inevitably have slithered overboard and the united efforts of the others to save him would in all likelihood have been in vain. Once, as the boat gave a tremendous lurch, I saw Vincent slide right across the icy sheathing of the canvas, and, horror-stricken, I threw myself forward instinctively to help him, only to find that he was beyond my reach. Fortunately he managed to grasp the mast just as he was going overboard. I recollect even now that in the momentary relief of seeing that Vincent was safe I felt the blood rush to my head. Furious with him, I yelled at him to "come in and give somebody else a chance." I know now why mothers invariably spank their lost children on recovering them. And whenever, since then, I have seen a Polar bear cuff her cub for wandering away, I have sympathised with her sincerely.

We had another anxiety too. An unlucky blow with knife or axe might go right through the canvas, which would add immeasurably to our danger by letting more water into the boat, to say nothing of the additional exposure it would mean. The decking was our only protection against the breaking seas and the searching wind.

After two hours of this damnable work we had removed the bulk of the dangerous top-weight. The *James Caird* had risen again and was riding the seas with her old buoyancy and swing. We felt that all immediate danger was over; but we knew that it was only an interlude of peace, for unless the wind shifted the same thing was pretty certain to happen again. The work had chilled us to the marrow: some of us were shivering uncontrollably. Never were men more grateful than we were to Shackleton for the boiling drink that he and Crean had prepared and which brought with its glorious heat new life into numbed and exhausted bodies.

It was now dawn—a dawn that broke with a hail squall and wind that blew more fiercely than ever. The few miserable rays of light that penetrated the gloom served only to accentuate the wretchedness of our condition. Shackleton, seeing that we all needed gingering up, told Crean to relight the little Primus cooker, so that we could sit round it and talk and smoke for a bit.

If you light a Primus stove in an ordinarily heated room you will notice very little difference in the temperature; but even the small amount of heat that it threw out, and the slight diminution of bitter cold that resulted, was of psychological value to us, for it gave us the impression that we were warm, consequently comfortable, and, to go a little further, comparatively happy. For two hours we smoked, yarned and coughed in the acrid fumes of the Primus, until the three men who had got into their sleeping-bags dozed off. Then, the stern necessity of conserving our fuel being ever present, the Primus was put out.

In the afternoon of that day, when the gale had freshened more than usual, we had to repeat the job of clearing the canvas of ice. I noticed that it was more trying to watch the other fellows go up than to do it yourself. When your own turn came you felt better than when you were merely an onlooker watching the most nerve-racking exhibition that any of us had ever seen.

The oars lashed outside on the decking were catching the spray and holding up masses of ice. Shackleton decided that we should have to part with all but two; so the rest of them were thrown overboard, and a trying moment it was when they splashed over into the sea; for we all knew that we might need those oars badly in days to come. The remaining two were pushed with some difficulty inside the boat.

By this time the sleeping-bags had been wet for so long that they had become just sodden masses, and Shackleton decided that, in order to relieve the boat of their weight, two of them should be thrown overboard. This was a drastic step to take, for it left us with four sleeping-bags to six men. However, as three were always on the watch while the other three slept, it did not matter much. We also had the advantage of crawling into a sleeping-bag slightly warmed by the previous occupant instead of into a stiff and frozen covering. Why anybody should look upon such a wretched bit of sodden wetness, hairy and chill, as a home I really don't know, but the fact remains that we all did, and I can remember even now the sad expression of two of the men as they watched their sleeping-bags floating away. They looked as if they had now lost the last thing on earth that mattered.

That evening the gale was still too heavy for us to run before it, so we remained riding to the sea-anchor. A great cake of ice had formed on the bows of the boat, and this chafed through the rope, with the result that we suddenly lost the sea-anchor. This was a serious matter as the boat immediately fell off into the trough of the sea, and had she been allowed to remain like this she would have rolled so violently that she would either have filled herself or have foundered under a heavy breaking beam sea.

Thus, right on top of the task of clearing the ice from the canvas we had the unpleasant work of first beating the ice off the jib and then crawling out on the canvas covering and hoisting the jib abaft the mast. The risk of slipping overboard was still present, though not so great as when the ice had formed a thick crust. As soon as we had accomplished this the boat again lay up to the wind, and we were in comparative safety.

A bad day.

That night we were so exhausted that Shackleton again had the Primus lamp lighted for a few hours. And in the early morning we found that the ice had formed a third time on the canvas decking, although, owing to the absence of the oars, more slowly than had been the case previously. Once more we had to go through the hateful work of removing it. The one bright feature of the situation was that the wind was dying down, the snow squalls were less frequent, and although the swell was still big, the sea was decreasing rapidly.

CHAPTER VII

We Reach South Georgia

ON the 30th April we set sail for South Georgia once more. That day turned out to be very fine, and we revelled in the unusual glow of sunlight. I took a sight and found that the distance we had covered from Elephant Island was three hundred and eighty miles, which was cheering. We also had the opportunity of hanging our sleeping-bags against the mast, so that a few rays of the sun might play on them and make them a little drier. Altogether things seemed to be brightening up a bit.

Such is the deceptive way of the Southern Ocean. Next day a gale was blowing again, and continued for three days. We were now assailed by a new torment. Owing to their continued wetness our Finneskoe boots and, worse still, our sleeping-bags, began to moult. The boots, which had become just soggy bits of repellent-looking grey skin, ceased to give protection to the soles of the feet. When we stood up to steer the boat we might as well have been wearing socks only.

This was as nothing, however, compared with the

discomfort caused by the moulting of our sleeping-bags. The hair penetrated everywhere. It got into our eyes, noses, and mouths when we wanted to sleep, making us splutter and sneeze and cough. It washed about under the ballast and choked the pump (which was, of course, essential to the safety of the boat) and forced upon us the unpleasant task of clearing it. It even got into the hoosh. One day while Crean was stirring the hoosh, all eyes as usual being turned on him, he suddenly stopped stirring and peered intently into the cooking-pot. A shudder of apprehension ran through us at any threat to our vital food. Next moment his great hairy grimy paw shot into it, and he triumphantly abstracted a handful of reindeer hair. Having carefully squeezed this over the pot so as to get all the hoosh out of it, he threw it away. We couldn't help dirt, but we did draw the line at eating hair.

I look back at this period as the worst that I have endured. None of the graver and bigger dangers ever caused me, personally, the torment inflicted by that ghastly moult. The thing irritated me to the point of fury, and it was infuriating also to realise that one was wasting one's precious energy in being angry. But it seemed so malignant on the part of Fate to intensify our miseries by causing hairs to tease our every nerve, baulk us when we wanted to sleep and defy us to eat the food that was life itself to men placed as we were. We never got rid of the hairs, each one of which seemed to me to assume a baleful entity of its own and crawl like a live thing, with malice aforethought, into everything I touched, ate, or wore, until we landed.

The one bright feature was that on the eighth day after we had started, in spite of all the set-backs and misfortunes that we had experienced, we had accomplished rather more than half the distance. It is a curious thing but common to seamen that when they have accomplished the first half of a difficult journey they feel that the job is almost as good as done. They argue "What we have already done, we can do again." Of course this may be fallacious, but that does not alter the feeling. In fact the only compensation we had in the days that ensued was the sense of achievement in reducing the miles that lay between us and South Georgia.

The chafing of our hands and knees as we crawled over the stones used for ballast was becoming worse. We now had raw and often bleeding surfaces, and our thighs were exceedingly sore from the constant rubbing of the briny clothing against our wet flesh. Shackleton to our distress, developed sciatica. He had made a gallant attempt to conceal it from us, but I noticed one day that his position was unnatural and strained, so I asked him what was the matter. He was in acute pain, and our powerlessness to do anything for him made us feel our situation all the more. He had enough to face without this added suffering. It was characteristic that his only concern was lest it should make him less efficient, and therefore less useful to us. Fortunately it seemed to leave him as we got nearer South Georgia, or possibly he was more successful in disguising it; I have never been quite sure which.

One night at midnight, when it was blowing hard from the north-west with a heavy cross sea, Shackleton, who was steering, saw a long line of white to the south-west. He shouted, "It's clearing, boys!" But next instant he cried out in alarm, "Hang on for your lives!" What he had taken for a clearance in the south-west was in fact a huge breaking sea—almost a tidal wave. We were very nearly swamped. We seized bowls and dipper, and worked hard at the pump. Everything loose was floating about in the water-logged boat. It was fifteen minutes before we felt safe again. Possibly this great wave was caused by the capsizing of some huge berg unseen by us in the darkness.

The next few days and nights we spent in ceaseless war with strong gales and heavy seas, but nothing startling occurred until we came to broach our one remaining breaker. It was on the eleventh day that we broached this, now our sole supply. We found that salt water had got into it.

I knew then that this must have happened when we were hauling it off through the surf from Elephant Island, but alas, my knowledge had come too late. Had I found it out in time we could have delayed our sailing to refill it. As though this were not bad enough, the wretched reindeer hairs got into this brackish water too. The stuff was not dangerous to drink, but the curse of it was that it made us thirstier. Naturally this irritated us, so that we were in no very good humour when we had to take a piece of gauze from our tiny box of medical supplies to strain out the hairs as well as some sediment that had got in.

On the thirteenth day we were getting nearer to our destination. If we made the tragic mistake of passing it we could never retrace our way on account of the winds and currents, it therefore became essential that I should get observations. But the morning was foggy, and if you cannot see the horizon it is impossible to measure the altitude of the sun to establish your position. Now, the nearer your eye is to the surface of the sea, the nearer is the horizon. So I adopted the expedient of kneeling on the stones in the bottom of the boat, and by this means succeeded in taking a rough observation. It would have been a bold assumption to say that it was a correct one; but it was the best that I could do, and we had to trust to it. Two observations are necessary, however, to fix your position, and my troubles were far from over; for at noon, when I wanted to observe for latitude, I found conditions equally difficult. The fog, which before had been on a level with us and therefore did not altogether obscure the sun, had now risen above us and was hovering between the sun and ourselves, so that all I could see was a dim blur. I measured to the centre of this ten times, using the mean of these observations as the sun's altitude.

With serious misgiving I worked out our position and set my course by it to sight South Georgia, near King Haakon Sound, the next day. I spent anxious hours that night, wondering whether we should make a landfall, and if so at what point. The fact that I had been able to take only four observations since leaving Elephant Island added to my perturbation. Weather conditions had made it impossible to get any more.

Next forenoon we sighted kelp drifting, which I hoped might have been torn off South Georgia, and soon after that we saw two shags, birds which, as I reminded Shackleton, were hardly ever found more than fifteen miles from land. Happily my calculations proved correct, for at one o'clock in the afternoon we saw the peaks of South Georgia straight ahead. It looked nearly as uninviting as Elephant Island.

As we came closer to the land the short winter's day was drawing to its end, and in many directions we saw blind rollers, indicating shoals, and breaking seas, pointing to reefs. I was anxious to sail on into King Haakon Sound, which lay ahead of us, even at the risk of landing in the dark; for instinct told me that there was dirty weather ahead and that if we did not take this opportunity we might find ourselves in worse plight. Shackleton, however, considered that the risk of going on amid the reefs was too great, especially in view of the blind rollers that we had seen. Blind rollers above shoals are more treacherous than deep sea waves. One huge undulation follows another, the size and steepness being increased by the shallowness of the water, until one roller bigger than the rest at last breaks, leaving acres of foaming sea. Any vessel caught in these undulations drives forward with the speed of a railway train, until, swept broadside on to the sea, she is rolled over and over.

We therefore stood out to sea to gain a safe offing for the night, and thus lost sight of the land. We were painfully thirsty, owing to the brackishness of the last few drops of water; but we knew now that since we were so near land it would be a matter only of a few hours before we could drink our fill. We were therefore greatly cheered. Unhappily we were to undergo further ordeals before we touched the land.

In the morning the wind shifted on shore and increased to a gale of the most extraordinary violence. None of us had ever seen anything like it before. We found ourselves suddenly in the thick of a struggle against elements that seemed to have been loosed from the infernal regions. We were in a welter of screaming winds that seemed to be rushing all round us with the speed of an aeroplane, and every few seconds the roaring seas dashed into the boat and sent up spray sufficient to thicken the air for a hundred feet above us. Our position was rendered more critical by our nearness to a lee shore: the wind was blowing us straight on to an iron-bound coast. It was impossible to sight the land, but we knew that it could not be very far off, and with an anxiety even more acute than that with which we had looked for it, we now hoped to avoid it.

Every exertion that we made increased our thirst. We were unable to cook anything as we had no water with which to do so. We could not therefore prepare a hot meal—our one defence against cold, wet and exhaustion. We peered constantly down wind through the murk of the storm, fearing that each hour would bring us nearer to the cliffs, and meanwhile we bailed or pumped continuously.

At about one o'clock, when we had been in this hell's de-light for ten hours, we saw, looming up through the spin-drift, a towering black crag. As therefore we were rapidly driving into a position of the greatest danger it was obvious that at all costs we must try to beat to seaward. To do this it was necessary to get some sail up. The mainsail, reefed to a rag, was already set, and in spite of the smallness of the reefed jib and mizzen it was the devil's own job to set them. Usually such work is completed inside of ten minutes. It took us an hour.

In striving to claw off the shore the boat struck the seas with a series of shocks as though she were beating herself against stone walls. One could hear the thud of the impact, as though the sea had been solid, every time. The bow-planks on each side opened and closed, so that long lines of water squirted into her. She was soon leaking all over from the tremendous strain, and this, added to the seas which swept continuously over us, filled the boat to such an extent that three men working the pump were not enough. Two men had to bail at the same time as the others were pump-ing. Only by strenuous efforts did we prevent the boat from foundering beneath us. The sixth man steered, and we took turns in changing rounds.

Yet in spite of every effort the gale and the sea were too much for us; we were rapidly driving inshore. Soon we could see the coast distinctly, and presently our position had grown so bad that it seemed inevitable that we should be wrecked. With alarming rapidity we were being forced nearer and nearer the great cliffs and glacier fronts against which a dreadful sea was battering.

At such a time, no matter how occupied with vital work every second may be, one's mind is peculiarly active. I re-member my thoughts clearly. I said to myself: "What a pity. We have made this great boat journey and nobody will ever know. We might just as well have foundered immediately after leaving Elephant Island." Then I thought how annoying it was that my precious diary, which I had been at such pains to preserve, should be lost too. I don't think that any of us were conscious of actual fear of death. I know that I did have, however, a very disagreeable, cold sort of feeling, quite different from the physical chill that I suffered. It was a sort of mental coldness. I felt, too, a sharp resentment that we should all be going out in such a way, and in sight of our goal, especially Shackleton. The recollection of the men on Elephant Island added a background of bitterness.

As we were being driven towards the coast, darkness set in. A new danger now threatened. We were bearing down straight towards a small island, Annenkov, standing off the coast. Behind it we could see reefs, and according to our imperfect chart these stretched across to the mainland. We knew that if we could not keep to windward of it the surf would dash us on to the reef. But after peering for a minute or two into the darkness at the black rocks and white slopes of the Island that now seemed to be towering almost above us, I said to Shackleton,

"She'll do it."

Said he: "Of course she will. She's damned well got to."

Probably neither he nor I believed it. But it did us good to cheer each other up.

We were actually on the outskirts of the backwash from the rocks, with a tremendous surf just alongside of us, when the wind suddenly shifted ahead. Some strange freak of a current then swept us slightly away from the island. It was easy then to avoid getting the boat wrecked on Annenkov, but we still had the difficult task of getting her on the other tack. Meanwhile much of our strength had gone, our thirst was truly dreadful, and the gale showed no sign of abating.

Yet we succeeded, somehow, and then gradually drew off shore into comparative safety. The gale moderating later, we spent that night making for the entrance of King Haakon Sound.

Early in the morning Shackleton signalled to me that he wanted to speak to me alone. As soon as possible I made an opportunity.

"We must get water or ice," he said. "Two of the men are weakening."

I nodded, and replied, "Wilson's Harbour, six miles north, is not bad. We can get a drink and a sleep there before making for the whaling stations on the east coast."

He listened thoughtfully, then blurted out,

"To tell you the truth, Skipper, I don't want to put to sea in her again. We are lucky to be alive, and I should be mad to risk losing everything by getting blown away to the east of South Georgia."

"Do you mean to cross the land to the whaling stations?" I asked.

"We'll try," he said briefly.

The very idea of crossing the interior of this bleak glacier-covered island that had never been explored before was sufficient to revive my spirits. "Good!" I said: "that will reduce the men's time of waiting." I knew that all his thoughts were on Elephant Island.

The condition of our mouths was now such that we were unable to eat, and we looked eagerly for floating ice to reduce the swelling of our tongues and allay, at least temporarily, the dreadful thirst that afflicted us. It was painful to us to reflect upon the vast ice-fields that we had left, and to realise that now, when we would have given anything for just one small piece, there was none to be had. We were not destined to make Wilson's Harbour, for the wind some hours later forced us into King Haakon Sound. After a long day's struggle we landed, beaching the boat in a tiny cove. It was then dark.

The little cove into which we had made our way with so much difficulty was bordered by rocky black cliffs close on a hundred feet high and topped with snow. At the head of the cove was a boulder beach. Above this, and between the cliffs, was a slope leading up into the interior through two swamps. The cove was about a hundred and eighty yards long and sixty broad, and the entrance was flanked by reefs—uncharted, of course—on both sides. Our relief was great when at last in the gathering darkness we succeeded in beaching the boat, in almost smooth water compared with the violent seas that were dashing against the shores outside and the constant roar of which penetrated to us.

As the *James Caird* grounded on the beach we leapt from her bows and hauled her up. With each succeeding wave we got her higher, and then, to our joy, we realized that we were actually standing in a stream of water that was running down from the interior. We followed this up a few yards clear of the sea, and while some of us held the boat, we took it in turns to have a good drink. This water came from the swamps above, and it may have been peaty or muddy, but to us it was nectar.

Meanwhile the boat was bumping heavily on the boulders, for even here there was considerable surf. Her stern swung round against the rocky cliff, and in the darkness her rudder was torn off, parted the lanyard and—was lost. We realised what this meant, but we had no time to worry about it, for it was imperative to haul the boat up out of the sea to prevent her from getting smashed. To do this we were obliged to throw out of her every atom of gear and stores as quickly as possible. We formed a chain and handed the stuff ashore. I well remember the unpleasantness of crawling along the bottom of the boat, under the canvas, in pitch darkness, with icy water sloshing over my legs, and thinking what a rotten job it was. We had slaked our thirst but were hungrier than ever; yet this had to be done before we could think of getting food, although we had scarcely been able to swallow anything for twenty-four hours. Moreover the work could only be done slowly, as we had almost lost the use of our limbs through the continuous wetting and lack of normal movement due to the confined space in the boat. It must be remembered that we had not been able even to sit upright for a meal, so that every muscle was cramped and we were in the condition that one might expect to find in sick or bedridden men.

We rested and ate only when we had stripped the boat of everything inside her; and even when we had hauled her up on the highest sea that broke, with all our united strength we were unable to get her clear of the water. We were obliged to watch our precious boat bumping about wildly, in spite of our efforts to hold her, until after a time I managed to make her painter fast to a large boulder, a job which took considerable time.

Under the cliff opposite the one where we had landed we found a cave. It was floored by a sharp slope of shingle, piled up by the gales, and although at any other time it would have seemed to us a most uninviting place, we looked upon it as very nearly perfection. Huge fifteen-foot icicles, like immense javelins, fringed the entrance. During the night we heard two of these come down with a crash. It was lucky that no one happened to be passing underneath at that moment. It will be realised, therefore, that our entrances and exits to the cave were more speedy than dignified.

Taking it in turn to watch the boat we snatched such sleep

as we could until two o'clock in the morning. Then Crean, who was hanging on to the painter, gave a shout. We all rushed out, and, stumbling in the darkness to his help, found that a big sea had torn from the ground the boulder to which the painter was secured, and that Crean, hanging on to it, had been dragged into the water which threatened to submerge him. We all hauled on the painter, and by the time that we had worked the boat up the beach again, the sea had swept her across until we were almost alongside the cave. There was no more sleep. All hands had to hold on to the boat for the rest of the night.

When our spirits were almost down to zero Shackleton got a laugh out of us by saying, with the most elegant formality, "I do hope that you are all enjoying my little party."

In the morning, after a hot meal, we managed, with tremendous labour, to get the boat above high-water mark. How desperate our endeavours were may be judged by the fact that we were forced to cut down the top-sides of the boat to lighten her sufficiently to do this. Later we utilised this wood for a fire, of which we were as badly in need as we were of food. And all through the day, working inch by inch, but taking our time about it and getting in plenty of short spells of rest, we got the boat up into a place of safety. In doing this we broke both the masts, but this troubled us very little; for we felt that we had had enough of sailing to last us a lifetime.

Next day we felt equal to having a look round. Shackleton, Crean, McCarthy and I went up on the plateau above the swamps, which we skirted, and there we found a small hill dotted with objects like snow-white sheep, which I immediately recognised as being baby albatrosses on the nest. The nests of these birds, made of turf and tussock, and built up year after year, sometimes exceeded a height of two feet.

It is rare for the albatross to lay more than one egg, and in each of the many nests that we explored we found only one chick. The egg is about seven inches long, a dull white, with reddish markings at the larger end. The chicks are fed in the nests for about ten months, and those that we examined were like giant powder-puffs, with dark eyes, and bills not hardened, so that although they snapped at us in the manner of older birds they could not hurt us. Their food consists of small fish, jelly-fish and euphausia (a species of shrimp) carried to them by their mothers.

We took three birds back to the cave, and each provided about fourteen pounds of delicious food, after being stewed in the pot with half a pound of sledging ration. The bones were so tender that we ate these as well as the flesh, and the soup from it was like super-chicken broth, forming a splendid jelly as soon as it cooled. We found this sort of food strengthening and nourishing, in fact just what we needed. I had brought into the cave some peaty substance and a few dead tussock leaves that I had found, and these, spread on the shingle, made a softer resting place than the uncovered stones. After the feast of albatross we lay back in our sleeping-bags, smoked some foul cigarettes made from sea sodden leaves of tobacco, and, because the conditions we had recently experienced had been so much worse, felt a glorious reaction.

Now that we were getting drier and had had some exercise our feet became painfully hot. It was a most uncomfortable sensation. I had been asleep for about three hours when the heat of my feet awoke me. Convinced that my sleeping-bag was on fire I woke Crean, who was sleeping next to me. I lifted my feet up and asked him to see whether my bag was burning. After a sleepy inspection he grunted, "No." Later I awakened McCarthy, who was sleeping on the other side of me, with the same result. At last becoming so uncomfortable that I could not endure it I awakened a third member of the party, and was reminded tersely that other people also had burning feet. Crushed, I subsided into slumber for the rest of the night. In the morning when I turned out I found that our little fire had eaten through the peat and tussock and burnt a hole eight inches wide in the foot of my sleeping-bag and that the heels of my socks had been charred off. Fortunately a wet skin does not burn well, so that I was not really hurt; but I was triumphant at having something to complain of after all.

Our first night of good rest was disturbed by Shackleton suddenly sitting up, clutching me by the shoulder, and shouting, "Look out! Look out, boys, and hold on! It will get us!"

I sat up and said, "What is it?"

He replied, "Look at that big sea breaking," and pointed at the black cliffs—snow-crowned—opposite which could be seen over the top of the sail that we had fastened across the entrance of the cave.

I said, "That is only the cliff with the snow on top."

He lay down again and I realised that he had been dreaming of the great sea that had broken over the boat and nearly sunk us during the journey. This incident showed me how acutely he had felt the strain to which he had been subjected.

When we awoke in the morning we missed the familiar sound of the sea breaking right alongside of us, and we noted with uneasiness that in its place a strange bumping and rustling was going on outside. We looked round the boat's sail—our only door—and saw that a change of wind had filled the cove with glacier ice, some of the lumps of which were prevented from falling into the cave only by the sail, which was bulging with their weight and was actually touching Vincent, the sleeper nearest the 'door.' This meant that we should be unable to launch the boat again to continue our journey until this ice had left the cove, a delay which might have serious consequences to the men of Elephant Island.

Later that day Shackleton and I prospected along the edge of King Haakon Sound, which ran eight miles into the interior. Although much of the higher country and the mountain ranges were obscured by swirling clouds and wreaths of mist, the glimpses we obtained made us think that a start from the head of the bay would not be very difficult. We traversed about five miles of very heavy country—tussocks, rocks, snow and swamps—until we came to an impassable glacier. To the north and south, as we looked up the sound, were steep mountain ranges, their flanks furrowed by fourteen mighty glaciers. These were the outlets of the great ice sheet which covered the interior. These glaciers effectually barred our way inland from where we stood. Shackleton named some of them—the largest after myself.

"Well, Skipper," he said, "we can't do it from here. We shall have to start from the head of the Sound."

While we were standing on that grim lonely beach we found among some wreckage a child's toy boat. I wondered what had become of the child who had lost it. Was it the sole relic of some shipwreck, or was it eloquent only of a minor tragedy—the loss of a treasured plaything?

We sat down for a while on a tussock, discussing plans for crossing the island, and Shackleton told me that he would take me with him when he went. As we sat there, we saw a seven-foot sea-elephant haul itself up on the beach— a pleasing sight to us, for it indicated the presence of food in abundance. These beasts are easily stunned by a blow on the nose, so I picked up a large stone and, going fairly close,

The glacier front
(ROYAL GEOGRAPHICAL SOCIETY)

stunned the animal; then, as it lay unconscious, cut its throat without difficulty. Having cut it up, we selected the best portions and carried them back to the cave. On entering our abode Shackleton asked the boys to guess what we had discovered. The guesses ranged from gold, diamonds and ambergris to a whaling station. But when we proudly produced the sea-elephant's liver there were more whoops of joy than the discovery of any of these things would have evoked.

The ice was in the cove for three days, so that we were detained in the cave for six days in all. Then some change in conditions swept the ice out of the cove. To see it leaving was an impressive and curious sight: it was like watching an army in full retreat.

During our detention we had rigged a steer-oar in place of our lost rudder, and this we hoped would enable us to sail the boat up the Sound and thus shorten our intended jour-

A bull sea-elephant
(*SCOTT POLAR RESEARCH INSTITUTE*)

ney across South Georgia by about eight miles. Accordingly on the seventh morning at daybreak, all our preparations being completed, we proceeded to launch the boat. As we were doing so I saw an object bobbing about in the surf and Crean waded out knee-deep to investigate. When he returned he yelled, "the rudder!" Thus, almost miraculously, we recovered the rudder that we had lost during our hazardous landing in the dark. After six days' wandering, with the vast Southern Ocean and all the shores of South Georgia to choose from, that rudder, as though it were faithfully performing what it knew to be its duty, had returned to our very feet. This incident strengthened in us the feeling that we were being protected in some inexplicable way by a Power of which we were aware but could not aspire to understand. We shipped the rudder, rejoicing, and pulled out of the sheltering cove. As we cleared its rocky headlands Shackleton exclaimed, "What a godsend that little shelter was to us, when we came in, exhausted, in the darkness!"

We hoisted sail to a fine west breeze, and as the sun came out and the waters of the Sound sparkled in the bright light we felt very cheery indeed. Half-way up the Sound we found a line of kelp stretching right across. I may mention that kelp, a giant seaweed of the South, sometimes grows to the surface from the astounding depth of a hundred fathoms, so that it is considerably longer than the tallest tree in the world. Unless it is in a neighbourhood of icebergs, which may tear it away, it is almost an infallible rule that kelp proclaims the existence of rocks, a fact which is a help to navigators. Consequently the moment I saw kelp I jumped into the bows to look for hidden dangers, while Crean steered the boat. Knowing, however, that there might be rocks from which the kelp had been ripped away by ice, I kept a sharp look-out continuously.

As we reached the head of the Sound we heard the raucous roar of the bull sea-elephant. We hauled the boat ashore and, after four hours' hard work, got her up against a rocky face, turned her upside down, sheltered her by building her round with turf and stones, and christened her 'Peggotty Camp.' This was to be our home until we could cross South Georgia. At one end we placed a large saucer-shaped stone, and lighted a blubber fire in this, in an attempt to dry ourselves. This fire, however, was not a success. The smoke nearly stifled us, so that we were forced to put it out and remain wet and cold. The oily soot settled on us, adding to our already fearsome appearance.

All round us were plenty of sea-elephants. The great roaring bull, lord of a harem of twenty or thirty wives, is a hideous, unwieldy brute reaching a length of eighteen or nineteen feet and weighing up to five or six tons. His colouring and hide, though not so wrinkled, resemble those of an elephant, but he gains his name from his large proboscis which rises and distends when he is annoyed or is in battle with one of his rivals. Though not aggressive unless they are interfered with, provocation will cause sea-elephants to attack a man, and one killed a seaman of Lord Anson's in the eighteenth century. These creatures live in the sea, but haul themselves up on the beaches of South Georgia and other southern islands in the breeding season. Sometimes they lie about on the beaches but they also go to the swamps nearby and wallow in the mud with only their noses exposed to the air. They nurse their young for about two months, and then, taking to the sea again, leave the pups to look after themselves.

The bulls are very quarrelsome among themselves, but this is due to sex jealousy. If a strange bull invades the harem, the fighting is so fierce that sometimes several pups get killed in the fray. It is therefore much to the benefit of the herd as a whole that many of the bulls be regularly killed off, and as some of these yield more than half a ton of blubber, it is worth while to slay them.

Shackleton, Crean and I were becoming feverishly anxious to leave this uninhabited coast and cross the unexplored land. Our thoughts were constantly with the men whom we had left eight hundred miles away, and it was all-important that we should obtain help quickly from Stromness Bay, where the principal whaling stations of the east coast were situated.

We sheltered under the upturned boat for three more days, which brought us to the ninth day after landing. During the greater part of this time it had been snowing, raining, hailing and blowing. The gales and blizzards that sweep across South Georgia incessantly in winter-time are perhaps the most violent in the world. The hurricane which had prevented us from landing was undoubtedly the fiercest that we had ever seen. But we knew that it must be less terrible, less furious than those that raged across the icy uplands and jagged mountain ranges which we now proposed to cross.

Close to the boat was a great pile of driftwood, about half an acre in extent—a graveyard of wreckage from ships. In places it was piled eight feet high or more, and there were ships' masts and timbers, a great mainyard, bits of figureheads, teak stanchions with brass caps, cabin doors, binnacle stands, broken oars, and harness casks. These had been swept before the westerly gales a thousand miles from Cape Horn, or farther, until the wild Southern Ocean had, by some strange freak of its eddies, thrown them up here to rot.

"Some day, Skipper," said Shackleton, "you and I will come back here and dig for treasure. Or, who knows, we may have to take our last sleep here with those who used these things."

That night the moon came out for a few minutes, and Crean suddenly yelled that he had seen a rat. We jeered at him, and with tears in my voice I implored him to give me a little of what had made him see rats; but when, some time later, the carpenter also thought he saw one, our derision was less pronounced. We recollected then that there were many rats on the east coast of South Georgia, and that it was possible that some had come ashore with the wreckage, and had bred continuously since.

Next morning we were unable to start because, as usual, it was stormy, with, however, a comparatively warm wind from the north-west, which caused the glacier at the corner of the Sound to calve frequently with noises like mighty thunderclaps. The succeeding day was still stormy, and we became anxious; for there was now a full moon, and unless we had the combination of fine weather and bright moonlight it would be impossible to cross South Georgia. Shackleton was more anxious and depressed than I had ever seen him. He and I started out to prospect for the best opening for our trek across the interior when we were driven back by a blinding snowstorm. As we fought our way back he exclaimed almost despairingly, "Skipper, I'll never make another expedition."

Knowing that the only thing that could prompt him to say this was nervousness on behalf of the marooned men, I answered his thoughts rather than his words by saying, "Don't worry, we shall soon have them off."

"I hope you are right," he replied, but with doubt in his voice.

I shall never forget the dreary hours that followed. All that day I watched closely the appearance of the sky and the direction in which the lower and upper clouds were moving. I tried to get indications of what was to come by observing the height and formation of the cloud-mists that swathed the upper mountain tops. Shackleton asked me repeatedly, "What do you think of the weather?" and "What is to-night going to be?" Before dark our spirits rose, as we had both concluded that the indications were favourable for making a start that night or in the early morning. The change in Shackleton as soon as he realised this was remarkable. He seemed to tauten and gain strength, and was vigorous and excited and talked of how soon we should be able to get the men off Elephant Island. He was the old Shackleton again.

Our preparations were few but effectual. The carpenter had fixed sixteen two-inch brass screws in our boot soles, point down, eight in each foot. These would give us a good grip on the ice and rocks. We turned in early, but Shackleton was too restless to sleep much, and he got up twice to look at the weather. The second time, I met him, having got up for the same purpose myself, and we saw that the moon was shining and that the clouds were clearing off. Everything promised well.

At two A.M. on Friday, May 19th, 1916, the moon was shining brilliantly, and the weather was fine and clear. Shackleton said, "We will start now, Skipper."

By three o'clock we had embarked on our pioneer journey across the island of South Georgia—an adventure destined to be far more thrilling than ever I had dreamed.

The Crossing of
South Georgia

THREE of our men were not fit to travel, so Shackleton decided that they should remain under the upturned boat until
we could return in a whaler and fetch them. These three
were McCarthy A.B., McNeish the carpenter, and Vincent
the bo'sun. We were especially fond of McCarthy, whose
optimism and cheerfulness during the boat journey were an
unfailing help to all of us, and we should have been very sad
indeed had we known that we were destined to see him only
once again, and that five months later he would go down in
his ship, in battle with the Germans. Shackleton who naturally did not want the men to feel the moment of separation
more than could be avoided, hastened the departure as
much as he could.

Our equipment was three days' food each, consisting of
two pounds of sledging rations, a pound of biscuits and two
cakes of Streimer's Nut Food, all of which we carried over
our shoulders packed into a Burberry sock. We also carried the Primus stove, a small bowl in which to cook our
hoosh, an adze to cut steps in the ice slopes, and a little sil-

ver compass that had been given to me ten years before in Switzerland. Shackleton had a sledging compass which had cost five guineas, but my little one, costing perhaps half a guinea, beat the more expensive one every time, for it was such a handy little fellow that I could rest it in my hand and, tipping it to one side sharply, stop the swing of the compass and, bringing it back, could get the bearing instantaneously. This was very valuable, as it enabled me to take bearings without ever halting the party for more than twenty seconds, and I often succeeded in doing it without stopping them at all.

I carried two compasses, binoculars, the Alpine rope, and the chronometer with which I had navigated the boat. This last was slung round my neck inside my sweater to keep it warm. I remember my load very well, because I felt half-strangled with the four cords and straps round my throat, even before the addition of the coils of the ninety-foot Alpine rope. Our arms had to be free, of course, to use our 'alpenstocks.' These last were pieces of wood five feet long which we had taken off the sledges that had been originally intended for the trans-continental journey and which of course had long since been abandoned. I had had the forethought to put a pair of socks (damp, naturally) on my shoulders inside my clothing, where the heat of my body dried them, and they formed a welcome pad against the load I was carrying.

Soon after we set out we were ascending the flank of a high mountain. This slope was littered with enormous boulders of every size, some as large as hay-stacks. It was obvious that there was danger of others rolling down the mountainside. In fact we saw one at some distance from us, travelling downwards in huge leaps and at a prodigious speed; so we kept our weather eye lifting until we were clear of that neighbourhood.

The backbone of the island of South Georgia consists of the Allardyce range, averaging five or six thousand feet in height and culminating in Mount Paget, which rises to nine or ten thousand. At the head of King Haakon Sound this range dips down into a saddle, which forms a diagonal pass running east and west, and gives a fairly easy passage to the interior. Great lateral ranges branch off at about right angles like ribs from the main backbone. An ice sheet hundreds of feet thick appears to cover most of the interior, filling the valleys and disguising the configuration of the land, which only shows through in rocky ridges, peaks, or nunataks. From this saddle of snow-ridden land where we started a great snow upland sloped skyward to the inland ice-sheet. This continued eastward on our course to one of the rocky ranges I have previously mentioned, which stretched athwart and threatened to bar our way.

Since we were travelling at night with only moonlight to guide us, our impression of the country that lay ahead could not be accurate. But what we saw in the distance could be described roughly as five rocky peaks with spaces between— like the four gaps between the fingers of a giant but stumpy hand—and it looked as though these might prove to be passes. Actually, none of them was worthy of the name, the one we finally came through being two almost precipitous slopes of snow and ice from a razor-back.

As we progressed the weather became misty, a very serious matter for us, since we could not see a step ahead. Suddenly we found ourselves on the very edge of a strange, dark pit that was more than a hundred feet deep. The formation of this pit mystifies me to this day, as I cannot see what could make a hole of that size in the ice. It looked as though an enormous meteorite had ploughed its way through the ice sheet.

By the time that we came to this pit, from falling into

which we certainly had a wonderful escape, the fog had thickened. Half-blinded by it, and with our view obscured, for one dreadful moment none of us knew that the other was safe. The relief of hearing Shackleton's voice, and then that of Crean, who was cursing softly, was indescribable. Never have I felt so puny, nor realised so clearly the help-lessness of Man against Nature. For a brief moment I felt that curious weakness about the knees that comes upon one when one has just gone through some fearsome ordeal. My skin prickled, and I became conscious of nerves in my body that I had not known existed.

"Better rope up, after this," said Shackleton, briefly; and as I had been carrying the ninety-foot rope all the time, I cheerfully assented. We roped up.

Shackleton went ahead, breaking the trail, Crean came next, and I, from the back, directed the course by my com-pass, calling out, "starboard!" "port!" or "steady!" as was necessary to maintain a straight course for Stromness Bay.

The moon was now shining through the mist, which re-sulted in a diffused light, rather trying and misleading, as we could not see properly where we were putting our feet. This was due not so much to the thickness of the fog as to the peculiar effect of the combination of moonlight, mist and snow. Moreover, our progress was slowed down by having to tramp almost knee-deep through upward-sloping snow, and since time was so valuable that every minute counted, this irritated us considerably.

After almost an hour we reached the top of the ice-saddle. The mist was clearing away to the east, and presently we saw the smooth surface of what we took to be a frozen lake. Shackleton decided to make for this, as he thought it would afford better travelling than the land to the south of it. As we made our way down the slope we came to a few small crevasses, which warned us that we were on the upper slopes of a glacier. Not liking the look of it, we went on with increased caution. Sunrise came, and the banks of mist, now rose-coloured, drifted farther away to the east. The 'lake' lengthened out to an extraordinary extent, so that I exclaimed to Shackleton in amazement, "What an astounding size! How is it possible for there to be such a big lake here?" Shackleton did not answer: he was looking anxiously eastward.

With the complete clearance of the mist we saw the straight line of the eastern horizon, and to our sharp disappointment we realised that what we had taken for a frozen lake was an arm of the sea. The light had deceived us, and we now saw that it was not even frozen over. Our mistake had cost us at least one valuable hour. We were obliged to retrace our steps—always a depressing business—and at length we got back to our original course and climbed the snowy upland that I have described towards the lateral range of mountains. The cold here was insufficient to harden the snow, which made our going heavy. As we got higher, however, the cold increased, and our progress was a little easier.

At about nine o'clock in the morning we had our first hot meal, having been on the march for six hours. The only nourishment we had taken *en route* had been a small piece of biscuit and a chunk of Streimer's Nut Food. After this we cooked a meal over the little Primus every four hours. Our procedure was as follows. We dug a hole in the snow with the adze, packed the bowl full of snow, lit the Primus and, placing it in the hole, Crean and I lay over it in turn to prevent the wind from blowing it out. As soon as the snow melted we broke in two blocks of sledging ration, and when it boiled, took it off and ate it as hot as possible, leaving the wind to extinguish the stove. On the breast of our sweaters we had sewn a patch of blanket, and in this pocket each kept his spoon, together with other treasures such as tobacco, half a biscuit and paper for cigarettes. We would set the pot in the snow, then, squatting round it, dip in our spoon in turn, which was a very fair way of whacking it out. At our first meal Shackleton, who was always fond of a leg-pull, said:

"Crean, you've got a bigger spoon than we have!"

"Doesn't matter," said the imperturbable Crean, "The Skipper has a bigger mouth!"

Having finished our first meal we marched on and soon reached the range that we had sighted from a distance in the darkness—the five crags or 'fingers' that I have described. Even from here it looked deceptively easy. We did not know what was on the other side.

I selected the right hand pass as being the lowest and nearest to our course. Shackleton agreed, and we made our way into it. The first part of it was between precipices but on an upward slope, so that for some time we could not see what lay beyond. When we came to the crest of it we found that it sloped sharply down, and following it a few yards further we found that it fell away in precipices and cliffs of ice to the chaotic surface of a glacier. Obviously it was impossible to negotiate this, and useless to get on to the back of the glacier, for we could never have crossed the hopelessly broken surface that we saw a thousand feet below. It was impossible to cross to the next pass, as a mountain crag towered in between. Therefore we had once again to retrace our steps part of the way, in order to outflank the mountain by working round it.

We were now at a considerable height, and the cold was intense. The going was so hard that we had to halt every twenty minutes for a short spell, when we would throw ourselves flat on our backs, with legs and arms extended, and draw in big gulps of air so as to get our wind again. During one of those halts my feet became so cold that I thought they were frost-bitten. I took off my boots and socks, and found that the latter were wringing wet from the snow that had worked in through the many holes in my worn-out Shackleton boots. Here was the need that I had anticipated for a dry pair of socks, and I now removed those which I had slung over my shoulders and put them on. The others I wrung out and wore as I had worn their predecessors. The boots I tied very tightly so that no more snow should come in over the tops and run down, and after this I had no more trouble with my feet. Shackleton was amused, but praised my foresight. He himself was wearing leather instead of the Shackleton boot (which was composed of a Durox sole with leather and canvas uppers, the canvas extending half-way up to the knee, and this, instead of lacing, was fastened with broad tape bands that were criss-crossed round the leg). The reason why Shackleton was wearing the colder leather boot was that there had been a shortage of footgear, and it was his rule that any deprivation should be felt by himself before anybody else. This matter of the shoes may seem a small sacrifice to those who have not experienced the severe conditions through which we had to pass; actually it was a matter of very great importance.

When we attained the crest of the second pass and again looked down, we found the conditions almost as bad as at the first. The beauty of the scene only intensified the irony of our position. In front of us stretched a truly magnificent view: the exquisite purity of Alpine scenery in a crystalline atmosphere with deep blue skies broken only here and there by a few soft, fleecy clouds which contrasted sharply with the brilliant sunshine that blazed into the valleys and over

"In front of us stretched a truly magnificent view"
(SCOTT POLAR RESEARCH INSTITUTE)

the icy uplands. We stood between two gigantic black crags that seemed to have forced their way upwards through their icy covering—dark and forbidding masses of bleak and barren rock. Before us was the Allardyce range, peak beyond peak, snow-clad and majestic, glittering in the sunshine. Sweeping down from their flanks were magnificent glaciers, noble to look upon, but, as we realised, threatening to our advance. And we were in a solitude never before broken by man.

Still a way had to be found. Shackleton said grimly, "We shall have to go on to the next, boys," and without a word we resumed the weary work of retreat from a hard-won climb.

Each of these successive climbs was steeper, and this third one, which brought us to about five thousand feet above

The country that we crossed
(SCOTT POLAR RESEARCH INSTITUTE)

sea level, was very exhausting. When we got to the third gap, which was nothing but a ridge of ice in the space between the two crags, it was four o'clock and the sun was setting, and in this altitude we immediately felt colder, a certain depression adding to our sensation of bone-deep chill. The position, seeing that our whole afternoon's labour had proved valueless, was becoming serious.

The third pass was little better than the first. Looking down further along the range, however, we thought that there might possibly be some way down from the fourth and last pass. Indeed there would have to be—in other words we should have to make one, whatever the ground might be like. So down again and up again!

Darkness was now approaching. As speedily as possible we zig-zagged our way, every now and then forced to cut steps in the ice with the adze, a slow process in the cold and gathering gloom. Thus did we struggle to the fourth—and last—pass.

At length we reached what appeared to be the lowest part of it and found ourselves on the brink of a gigantic chasm that had been carved out of the solid ice round the base of the fifth 'finger.' The forces that had ripped away thousands of tons of ice, leaving a ravine more than two hundred feet deep, two hundred feet broad, and two thousand feet long, were the terrific gales that for countless centuries have swept the uplands of this Iceland of the South. We lay face downward where the overhanging cornice had been broken away, and with a thrill of awe at the elemental power of Nature peered into this dark and sinister gulf in which a couple of battleships could easily have been hidden. As we drew back cautiously we looked at each other and knew that each was thinking the same thing—that if a blizzard should spring up nothing could save us from being hurled into the depths below. From this chasm a razor-back of ice sloped upwards towards the last crag that we had passed. We cut steps diagonally up this, anxious to put a distance between ourselves and the gulf. Into my mind at least there had crept a most disturbing uncertainty as to what we should find next in that treacherous pass.

I had now changed places with Crean on the rope and was between him and Shackleton when we reached the ridge of the razor-back. It was so sharp that we were able to sit astride it with our legs hanging down. We had not lost our way, but it was exceedingly difficult to gauge the best line to take across the country, despite the aid of my compass.

As we sat there we turned and saw that behind us a heavy sea-fog had come up and blotted out the country we had traversed as completely as though it had never existed. The fog had been creeping up unnoticed as we had been cutting steps in the slope, and so quickly did it overtake us that as we sat there wisps of it actually swept in between Shackleton and Crean and myself.

Crean said, quaintly, "You won't be able to do much navigating in this, Skipper"; but Shackleton, who was usually amused by his remarks, did not smile. He said tersely, "I don't like our position at all. We must get out of it somehow; we shall freeze if we wait here till the moon rises."

Down below us was an almost precipitous slope, the nature of which we could not gauge in the darkness and the lower part of which was shrouded in impenetrable gloom. The situation looked grim enough. Fog cut off our retreat, darkness covered our advance.

After a moment or two Shackleton said, "We've got to take a risk. Are you game?"

Crean and I declared that anything was better than delay.

"Right," said Shackleton; "we'll try it."

We resumed our advance by slowly and painfully cutting steps in the ice in a downward direction, but since it took us half an hour to get down a hundred yards, we saw that it was useless to continue in this fashion.

Shackleton then cut out a large step and sat on it. For a few moments he pondered, then he said:

"I've got an idea. We must go on, no matter what is below. To try to do it in this way is hopeless. We can't cut steps down thousands of feet."

He paused, and Crean and I both agreed with him. Then he spoke again.

"It's a devil of a risk, but we've got to take it. We'll slide."

Slide down what was practically a precipice, in the darkness, to meet—what?

"All right," I said aloud, perhaps not very cheerfully, and Crean echoed my words.

It seemed to me a most impossible project. The slope was

well-nigh precipitous, and a rock in our path—we could never have seen it in the darkness in time to avoid it—would mean certain disaster. Still, it was the only way. We had explored all the passes; to go back was useless: moreover such a proceeding would sign and seal the death warrant not only of ourselves but of the whole of the expedition. To stay on the ridge longer meant certain death by freezing. It was useless therefore to think about personal risk. If we were killed, at least we had done everything in our power to bring help to our shipmates. Shackleton was right. Our chance was a very small one indeed, but it was up to us to take it.

We each coiled our share of the rope until it made a pad on which we could sit to make our *glissade* from the mountain top. We hurried as much as possible, being anxious to get through the ordeal. Shackleton sat on the large step he had carved, and I sat behind him, straddled my legs round him and clasped him round the neck. Crean did the same with me, so that we were locked together as one man. Then Shackleton kicked off.

We seemed to shoot into space. For a moment my hair fairly stood on end. Then quite suddenly I felt a glow, and knew that I was grinning! I was actually enjoying it. It was most exhilarating. We were shooting down the side of an almost precipitous mountain at nearly a mile a minute. I yelled with excitement, and found that Shackleton and Crean were yelling too. It seemed ridiculously safe. To hell with the rocks!

The sharp slope eased out slightly toward the level below, and then we knew for certain that we were safe. Little by little our speed slackened, and we finished up at the bottom in a bank of snow. We picked ourselves up and solemnly shook hands all round.

"It's not good to do that kind of thing too often," said

Shackleton, slowly. "Thanks be that the risk was justified this time."

We turned and looked up at the mountain down which we had just sped. I judged that we had travelled down about three thousand feet, and it was difficult to realise that we had reached the bottom in less than three minutes after we had left the top. This of course included the slowing down at the bottom.

As we dusted the snow off us, I looked ruefully at my trousers, which happened to belong to an old dress suit. They were badly torn in spite of the pad of rope. Shackleton laughed, but when I pointed out to him that his own were in equally bad case his laugh eased up a bit.

We then turned and tramped on in the darkness for about half a mile, on a fair level upland, but finding the going heavy and difficult in the dark, Shackleton said, "We'll halt here and have a meal." As we were cooking the hoosh a faint but beautiful glow showed behind a ridge of weird and jagged crags to the southeast—great peaks thousands of feet above us reared like titanic fingers. It was the light of the rising moon. In the gaps between the peaks the glow became stronger and, as time went on, the moon seemed almost to be playing Bo-Peep behind the black pinnacles of rock. At last she emerged, clear and brilliant. We should now have her all-important light to enable us to find our way across the snowy wastes. The scene was majestic. The great snowy uplands gleamed white before us, enormous peaks towered awe-inspiringly round about, and to the south was the line of black crags, while northwards lay the silvered sea. The silence, utter and complete, was broken only occasionally by the thunderous reverberations from distant glaciers 'calving' into the sea.

We resumed the march, and at about midnight we started

on a long downward slope. Along this we strode and swung with joyful exhilaration, for the snow was hard and we were making great progress. By two o'clock in the morning the going had been so good that we were drawing close to the bay below us, which we took to be our destination. Then suddenly we found ourselves among crevasses. We were on a glacier. Our joy gave place to consternation, for we knew that there were no large glaciers at Stromness Bay.

"We've made a mistake," said Shackleton, grimly, when we had taken stock of the situation, "and we shall have to go back on our tracks."

It was easy enough to take a bearing with my little compass, but to decide which was the best route was a much more complicated matter. And we had to face the fact that whichever way we took we should have to retrace our steps for miles and wearily climb up slopes that it had been so easy to descend. Too late I realised that the smoothness and easiness of that long slope to the bay had lured us on and deceived us. After the difficulties and hard climbing that we had experienced we had accepted too readily the promise held out by what appeared to be the easiest way. Now we had to pay for it. It was not until five in the morning that we regained our former altitude and resumed our proper course.

At this time I was the last on the rope, and every now and then the two men ahead of me were obliged to go so slowly that the rope slackened and trailed in the snow, and I had to be very careful of my steps to avoid treading on it. It does not do for an exhausted man to be jerked back harshly, and perhaps thrown over. When men are as tired as we were—beset and harrassed by difficulties—their nerves are on edge, and it is necessary for each man to take pains not to irritate the others. On this march we treated each other with a good deal more consideration than we should have done in normal circumstances. Never is etiquette and 'good form' observed more carefully than by experienced travellers when they find themselves in a tight place.

At dawn we reached the top of another great transverse range. Looking over the dark waters of Fortuna Bay, some thousands of feet below us, and beyond two distant mountains, we recognized the Z-shaped stratification that told us that Stromness Bay was in that direction. Seven o'clock came, and we listened intently. Then, clear across the mountains, in the still morning air, from eight miles away came the sound of the steam whistles of the whaling factories bidding the men turn-to. It was the first signal of civilisation that we had heard for nearly two years. For the second time on that march we shook hands; for each of us recognised that this was an occasion on which words were inadequate.

After breakfast we began to descend the range, with the intention of going round the head of Fortuna Bay. Everything looked so smooth and straightforward that I remarked to Shackleton,

"I am afraid that this is too good to be true."

Shackleton, for the one and only time in my memory of him, seemed to be less cautious than I. I suggested a route which I judged would be the safer though longer one; but at that moment he was ready to risk everything for the saving of time.

Sure enough, the mountain side soon became alarmingly steep, and presently we found ourselves on an ice slope above what was, virtually, a precipice. Very carefully we cut steps and made a diagonal traverse to avoid the danger of falling.

The ice slope was now so nearly sheer that apparently the only way down was to cut steps with the adze. This would have taken us hours, and there was the ever-present danger of a blizzard, for gales rarely hold off for any length of time at that season of the year. It was vital for us therefore to hurry our movements. Had a blizzard caught us on that exposed mountain face we should have been lifted clean off our feet and whirled away, and nothing on earth could have saved us.

We could neither walk nor crawl, and as we crouched and clung, and with much toil went on cutting steps in ice that was nearly as perpendicular as a church steeple, we found that the snow had been plastered there by the gales. It had melted and then had frozen on the surface, so that a layer of snow was lying under the skin of ice, which was about an inch thick. Shackleton was sitting with one leg bent under him, when raising the other leg, he chanced to smash through the ice with his heel. This immediately suggested an idea to him. Lying on his back, with one leg under him, he stretched forth the other and smashed through the ice again with his heel. He went on doing this, using first one leg and then the other, each time, of course, going a little lower. Holding his weight up with the rope, I followed behind him, also driving my heel through the ice, enlarging his steps. Crean followed in my wake. Whereupon we progressed down that seemingly unending steepness by literally walking on our backs. It was not an agreeable experience. I was afraid to lift my head off the ice, feeling that if I did so I might fall outwards.

This method of advance, however, was extraordinarily rapid compared with that of cutting steps in the ice, and by ten o'clock we had got down to the desolate and uninhabited shores of Fortuna Bay. A mighty curved glacier reached down almost to the sea, and we found ourselves ankle-deep in the mud flats that it had pushed out.

We climbed the slopes on the far side of Fortuna Bay, but the going was very heavy; and our spirits rose when we found ourselves on a fine piece of level country with a hard surface. Suddenly Crean broke through the ice, and we discovered that what we had thought such good ground was in reality a frozen lake. Having hauled him out, wet up to his waist, we made our way gingerly to the shore. Soon after we reached the top of the last range. Far below us we could now see the factories and two whale-catchers towing in whales. Unconscious of the absurdity of our actions we yelled and waved, but of course no one saw or heard us.

We then prospected a little, and finally made our way down a ravine, but as we went along it became gradually steeper and narrower, and we were forced to walk ankle-deep in a stream of water, coming possibly from some small glacier. A little further on this stream ended in an icy-cold waterfall. But by this time we were too exhausted to go back. Shackleton said, "If the rope's long enough we'll risk it, and go right through the waterfall."

With some anxiety we lowered the rope, and were relieved to see it touch the rocks below. It was not only long enough but we had a few feet over. There was nothing whatever to which we could make the rope fast, but the rock on which we stood domed upwards, and, being rough, it was easy to hold the rope across it. As I was the lightest I volunteered to do so.

Shackleton slid down the rope in the waterfall, Crean after him, and when my turn came they stood one on each side of the waterfall with their arms stretched out to catch me. I stamped the rope well into the inequalities of the rock, but I had no faith in its holding. Then, sailor-fashion, I eased myself carefully over the rock and shot down without putting my full weight on the rope, letting it slide freely through my hands until just before I reached their out-stretched arms. I expected to crash, but didn't. They pulled me clear, and then the three of us tailed on to the rope to pull it down. Nothing would budge it: I wished I had known that a little earlier. . . . Anyway, we left our rope twirling in the waterfall.

The sixteen two-inch brass screws which the carpenter had fixed in the soles of our boots before we set out had by this time worn down level with the soles, so that now, when we came to smooth ice, we slipped and slithered all over the place. Each of us collected a number of tumbles, some of them rather heavy ones that jarred unpleasantly. I suppose the fact of the matter was that our legs were a bit tired. But in spite of all our troubles, at three o'clock that afternoon of May 20th we came to a large shed—a whaling factory. Our tramp was over. Without sleep, and halting only for meals, we had crossed South Georgia in thirty-six hours. True they had been hours of unremitting effort, of risks, anxiety and misadventure, but we had succeeded, and that was all that mattered.

CHAPTER IX

The Rescue

THE excitement of winning through being over, we realised that we were red-eyed from want of sleep, and wet from our immersion in the waterfall. We were cold with that peculiarly penetrating chill which comes from physical exhaustion. But we did not trouble about these things. All we wanted was to see somebody, to hear the sound of a strange voice.

The first human beings outside of our own party whom we had seen for upwards of eighteen months were two lads, who bolted at the sight of us. We were grimy-faced and bearded, ragged and uncouth—perhaps rather more terrifying than primitive savages. Our old friend Captain Sorlle, who had entertained us two years previously when the Expedition had touched Stromness Bay, failed to recognise us as we stood on his doorstep. But after food, hot baths and clean clothes we became civilised beings once more. I don't think I have ever appreciated anything so much as that hot bath: it was really wonderful and worth all that we had been through to get it. After the bath came the somewhat difficult operation of shaving. When we were through with it we hardly knew each other.

Naturally we had heard nothing of the War for over eighteen months, and we were greedy for the news that Sorlle poured into our ears. But we had been away too long to grasp all that had happened, and we were too distant for it to seem real. The one thing of paramount importance to us was the rescue of the men on Elephant Island.

That night, I started out on a whaler to bring in the three men whom we had left under the upturned boat at King Haakon Sound. I was content to leave the navigation to the Norwegian Captain, and the last sound that I heard as I fell asleep while we were steaming out of the harbour was the scream of a blizzard blowing down from the mountain range we had just crossed. It could blow as hard as it liked up there—now. Incidentally I learnt afterwards that we had crossed the island during the only interval of fine weather that occurred that winter. There was no doubt that Providence had been with us. There was indeed one curious thing about our crossing of South Georgia, a thing that has given me much food for thought, and which I have never been able to explain. Whenever I reviewed the incidents of that march I had the sub-conscious feeling that there were four of us, instead of three. Moreover, this impression was shared by both Shackleton and Crean.

Next morning I went ashore at King Haakon Sound, accompanied by two Norwegians from the whaler, and greeted the occupants of the upturned boat. They said they thought that one of their own party would come back for them. I said, "Well, I'm here, am I not?" They looked at me in amazement. They had been in my presence daily for two years, but failed to recognise me after a bath, a shave, and a change of clothing.

By the time I had got McCarthy, McNeish and Vincent

aboard the weather had cleared, but when we reached Stromness Bay a gale was blowing again, and a snowstorm through which it was impossible to force our way kept us out at sea for two days. But they were not unhappy days. All the time that we were on board the *Samson* the kindhearted Norwegians were competing with one another as to how much food, drink and tobacco they could force upon us. It is not on record that they met with any rebuffs.

I had brought the *James Caird* along with our three men in the *Samson,* and when we landed at Leith Harbour in Stromness Bay every man in the whaling station wanted to share the honour of hauling the boat ashore. We were not allowed to touch it. That evening the manager of the whaling station assembled all his captains and officers of the whaling fleet in the big club-room which they used for social purposes, to give Shackleton and his men a reception. I think I enjoyed this more than any honour bestowed upon us afterwards; for these fine seamen were men of the Viking brand who for years had been weathering the self-same storms through which we had come in our little boat. Congratulations from them meant something. When we entered the room it was blue and hazy with tobacco smoke. Everybody stood up, and a fine-looking white-haired old Captain, who had been chosen to represent the others, came forward and shook hands with Shackleton and each of us in turn. He then made a short speech in Norwegian, which was translated by the manager. He told Shackleton how greatly he and his brother seamen admired the boat journey that we had made and the crossing of South Georgia. As fellow seamen they knew well the storms and seas of that region, and they thought it a great feat to have brought the *James Caird* so far.

When I returned from King Haakon Sound with Mc-Carthy, McNeish and Vincent, I found that Shackleton had made arrangements to charter a whaler, the *Southern Sky*, owned by a British company, with which to rescue our men from Elephant Island. Captain Thom, a fine type of Norwegian, and a crew of his countrymen immediately volunteered to take us. Shackleton sent the three men, McCarthy, McNeish and Vincent, home to England, and we set out as soon as we could, sailing on May 23rd.

The *Southern Sky* was deeply laden with coal, as she had to make sixteen hundred miles if she was to get to Elephant Island and back. She was so deep in the water that the deck was almost awash as we left, and we went through an anxious time until some of the coal was used, and she rose a little, after which we felt easier.

After being on short rations for so long we had developed a positive passion for food, and we had five good meals a day, and at least as many snacks. The Norwegians seemed to think that they could make up for all that we had gone through if they could only persuade us to eat continuously, and they did their best.

We drove the ship steadily against the westerly gales, and presently, as we came within a hundred miles of Elephant Island, it became bitterly cold and the sea grew smooth. That is always a bad sign in these latitudes, as it gives the sea a chance to freeze over and allows the pack-ice to consolidate. Indeed to our annoyance we now saw bits of it floating about, and we knew that it might prevent us reaching our shipmates. An hour or two after we first sighted pack-ice the weather changed suddenly, and a southerly gale sprang up, with thick snow. We could see only a short distance ahead, and we found the ice gradually growing thicker and more dense.

At about sixty miles' distance from Elephant Island our way was barred. To attempt to force the unprotected steel whaler through the masses of pack-ice that now confronted us would have been suicidal. Through the unceasing snow-storm we skirted the ice for many miles to the westward, until at last Shackleton, seeing the hopelessness of trying to get through it, and realising that our stock of fuel was running low, reluctantly changed our course and made for the Falkland Islands. He did not attempt to conceal his disappointment from me. For many an hour we tramped the decks together, and every now and then he would say to me, "They can't be starving yet, can they?" and each time I would reply, as though the question had not been put a few minutes before, "Certainly not. Remember their food reserves and the seal and penguin on the island." We made for the Falklands instead of returning to South Georgia as Shackleton wanted to get in touch with the outer world and to obtain another vessel. Moreover the total distance of the return journey to Elephant Island and back would be nearly five hundred miles less—a matter of very great importance when there is limited space in which to stow coal.

We had three days of very heavy weather before we made Port Stanley, and directly we had landed Shackleton cabled to London a message to the King, informing him of the loss of the *Endurance*, of the boat journey, and of the plight of our men on Elephant Island. The same afternoon he received a reply as follows:

> "Rejoice to hear of your safe arrival in the Falkland Islands and trust your comrades on Elephant Island may soon be rescued.—GEORGE, R.I."

Cables also passed between Lady Shackleton and her husband, and it cheered him enormously to know that she was doing everything she could on his behalf in England, and was trying to secure a vessel for him.

The next ten days were bad ones. In addition to our own

troubles the first news we heard on arriving were the exaggerated and garbled reports that were current concerning the battle of Jutland. According to these it seemed as though the British Navy had been almost wiped out, and although I did not for a moment believe this, nevertheless it was depressing to hear that we had not achieved a victory. Then the Admiralty cabled to Shackleton that it would be impossible to get a vessel out before October. He knew that the Admiralty, in spite of the magnitude of their task at such a time—a task that comprised within its ambit every British ship afloat—would do their utmost to help him; but five months would be too long for the men on Elephant Island. He cabled back that October would be too late.

At this time there were no means by which we could leave the island, as the whaler had returned to South Georgia. To pass the time I rambled about the islands, which consist mainly of low, tussock-covered hills and downs. There are no trees, but under the tussock is about five or six feet of peat, which the inhabitants cut out and dry for fuel. To cultivate a garden the peat has to be removed first of all.

After a few days the Uruguayan Government offered Shackleton their trawler *Instituto de Pesca* No. I. He gladly accepted this generous offer, and the trawler was despatched at once from Montevideo, arriving at Port Stanley on June 10th. Shackleton, Crean and I were thankful to step aboard her, for the time we had spent in kicking our heels about the cable office and trying to find a ship had got on our nerves, and Shackleton himself was in a fever of impatience.

We were now at the height of the Southern winter, and on this, our second attempt to reach Elephant Island, we had stormy weather all the way. On the third day at dawn we sighted the island, but when we arrived within twenty miles of its northern shore we found that the whole of the area between ourselves and the land was filled with impenetrable pack-ice. For hours we searched to the eastward, and at length were successful in finding some looser pack-ice, through which I attempted to force the vessel. I hoped that the little open water which I saw might mean that we could outflank the pack. Once we got into it, however, we saw that if we were not quick in getting out we should be beset, and a small unprotected steel vessel like this would have gone down immediately the ice pinched her. In addition we were running short of coal, for the little ship could not contain enough for a long journey. Therefore, although Shackleton was nearly heart-broken, we were compelled to return. It was a dreadful experience to get within so short a distance of our marooned shipmates and then fail to reach them. At one time we were actually facing the camp, and had it not been for a white low-lying mist they would have seen us. With each mile that we put between the island and ourselves our spirits sank lower, and we were not altogether sorry when a gale sprang up and took our minds perforce from the waiting men.

We returned to Port Stanley, and from there Shackleton sent the trawler home, to the disappointment of the captain and crew, who were anxious to try again. Unfortunately her engines had been giving a certain amount of trouble, and she proved to be too slow for the job. She was supposed to do ten knots on six tons of coal, but actually she did six knots on ten tons, which completely ruled her out of court for our purpose. It was now past the middle of June and we were no nearer Elephant Island.

The residents of the Falkland Islands were most sympathetic to us in our plight, and Shackleton was the guest of the Governor, Mr. Douglas Young, while I stayed with Commodore Luce, who lent me his cabin in H.M.S. *Glas-*

gow. But not even the wonderful kindness that was shown to us could lessen the strain under which we laboured.

After a few days the mail boat *Orita* put in, and Shackleton decided that we should go in her to Punta Arenas, in the Straits of Magellan, where he hoped to get a more suitable vessel. At Punta Arenas, which is Chilian, there are large numbers of British residents, and they treated us royally. Headed by Mr. Allan MacDonald they raised fifteen hundred pounds and chartered the little seventy-ton schooner *Emma* for us. She was rather a well-known little craft, about forty years old, and had been a seal-poacher. She was of oak, strong and well-built, and had auxiliary oil engines of a sort. I never took very kindly to the engines, and later these proved to be nearly as much of a nuisance as a help. We signed on seven seamen of varying nationalities. One of the newcomers had done twelve months in jail for seal-poaching in this self-same schooner, but this did not worry us as we found him a good and cheery seaman. As an extra officer we took a very dashing little Chilean lieutenant, Ramon Aguirre, who came aboard with a pair of sea-boots, an oil-skin coat and a guitar. The Chilean Government lent us a steamer, the *Yelcho,* to tow us the first part of the way; but as soon as we got outside the Straits of Magellan the tow-rope parted, and Shackleton told the tug to go back. She left us, but to our surprise rejoined us next day, as we were heaving up anchor from a small bay in Staten Island. She threw us a rope and towed us for fifty miles, but then returned, as a heavy gale was springing up and she could have been of no more assistance to us.

I had had command of schooners in the South Pacific and rather looked forward to the voyage. I soon found, however, that this was a very different proposition. In a seventy-foot schooner far south of Cape Horn in the depth of the winter you can have quite a lively time. We did. On the second day of the gale we had to heave-to, but forty-eight hours later we had worked down to comparatively smooth water along the edge of the pack-ice. Unfortunately the pack-ice now extended to a hundred miles north of Elephant Island. We searched along it under sail and finally, seeing an opening in the ice, we headed into it and started up the engine. There was a heavy swell running and the ice was swinging and bumping heavily, but since the *Emma* was of oak we could take more chances than with her steel predecessors. When we had worked a few miles into the opening, however, avoiding many heavy and dangerous masses of ice, she lifted high on a swell, and swinging her bowsprit hard down on a heavy floe carried away her bobstay and nearly lost the spar.

As it was obvious that we should meet with more serious damage if we continued we were forced once again to turn back, with the ice getting more closely packed round us all the time. The intake of the engine was choked by the ice, which stopped it running, so that I was compelled to take her out under sail alone. Finally we escaped from the ice, and for three days longer we worked our way along the pack, trying to see whether there was any way of getting round it to reach Elephant Island. At last we were driven to recognise that at this time of the year it could not be done.

This last disappointment was a bitter one to Shackleton. It was hard enough for Crean and me, but on Shackleton's shoulders lay the main responsibility, and so deep were his emotions that, in contradistinction to his behaviour after the first two attempts, he did not even speak of the men on the island now. It was a silence more eloquent than words.

We hove-to for one more night in the faint hope that the gale which was then blowing might open up the ice; but in the morning the pack was closer than ever. The schooner was one mass of ice from freezing spray. The ropes had accumulated ice until these were thicker than a man's arm, and the sails were sheets of it. This was a dangerous state of affairs, as it might have meant having to cut the sails away should it become necessary to take them in. An added difficulty was that some of the crew were pretty well done in, being unaccustomed to the piercing cold and the continual bumping, tossing and jerking of the little vessel. Indeed her careerings were wild enough to upset the most hardened seaman. But despite all these hardships, Aguirre, the little Chilean officer, was as gay as ever, and played to us on his guitar whenever he had a spare hour.

When it became obviously impossible to go on we set to, once more, to face the dreary business of turning away without our men. I dreaded the landing, for I knew that to return to port would be so very different from all that Shackleton had hoped, and that to step ashore without having accomplished our object would be like rubbing salt into an open wound. Yet there was nothing for it, and we were forced to reconcile ourselves to a situation that was, to put it mildly, nerve-racking.

For the first twelve hours I headed the ship north-west for Cape Horn, but a gale of wind coming on from ahead we had to beat against it. Any seaman can imagine what this was like—trying to beat up to Cape Horn from the south, in winter, in a tiny schooner with a fifty-foot boom continually trying to take charge, while we rolled and pitched everlastingly. Day after day, as I worked out my observations, I found that we had made no headway. This continued until we were three weeks out.

The wear and tear of this period was dreadful. To Shackleton it was little less than maddening. Lines scored themselves on his face more deeply day by day; his thick, dark, wavy hair was becoming silver. He had not had a grey hair when we had started out to rescue our men the first time. Now, on the third return journey, he was grey-headed. Shackleton was very human—human enough to become irritable with me and to treat me rather as though I could have prevented the gale had I so chosen. So far from minding this I was glad that he should have some little outlet for his misery.

On the twenty-fourth day that we had been on board we got a fair enough slant of wind to enable me to head the schooner once more for Port Stanley. This held for two days, and on the twenty-seventh day of our journey I was beating her up through Port William into Port Stanley. We got in just after dark.

Shackleton was taking his disappointment very badly. As I had feared, the sight of the land to which he had counted on bringing his men, and to which he had to return without them, cast him into the depths of despair. For the first time in three years I saw him take a glass of whiskey. He was unaccustomed to it and it affected him at once.

We reached Port Stanley on August 8th and news was awaiting Shackleton that the *Discovery* was about to leave England and that she could be out in about six weeks. In his present mood this seemed as bad as if he had heard that she was to reach us in six years. He was in an acute fever of mind about the condition of his men away in the south, and every day increased that fever. His days were bad; what his nights were like I can only imagine. He had already had a difference with the Admiralty when he was in Punta Arenas, over what he considered the irksome restrictions that were being placed on him in regard to the rescue of his men. In fact he had let his feelings so far get the better of him as to cable scathingly to the authorities that they were winding his men in a shroud of red tape. His anger, intensified by his impatience to reach his men, caused him to decide to appeal to the Chilean Government for help. His first step was to cable to them, asking them to lend him the *Yelcho* to tow the *Emma* back to Punta Arenas. His plan was to go to Chile himself, where he would be in close touch with that Government, and persuade them to lend him the *Yelcho* for a final attempt to reach the marooned men. He much preferred this to waiting for the *Discovery*. Waiting, in fact, had become impossible for him.

As soon as we arrived at Punta Arenas he enquired whether there were any suitable vessel to be had, and finding that his only chance lay in the *Yelcho*, he approached the authorities. The Chilean Government were aware that they were being asked to lend the vessel for what was little better than a forlorn hope, but they agreed at once. The *Yelcho* was a small steel vessel used in their lighthouse service, and, like the three other vessels that we had employed, was unprotected and unsuitable for ice work. Shackleton therefore thought it only fair to promise the Chilean Government that he would not take her into pack-ice.

It took only twenty-four hours to get the little vessel ready. Her Captain, Luis Pardo, and the crew of the *Yelcho* volunteered to a man. These Chileans are, in my opinion, by far the finest seamen in South America. Probably they are the best Latin sailors in the world. Our friend Ramon Aguirre, complete with guitar, came again of course, and very glad we were to have him. He was a most amusing character, completely indifferent to everything but the pleasure that he could extract from the moment, and always in high spirits. He had never seen ice before he joined us, but he simply ignored its presence and carried on as though he were

The rescue (ROYAL GEOGRAPHICAL SOCIETY)

in home waters. We had ample equipment and provisions, all of which were presented to Shackleton by the Chileans and English settlers, whom we now looked upon as brothers.

On August 25th we started out on the fourth attempt at rescue. We steamed through the Beagle Channel and the following night anchored off Ushuaia, the most southerly town in the world. The township contained an Argentine convict station, the streets had boarded pavements and were lit by electric light, and although the great mountains at the back and the whole countryside were covered deep in snow, we found great comfort when we enjoyed the hospitality of the Governor of the jail.

Next morning at daylight we proceeded to Woolaston Island, just north of Cape Horn, where, by arrangement with the Chilean Government, we were to fill our bunkers with coal so that we should have a sufficient supply for the nine-hundred-mile journey to and from Elephant Island.

As soon as we left I set a course east of Cape Horn,

straight for the North-West Breaker of Elephant Island. In the matter of weather we had the first bit of good luck that had come our way for a long time, for it was fine and clear, and the sea was almost smooth. Our spirits rose, and Shackleton was confident that at last we should get our men off the Island. He was a different man—vigorous and alert, urging the engineers to drive the little ship hell-for-leather.

A day and a half's hard steaming brought us close to Elephant Island. All went well until midnight, when a thick fog came up and made us uneasy. We wanted no set-back now.

Shackleton, very anxious, came to me on the bridge.

"How far do you make it to the North-West Breaker?" he asked.

"Sixty miles," I replied. "We should reach it at daybreak."

"That's dangerous," he said. "Supposing we have a strong current with us?"

"I've allowed for that," I answered; "and I think we ought to push on."

"No," he said slowly; "we won't run any risk—especially at this stage. If it doesn't clear by two o'clock put her at half-speed."

Being so close to our marooned shipmates we were considerably excited, and we anxiously watched for the fog to lift. But it didn't, and at two o'clock, with very great reluctance, I carried out Shackleton's orders and rang half-speed. In fact it would have been less trying to me to press through the fog than it was to slow down the *Yelcho*. We were heading straight for the North-West Breaker of the Island—an area of about two acres of submerged rock over which the sea broke furiously at all states of the tide. It was ten miles from the shore and twenty-five miles distant from the camp on Elephant Island. On two or three occasions before we had left the Island I had watched, from the top of the hundred-foot promontory in front of the camp, the seas shoot up to a great height from this ledge. A more forbidding place is difficult to conceive and it may be thought that for us to approach such a reef in a fog was a highly dangerous thing to do; but I knew the exact position and that ledge always manifested itself by breaking seas. Moreover there were no rocks outside it, and our little vessel was so handy that I could swing her round in less than a hundred yards. If we did not hold on our course, there was a possibility of striking other dangerous rocks off the north shore. The ledge would give us our exact position, and as I knew the course and distance from it to the camp, it was better than heading straight in for the coast, a proceeding which might have lost us time in locating the camp.

At daybreak it was still foggy. Shackleton and I had spent the night together on the bridge. We were, as may be imagined, considerably on the *qui vive*; for we had promised the Chileans not to take the vessel into pack-ice, and so we dreaded above all things the sight of floes coming through the fog. As it began to grow light, I said:

"I'll go up into the bows, so that I can see anything that's coming along. At the same time I shall be able to look down into the water and see if it changes colour for the depth."

Shackleton hesitated for a moment and then said, "You have been trying to get me to go full speed ahead. Well, we'll do it now, if you think it's good enough."

"Splendid," I replied. "We'll soon have them on board."

We now saw a few small patches of floating pack-ice, which we knew were the vanguards of the great masses farther south that are continually drifting north. It had become a race between the *Yelcho* and the ice. I went into the bows and scanned alternately the water beneath us and the fog in front. Suddenly I saw what appeared to be a great mass of pack-ice looming up through the fog dead ahead. As I pointed to it and waved for the helm to be starboarded Shackleton also spotted it. But even as we gazed at this pack-ice we realised that there was something extraordinary about it, and a few seconds later it sent up a great foaming sea. It was not pack-ice, the fog had disguised it: it was the sea breaking over the north-west ledge. Depression changed to relief indescribable. I knew exactly where we were, and shouted out to Shackleton.

"East by south is the course for the camp," I yelled, and by the time that I had got back to the bridge he had steadied her on her course.

It was a happy moment, and when I came alongside of him he said nice things about the accuracy of my landfall— if such it could be called.

"How long before we land?" he said eagerly.

"A little over two hours, if we are not checked by the pack."

"Pray Heaven we won't be," he said, fervently.

An hour later the fog cleared enough to enable us to see the tops of the mountains of Elephant Island. But the whole of the coast line was still shrouded. We had no great difficulty in clearing the numerous stranded bergs that were perched on shallow banks around us, and by noon the coast line was beginning to define itself. As the fog lifted still more, Shackleton and I searched the coast with our glasses. We were perplexed at not seeing the camp, as we were now drawing very close in shore. Presently I glanced back a little and saw the familiar shape of the little peninsula, so much clearer in profile. I shouted to Shackleton and ordered the helm hard a-port, for I realised in a flash the agony of mind that would be experienced by the marooned men as they watched us go past them.

As I was turning her, Shackleton was peering with almost painful intensity through his binoculars. There were reefs and shoals about and all my attention was on the ship, when I heard him say in a low strained voice:

"There are only two, Skipper!" Then, "No, four!" A short pause followed and he exclaimed, "I see six—eight—" and at last, in a voice ringing with joy he cried, "They are all there! Every one of them! They are all saved!"

He put his glasses back in their case and turned to me, his face showing more emotion than I had ever known it show before. Crean had joined us, and we were all unable to speak. Then Shackleton galvanised into life. It sounds trite, but years literally seemed to drop from him as he stood before us. In that moment he had sloughed the never-ceasing anxiety of four months.

I was obliged to bring the ship in very slowly, for navigation there required considerable care, but as soon as the boat was lowered Shackleton leapt into it. And as he drew close into the shore I heard him shout: "Are you all well?" Back came their answering yell, "All well!" followed by his wholehearted "Thank God!" It was a wonderful little drama and their cheers were good to hear.

Next time that I could take my eyes off the ship I saw them crowding round him, wringing both his arms.

Northwards
Once More

WHEN I got near enough to the shore I stopped the ship and watched the men embarking in the *Yelcho's* little boat to come aboard. Shackleton, fearing that the pack might close round us and imprison us, was determined not to lose a minute in getting all the men off Elephant Island. It was imperative, too, to get on board the records of the Expedition and the photographs and films that Hurley had made, as herein lay his only chance of paying off the expenses of the Expedition, which fell on his shoulders.

Greenstreet was the first to leap on board and clasp my hand. He exclaimed, "We all knew that it would be all right if you were on board, Skipper." "Why, how's that?" I asked, and he replied: "Don't you remember when we were seeing you off we said that you weren't born to be *drowned?*" I laughed at the inference, as the scene of our departure suddenly came back to me.

The boat had to make three trips to bring all on board, but so swift was Shackleton that within an hour we were steaming away in the direction of Cape Horn. This was at 1 P.M. on August 30th, 1916—a hundred and twenty-eight days since we had left them—days covering the worst of the Antarctic winter.

Frank Wild, who had been in charge of the marooned party and had held them together all this time, was soon giving us his story. I cannot, of course, quote it word for word, nor can I put in any of our own numerous interpolations and comments, but, so far as I remember, it was something like this:

"You know, Sir, when you left, I was always sure you would get through—so much so that about two weeks after you sailed I rather amused the men by starting to say every morning, 'Roll up your bags, boys, the "Boss" may be coming back to-day.' I don't mind telling you, though, that it got pretty wearisome saying it, and I admit that I became a bit doubtful about it myself at times, but of course I never let anyone else know that. And to tell the truth I little thought that it would be to-day when, almost as a matter of routine, I sang it out this morning.

"The day after you left in the *James Caird* the Island was surrounded with heavy pack-ice, so you got away only just in time.

"My first consideration after you left was to make really good shelter for the men. I looked upon that as being almost as important as the food supply. You remember that hole we started to dig in the ice-slope before you left? Well, I went on, and made a cave there in which we could have lived if I found that it became too dangerous to remain under the boats. I was very thankful that we did not have to try it, since with twenty-two men living in it the temperature would generally have been above freezing point, and then we could never have kept the place dry. Anyway, digging it was an occupation for the men and took their minds, for the time being, away from your departure.

"After that we collected big flat stones and built two walls on which to rest the ends of the boat. These walls were four feet high and nineteen feet apart. On top of these we put the two boats upside down and side by side. We lashed them securely to the rocks and laid all the wood we had across the boats from keel to keel. We made all the improvements we could and effectually closed in the space underneath the sides of the boat. The work was very hard against the wind and snow, especially as we were all ridiculously weak and our fingers got frost-bitten continually.

"At the end of April we had a tremendous storm, which nearly destroyed the hut and finished off young Hussey. The wind was terrific. It came in a succession of hurricane gusts that swept down the glacier. All these gusts were heralded by a low rumbling which suddenly increased to a thunderous roar. Snow and stones came whizzing through the air, and we piled heavy rocks on everything outside, as otherwise it would have been blown into the sea. This actually happened to those things that we didn't have time to weight down; we lost a lot of our cooking-pots and two bales of sennegras in this way. Six of the men were shaking the snow off a floor-cloth of the tent when a sudden gust tore it out of their hands and swept it away to sea.

"Hussey was digging up frozen meat with a pick-axe and the same gust forced him down to the beach; but there, fortunately, he managed to drive his pick into the shingle and hang on for dear life until the squall was over. The force of the wind was extraordinary, and ice-sheets up to two or three feet across and a quarter of an inch thick were being hurled about and splintered, so that everybody had to rush into the hut, for it was like being in a shower of broken glass.

"A little later on we had another remarkably heavy gale from the north-west which brought up such a tremendous sea that it broke within four yards of the hut.

"One day during a heavy blizzard I decided to try to cook inside. You know what Green is—he would manage to make shift with anything. He did cook a meal all right, but the blubber smoke was enough to poison us, and we all had a bad time. Some of the fellows got smoke blindness, which was very like snow blindness. It was very painful and Micky and Mac had to attend to them. Kerr made a chimney out of the tin lining of one of the biscuit cases, and after that our little home was a happier one. Anyway, there was much less smoke.

"Some time after you left we gradually got everybody's clothes dry with the help of the stove. That cheered us a lot. The men who had changed clothes with Vincent and McNeish when they fell into the water just before you left took a fortnight to get dry.

"One of the most annoying things was the perpetual darkness inside. It wasn't much better outside, and most of the time we could not tell whether the sun was up or not. I was determined, however, that we should be able to see each other inside the boats. We therefore made lamps out of sardine tins, with bits of surgical bandage for wicks. We used oil from seal blubber. At its best it only gave a very poor light, but it was better than the total darkness in which we had been living. To improve matters in the daytime, I sewed the glass lid of the chronometer box into the canvas under the side of the boat. Later on I made three more windows with celluloid panels from that photograph case that you left behind.

"The fellows who were on the floor could read and sew, which relieved the monotony considerably. The library, as you know, consisted only of two books of poetry, one of which was yours, one book of Nordenskjold's Expedition, and two volumes of the Encyclopædia Britannica, and a penny cookery book of Marston's. The cookery book was sometimes dashed annoying, because it reminded us of all the things we couldn't get. Of course our clothes were in such a state that it took nearly all our spare time to repair them.

"When the temperature rose a little the water from all round ran down into the hut. So we dug a hole in the floor, and from this we had to bail water for hours. This went on for three days. We got rid of a hundred gallons the first day, a hundred and fifty the second, and on the third a hundred and sixty. In the end we removed a bit of the wall and dug a long channel down to the sea. After that we had no more trouble with water.

"You remember that big glacier across the bay at the back of the camp? Well, that calved twice. Thousands of tons of ice fell into the sea and raised a huge wave that swept right across. If it hadn't been that there was a lot of ice floating about the bay which checked the swell, I think it would have carried us all away into the sea. As it was the water came surging under the hut. If it had been over it instead of under, probably we shouldn't be here now.

"The weather has been hellish. It seemed to be an unending series of blizzards, hurricanes, snowstorms and gales. That big glacier, as you know, was moving down the gulley and seemed to funnel the wind down. The air was hardly ever free from spindrift, and great lumps of ice were tossed about. Whatever we had in our hands—cooking-pots, clothes or anything else—would be blown right out of our grasp. What worried me was the danger of some of the men being blown into the sea.

"During the first fortnight the wind reached a force of over a hundred miles an hour. We had to shout to make ourselves heard. The noise of the wind was appalling. The sky was continually overcast and the land was shrouded with mist and snow. In fact, it seemed to us that almost the only time it was ever clear was when the pack-ice surrounded the island.[1]

"Whenever the pack-ice hemmed us in we got a bit depressed," went on Wild, "because we knew that it would cut off your return. Also, it stopped the seals from coming up on the beach. That, of course, produced a shortage of food. The penguins and seals migrated north at about the time you left. After that it was rarely that we got them in any numbers. I laid in as big a supply of seal and penguin meat as I could, for I knew, of course, that a scarcity of seals meant a shortage of fuel as well as of food. These precautions were not so successful as I could have wished, for we had a warm spell, and a lot of the meat went bad. We got so short of food that we had to scrape about in the snow for bones and pieces of meat that we had previously considered unfit to eat. We stewed them up with limpets off the rocks and some of that dulse sea-weed that you remember we ate when you were there. By this time everybody was rather run down, partly through the conditions and partly through the monotony. It will give you an idea of our condition when I tell you that even Greenstreet and Clark—as you know, our star turns—had lost their appetite. The effect of the dulse, however, was so stimulating that it gave everybody such an appetite that we had to go easy with it. Occasionally we snared some paddies, and these were a boon.[2]

"We thought ourselves very lucky when we caught some penguins with undigested fish in their gullets, and we used

---

[1] When pack-ice covers the sea, the latter cannot give off vapour and mist, and therefore the air becomes much clearer.

[2] Paddies are white birds, superficially something like pigeons and about the same size.

to cook these in tins hung up over the stove. We got very fed up with a meat diet, especially as it was such a restricted one, and we all longed for cereals. The men used to curse themselves when they remembered that there had been times at home when they had refused second helpings of pudding! Out of curiosity, one day, I asked each man what he would most like to eat. The majority wanted suet puddings. It was interesting, because it showed their craving for carbohydrates.

"On Saturday nights we drank the old toast of 'sweethearts and wives'—in methylated spirits, mixed with hot water, ginger powder and sugar. It sounds a ghastly drink, but a couple of the men got quite merry on it one Saturday. Of course it was a case of anything for a diversion.

"On midwinter's day we had a regular celebration— Hussey gave us a concert on his banjo. He has been consistently cheerful all through, and his songs and the entertainment we got out of it were at times the only things that kept our spirits up. The waiting naturally wore us down.

"I had a bit of trouble with the health of some of the men. One or two had heart attacks, and all of them were weak. Occasionally one would get lightheaded. The whole lot of us were frost-bitten, and Blackborow's condition was a great worry to me. You remember the state he was in when you went? Well, he got worse. Finally he was threatened with gangrene. Macklin and McIlroy had to amputate his toes. Under the circumstances it was really a wonderful operation. We boiled up all the water we could, but in the condition we were in it was difficult to keep things antiseptic. Happily they had just enough chloroform left. One of our great difficulties was to get the place warm. We were afraid that after the anæsthetic the shock of cold might kill him.

Our arrival at Valparaiso
(SCOTT POLAR RESEARCH INSTITUTE)

When everything was ready we cleared out of the hut and closed up the entrance and plastered snow all round so that no cold air could get in. The blubber lamps then raised the temperature to about sixty degrees. Mick and Mac said they found it very difficult work, being hampered by the smoke and the poor light. Nevertheless, the operation was successful.

"Sometimes, for as long as a fortnight at a time, the island was surrounded by heavy pack-ice, and then it would break up and clear away for a few days. Whenever this happened we used to keep a very sharp look-out for you, hoping every day that we should see you. The disappointment at each sunset when it was realised that another day had gone and that you had not appeared had a depressing effect on every-

Blackborow and 'Mrs. Chippy'
(SCOTT POLAR RESEARCH INSTITUTE)

body. At times frayed nerves got the better of some of us—it certainly was hell when we ran out of tobacco.

"Toward the end of this month we had a series of south-west gales that got the ice on the run. And two days before you came along the last of the pack disappeared to the north-east, leaving a comparatively clear sea. For some reason I thought you would come this time. God knows we needed you. We had become terribly anxious about you as week after week went by, and I personally, as the man left in charge by you, was worried because we had only two days' seal and penguin meat left, and no signs of any more coming along. I was determined, of course, not to touch the fourteen

days' reserve stores unless absolutely driven to it by actual
starvation. I was keeping these stores, as you know, for the
early summer, in case you did not return. If things had
panned out like that I should have attempted a boat journey
to Deception Island as soon as the ice had cleared off sufficiently for the whalers to start there. But I doubt whether we
could have lasted out till summer.

"To-day we collected limpets, sea-weed and seal bones
for a stew. I was dishing out the lunch, and Hurley and
Marston were outside taking a long look to seaward for you,
a thing that some of us were always doing when we were
not surrounded by the pack. The mist was just clearing
away, when Marston suddenly saw you and yelled out,
'Ship, O!' Inside the hut we thought that it was a call for the
lunch, and took no notice. Then I heard him running along
as hard as he could, and as he ran, gasping: 'Wild, there's a
ship. Let's burn a flare.'

"We all made a dive for the narrow door and those that
could not get through recklessly tore down the canvas sides
in their haste. The hoosh pot was kicked over and the stew
spilt, and it will show you how excited we were when I tell
you that nobody paid any attention to that.

"It was a cheery sight to see this little vessel coming along,
but not so cheery when we saw that she was passing us and
going on. I drove a pick through a petrol tin, and poured it
over my waistcoat to set fire to it and make a smoke. If our
thoughts had been less confused we should probably have
realised that you must be on board, since no one else would
come within a radius of hundreds of miles: but we were too
worked up to think very clearly.

"Macklin dashed to the flag-staff to hoist the flag, but
everything was frozen up, so he hoisted his sweater instead.
The rest of the men were dashing about and yelling, al-

though they must have known that their voices could never carry that distance. And then, just before my waistcoat blazed up, to our utter joy, we saw you turn and head straight for the camp. I was a bit puzzled about the Chilean flag, but when I saw the boat lowered, although I couldn't make out your face, I recognised your figure. You must have heard us cheer then? And the first thing that everybody said was 'Thank God, the Boss is safe.' As a matter of fact we were really more worried about your safety than our own. We knew that you would be taking pretty long odds to reach us."

As a matter of fact, Wild was right. Both at Port Stanley and at Punta Arenas many people thought that Shackleton was mad to go down to the pack-ice, in the dead of winter, in small, unprotected vessels. But these people did not re-alise that suspense was ravaging him so that he could not rest, that he thought no risks could be too great if they of-fered any chance, however faint, of getting his men back in safety. I may add that Crean and I, who had been through it all with him, thought that he was absolutely right.

Wild finished his story by telling us how, as we ap-proached, they had carried Blackborow, who could not walk, to a high rock and propped him up in his sleeping-bag so that, as Wild put it, he should have a front seat in the stalls and not miss any of the wonderful show. This act was typical of Wild. It was a wonderful tribute to him that the men should be in such splendid condition after all they had endured, and it was owing to his efficient discipline and ir-repressible optimism that the party had been held together in such shape, and their spirits maintained throughout that long, black period of waiting. Wild was the kind of man who was at his best when everything was against him and he had his back to the wall.

All the time that Wild was telling his story the men, still very excited, were wandering round the ship, talking, laughing, even singing. They had had no news for four and a half months, and none of the outer world for nearly two years. Now they were trying to make up for it. A good many were surprised to hear that the War was still going on. They seemed to have great difficulty in grasping what had happened, which was natural enough considering that they had not been able to follow any of the developments and, so far as the War was concerned, were in the condition of Rip Van Winkle when he woke up. They all smoked like chimneys, but they had been on short commons for so long that this, on top of the first really hearty meal they had had for months, upset most of them. Moreover they were unaccustomed by now to the motion of a ship; so the groups gradually dispersed. But our dinner that night was a cheery one, and it was midnight before we turned in.

Next day it blew a gale from the west, and after consulting with Shackleton I took the ship through the Straits of Le Maire between Staten Island and Tierra del Fuego, and so we came to anchor at Rio Secco at 8 A.M. on Sunday, September 3rd. Shackleton went ashore and telephoned to his friend the Governor of Punta Arenas that his men were safe. We then hove up our anchor and arrived off Punta Arenas while most of the population were at church.

The news of our arrival spread rapidly. Bells were rung, fire alarms were sounded, and the police were instructed to broadcast the news that the *Yelcho* had arrived with every man of the party safe. Services were curtailed and the whole population of Punta Arenas streamed down to welcome Shackleton's men as we landed on the wharf. It was proclaimed a fête day.

The Chileans were delighted at the fact that it was on a

ship flying their flag, built by them and lent by them, that Shackleton had rescued his men. Nothing would content them but that we should march through the town with a band playing, not their own national anthem as might well have been expected, but "God Save the King." Each one of the men from Elephant Island, despite the fact that he was dirty, bearded and ragged, disreputable looking to the last degree, was seized upon by the various families of the *élite* of the town and carried off in triumph to be their guest. The local hospitality seemed to know no bounds, and I look back at my stay at Punta Arenas as one of the most wonderful times I have ever had. Shackleton, Crean and I, of course, had already made friends there.

On the evening of our arrival we were entertained by the British residents at their club. The Chileans, however, decided that they would welcome us on the following night at theirs. And they were set upon outdoing our own countrymen in hospitality if possible.

The Chilean dinner started at eight in the evening and did not finish until one in the morning. It was interspersed with a few short speeches, but it was mainly devoted to "taking wine." From different parts of the table, at short intervals, a Chilean would rise and say, "A glass of wine with you, gentlemen," and we, of course, would fill our glasses and drink. About half-way through the dinner it dawned upon me that Chilean hospitality was hospitality indeed; for by making us take wine with individuals at frequent intervals, our hosts were ensuring that we should drink six or eight glasses to their one! For a time we managed to hold our own by leaving large "heel-taps," but this was soon noticed by our hosts, who roared "Al seco!" to urge us to drain our glasses. Realising that there was heavy weather ahead, Shackleton, who according to his rule was not drinking, excused himself and slipped away. Shortly afterwards Greenstreet and I did the same. As we came out of the club, a magnificent and most luxurious place, the moon was shining brightly. Sailor-fashion, I looked up at it for a moment or two, and when I lowered my gaze I saw to my amazement that we were surrounded by men with fixed bayonets.

I said to the Chilean officer in charge, "What is the meaning of this?"

He stepped forward, bowed and saluted, and said, "Pardon, señor. Ze orders are: 'No sober *gringo* (foreigner) leaves ze building!' "

"But we're not sober," I protested.

He scrutinised us carefully, and not wishing to give us the lie direct, replied tactfully, "But you are not drunk enough!"

So we were compelled to return to the dining-room.

The next night Shackleton related our Antarctic experiences at a public lecture. He had a peculiar aptitude for learning just as much of a language as he needed, consequently we were not greatly surprised when he delivered a lecture lasting forty minutes in fluent—and, I trust, pure—Castilian to our delighted friends the Chileans.

Now that his anxieties concerning the marooned party on Elephant Island were over, fresh troubles began to assail him. The *Aurora*, his ship on the Ross Sea side, south of New Zealand, which was to have come in to McMurdo Sound and taken him off after his trans-Continental journey (had that succeeded) had been drifting to and fro in the Ross Sea pack-ice all the time that we had been drifting in the Weddell Sea in the *Endurance*. Fortunately the Ross Sea ice is not quite so bad as that of the Weddell Sea. Even so, Stenhouse, the captain of the *Aurora*, had avoided disaster only by his skilful seamanship. Twice he had made all preparations to abandon the ship, though fortunately he was not forced to do so. But he went through a very bad time. After months of drifting the rudder was torn off by the floes. Stenhouse, with great skill, then rigged a jury-rudder from the spanker gaff weighted with steel plates. As the ship gradually drifted out into the open through the pack-ice he lowered this over the stern, and with a tackle on each side hauled the rudder to starboard or port as necessary, and so steered his ship and brought her safely to New Zealand across one of the stormiest oceans in the world. This great feat of seamanship saved his crew and ship, and by this accomplishment he made it possible for Shackleton to rescue the men left behind on the Antarctic Continent when the *Aurora* was driven out of the McMurdo Sound by a blizzard. But I must explain the situation regarding the Ross Sea Expedition.

Shackleton had sent out the *Aurora* under Captain Mackintosh, who, on arrival at McMurdo Sound, left the *Aurora*, and laid depôts of food out to the Beardmore Glacier. This was done in readiness for Shackleton's crossing the continent, so as to provision him for the last stages of his journey. It was while Mackintosh was occupied with this work that the *Aurora*, during a heavy gale, was torn by the ice from her moorings and started out on a long twelve-months' drift.

Now that Shackleton had time to attend to this branch of the Expedition he learned that a committee, the Ross Sea Relief, had been formed in Australia. This committee, which was responsible to three different Governments, British, Australian and New Zealand, had most amazingly decided that Shackleton's presence was not necessary on board his own ship the *Aurora*, which had returned to port and which it was proposed to send out again to rescue the Ross Sea party as soon as possible. Whatever the reason for this action against Shackleton, it seemed to me the most egregious piece of foolishness which I had yet come across, and I can only imagine that it was prompted by a petty spirit of resentment at Shackleton's outspoken remarks and criticisms. He had never been a man who brooked interference with his most carefully thought-out plans, and he had never suffered fools gladly. On top of this he now received the news that the command had been taken from that splendid seaman Stenhouse, in spite of his obvious suitability and experience and knowledge of Antarctic conditions, and handed over to Captain J. K. Davis.

The situation made Shackleton once again blaze up with impatience. His one thought was to get to New Zealand as quickly as possible, to attend personally to the rescue of the stranded party. It was a repetition of the anxiety that I had witnessed when our men were stranded on Elephant Island.

He now availed himself eagerly of the Chilean Government's offer of the services of the *Yelcho* to convey the whole party up to Valparaiso, where the Chileans desired to give us a national welcome. We steamed up the west coast of South America through nearly two thousand miles of the wonderful series of natural channels that exist here. There are thousands of islands, inhabited by only a few wandering natives, and these islands act as natural breakwaters against the heavy gales of the South Pacific. They are covered with forests of evergreen trees that continue almost up to the snow line. To the eastward the towering Andes shed enormous glaciers into the deep Sounds below. Little icebergs and large lumps of ice have to be guarded against frequently. Navigation had to be suspended a good deal in the darkness, as these channels were intricate and were continually swept by storms of wind and rain. This region has the second heaviest rainfall in the world.

The natives on this coast are a miserable and stunted lot. One day a canoe made from a hollowed-out tree came alongside while we were at anchor. This contained a family—father, mother, a baby, small boy and a young girl. All were naked except the old man, who wore a ragged old coat. They had a small fire burning in the bottom of the canoe, over which mother, daughter, and son sat huddled. We gave them some food and a lot of old clothes, with which they were delighted and which they put on in our presence. Generally it is thought that these people wear skins of some sort in winter, but actually here were these unfortunates without any clothing whatever. Physically they were of a low Indian type. In their boat were two beautiful sea-otter skins, about two feet long. These they sometimes get by diving, catching the otters under water with their hands. They also catch fish by this method.

We arrived at Valparaiso on September 27th, and here we were given a magnificent reception. The whole of the Chilean Navy was in the Bay, every ship was dressed with bunting, and they manned ship as the little *Yelcho*, with all her flags flying and all our party cheering back in reply to the Chileans, steamed proudly along. Every craft and little boat that would float appeared to be out, and the Chilean and British flags were everywhere in evidence: it was amusing to note that every little boat had a flag with "Shackleton" at one end and "Pardo," the captain of the *Yelcho*, at the other. Captain Pardo, by the way, had his work cut out to avoid ramming some of these small boats, so closely were they swarming round us.

When we came alongside the quay we were greeted by a cheering, roaring mob of over thirty thousand people, who welcomed us so heartily that they nearly pushed us off into the sea again. Shackleton was carried away and we lost him for a full half-hour. To get to the Town Hall, where we were expected, we were obliged to form a football scrum and almost fight our way through.

The following night the Chilean Minister for Foreign Affairs publicly decorated Shackleton, who presently called upon the President of the Republic and thanked him for his help. The President very charmingly reminded him of the part that British sailors had taken in building up the Chilean navy.

Later we were provided with a special train to take us over the Andes. A platform had been built in front of the engine especially for us. At Rosario, on the Pampas, when we had crossed the mountains, a reception was given to Shackleton, and a railway carriage in which we dined was decorated for the purpose of honouring him. It was literally a bower of pink and red roses, a most wonderful sight.

From Buenos Aires Shackleton went on to Montevideo and personally thanked the President of the Republic of Uruguay for the generous help that he and his Government had given in the second relief voyage.

All our party were now eager to get home and take their share in the War, so Shackleton made arrangements for their passage to England. Then he and I started for New Zealand.

During the journey, which by the way involved crossing the Andes again, we would talk for hours on end of what we would do for the Ross Sea party. Now that Shackleton was travelling towards his men his mind was much easier. I persuaded him that since there was nothing he could do until we reached New Zealand he might as well enjoy himself while he could and approach his fresh task in a care-free spirit. All the way up the coast, therefore, we had a splendid time. At each port that the mail steamer called at we had a jollification with the British and Spanish residents.

At Panama we stayed three days, waiting for a steamer to New Orleans, and from there by rail to San Francisco, whence we made our way to New Zealand.

CHAPTER XI

The Ross Sea Party

WE landed at Wellington at the beginning of December. All the way out there, knowing that troubles were brewing ahead, and irritated by the fact that Shackleton's captain had been displaced and that efforts had even been made to prevent his rescuing his own men, I had tried to persuade him to let Stenhouse and myself pirate his own ship with him aboard! The idea undoubtedly appealed to him, from its humorous as well as its practical side. But finally, lest his friends should be placed in an awkward position, he decided against it.

As soon as Shackleton came in contact with the New Zealand Government his magnetic personality won everybody over to him. His one idea was to hasten to his men, and he did not care enough about himself or his rights to delay for an hour to alter details which appeared to his great spirit as being of secondary importance. Therefore he accepted the arrangements that had been made, although by these arrangements he was no longer leader of the Expedition. His unselfish devotion to his men was sufficient to in-

duce him to sign on under Davis on his own ship. Nevertheless, Stenhouse and I felt deeply aggrieved that the Relief
Committee had barred Shackleton from taking either of us
with him, despite our experience, for the sole reason, apparently, that we were Shackleton's men. We felt also very
keenly the indignity to which our leader was being subjected. Had I, as an outsider, been appointed to this command, I should have resigned the position and gone with
Shackleton in any capacity other than as his superior. Captain Davis did resign, but this proved to be only a gesture,
since in the end he sailed in command. I felt sharply, too, the
contrast between the treatment of Shackleton by his own
people and the generous friendship and recent support given
by the Chilean Government.

To obtain a thorough grasp of the situation Shackleton
asked Captain Stenhouse for an exhaustive account of his
adventures in the Ross Sea. I will repeat some of that story
here for the benefit of my readers, asking them to assume
that Captain Stenhouse is speaking:

"As you know, we sailed from Hobart on December
24th, 1914. The *Aurora* was in good shape and things went
pretty well. We landed stores on Macquarie Island for the
meteorological party that occupied the hut erected by Sir
Douglas Mawson's Expedition. Three days later we came
to a belt of pack-ice in 179° E., and six days after that we
were off Ross Island, where it joins the great Ross Barrier."

Here I would explain that the gulfs which penetrate the
Antarctic Continent are hidden under huge ice-barriers
nearly a thousand feet thick. The southern part of the Ross
Sea is covered by one of these. It is a sheet of ice extending
over an area as big as France, and it fronts the Ross Sea with
a cliff of ice four hundred miles long. In places it is two hundred and fifty feet high, whereas at others it is not more than

ten or fifteen feet above sea level. Wherever the depth of water is sufficient—that is about eight hundred feet—these monstrous sheets lie afloat. The surface is then flat, resembling a frozen sea cutting a level line along the foot of the mountain ranges behind. There are no such barriers in the Arctic or elsewhere, although thousands of years ago there was one most probably near North-West Europe, perhaps extending across to North America.

The Ross Barrier has been the highway by which explorers have penetrated to the interior of the Continent. To look at, it is just a barren plain of perfectly flat or slightly undulating snow-covered ice, extending over shallow seas and low-lying land. The presence of land beneath is shown by deep crevasses and the broken-up state of the ice. These conditions are also met with along the mountain ranges on both sides where great glaciers descend into this sea of ice.

To continue with Stenhouse's narrative:

"We were off Cape Crozier on January 9th, 1915. I took a boat ashore with five men to search for a landing place. We were anxious to land that hut that you had sent down to be erected on Cape Crozier for the winter party collecting the Emperor penguins' eggs."

(The Emperor penguin lays its eggs and rears its chicks, strangely enough, in the depth of winter. The conditions then are so hard that the mortality among the chicks is seventy-five per cent. No other creature in the world breeds in such incredibly severe and unfavourable surroundings. The bird lays but one egg, which is five or six inches long and of a dull white colour. It is flattened at one end and pointed at the other, and takes three or four weeks to hatch. As has been already told, it carries this egg in a depression on its feet. There is a penguin rookery at Cape Crozier to which the birds return every year. This rookery has only once been visited, and that was by Captain Scott's party. It has been described in detail by Cherry-Garrard. Shackleton's intention had been that a hut should be landed near the rookery to be utilised by a small party that would cross Ross Island and winter there to study those birds.)

Stenhouse continued:

"We pulled into a bight in the Barrier but failed to scale the steep ice foot under the cliffs, and so we went farther up the bight. In a bay in the ice-cliff was a cul-de-sac with a grotto at the head of it. Here on a ledge of snow were perched several Adelie penguins. It was a wonderful picture we saw, with these birds dotted all about amid the beautiful green and blue tints of the ice colouring. Then we came back to our first landing place. We were only just in time, for no sooner had we cleared the ledge, where one of the men had been hanging while catching a penguin, than the Barrier calved and hundreds of tons of ice toppled over into the sea. It was a pretty narrow squeak.

"We found a slope in the ice-foot and cut steps, and climbed up to a ledge between the ice-foot and the cliffs. For about a mile we walked along the foot of the cliffs. It was terribly rough going—up and down, over gullies and through rocks and *débris* which had fallen from the lofty cliffs towering above. We couldn't find the rookery. There was a narrow space between the cliffs and the Barrier which had broken up and showed signs of heavy pressure, and rounding a turn in the cliffs we saw a most wonderful sight. The Barrier had forced right up against the cliffs and it looked as if icebergs had fallen down into a huge cavern and lay jumbled together in mad confusion. It made one realise the immensity of the forces of Nature.

"On January 16th we reached Cape Evans, and landed ten tons of coal and ninety-eight cases of oil. By January

24th Captain Mackintosh had worked the *Aurora* within nine miles of Hut Point, where we made the ship fast. We then proceeded to arrange sledging parties in readiness for depôt-laying. We knew, of course, that it would be months before we could hope to see you. After Captain Mackintosh had landed with the sledging parties I was in command and had a bad time with the heavy gales continually blowing us away, and ice all about.

"On March 11th I worked the ship into Hut Point, took off some of the party and left a letter for Captain Mackintosh. A heavy southerly gale sprang up and we dragged the anchor out to sea. We drove north past Cape Barne and Cape Royds in very thick weather with a heavy sea running. The ship and everything alow and aloft was cased with ice from frozen spray, and all the time I had to keep dodging bergs and heavy drifting floes. It was a rotten time and I could not get back to Cape Evans until the evening of the 13th. At the Cape I moored the ship close to the shore for winter quarters, with the bows out to sea. We got two anchors ashore and buried them in the heavy stone rubble. We made six steel hawsers fast to the anchors to hold the stern in, while the bow was secured by the ordinary ship's anchors. The ship's heavy cable was also dragged ashore over the ice and made fast to the stern. Your orders had been that the ship was not to winter south of Glacier Tongue on account of the *Discovery* having been unable to break out from there in 1902.

"On the 23rd March I landed Stevens, Spencer-Smith, Gaze and Richards to carry out observations ashore and kill seals for meat and blubber. They took up their quarters in Captain Scott's old hut, with Stevens in charge. I landed coal and a certain proportion of stores and gear.

"I would like you to know that I had taken great pains to

work out the best place to winter the ship. Heavy bay-ice prevented me from getting the ship anywhere near Scott's winter quarters. I had already tried the glacier-tongue and two other places. But at each of these she was in a very exposed and dangerous position, and this, though not my free choice, seemed the best. The ship stood several heavy gales and there was no sign of the ice moving.

"On the 20th I had the fires drawn and the boiler blown down to conserve coal. All through April I was continually nursing the moorings against the onslaughts of the ice.

"On May 6th, in the afternoon, a very strong blizzard came on. At eight in the evening there were very heavy strains on the after-moorings. I could do no more for her then. An hour and three quarters later the ice broke away from the shore. The upheaval caused by the blizzard and the breaking ice was terrific. Our heavy moorings snapped like threads. No moorings ever made could have held her. Through the haze I looked over the stern of the ship and saw the ice breaking up everywhere and the shore rapidly receding into the gloom.

"All hands were instantly on deck and clapped relieving tackles on to the cables forward. I was afraid that with the fearful strain the anchor and cables would tear the windlass out of her. Luckily that did not happen. The bottom sloped steeply so that the anchors did not hold, and we dragged straight out to sea. I ordered steam on the main engines and this was carried out with all possible speed. As we disappeared in the blizzard the light in the little shore hut, towards which I looked quite often, became dimmer and dimmer until at last I could not see it.

"The ice round the ship was breaking and piling all over itself and striking the ship with tremendous thuds. The gale continued fiercely, with a heavy swell out of McMurdo

Sound. I had still every hope, however, of driving her back before the ice had time to freeze over again, though of course I knew that this would be a quick process. All next day the gale was heavy and we drifted helplessly to the north-west. There continued a series of violent blizzards of such force that it was exceedingly difficult to get along the decks at all, and these conditions lasted right up till the 12th—nearly a week of it.

"That day we succeeded in heaving up the two anchors and the seventy fathoms of heavy cable that were hanging down. You can imagine what a job this was in the pack. Both of the anchors were broken.

"By this time I was terribly worried about the men that we had left on shore. I knew that they must be most anxious about what had happened to us. It was impossible that they should have any way of knowing whether we had or had not got through all right.

"All told, there were ten stranded ashore, including Captain Mackintosh. On the *Aurora* there were eighteen of us. As we found ourselves closely beset in the heavy pack-ice it was impossible to do anything whatever with the ship. All my time was devoted to trying to prevent her from being crushed or over-ridden.

"Gradually we realised that we were to be imprisoned for the whole winter. We had a bare supply of winter clothing and so I had to take every care of it and issue it very sparingly indeed.

"Week succeeded week with the most deadly monotony as the *Aurora* drifted slowly north, and sometimes I felt that we should go on like this for ever, until our food gave out. It was impossible not to worry about the men at the hut, although I knew that worrying did no good. I worried about their stores, about their clothes, and as to how the sledging parties had got on. I had got into that state about them in which you worry as much about details as about important things.

"We kept Midwinter's Day as a holiday and had all hands aft to drink the health of the King and the Expedition. For five or six weeks we had seen nothing of the sun, and had lived in the darkness of a winter's night. The men were kept pretty cheerful in spite of this, but we were glad to know that now every day the sun was coming back towards us.

"On July 21st we got into very violent pressure and then the ice opened up into lanes and then closed again on the ship. Unfortunately they closed on her endways. The stern was pushed heavily over on to the ice and the floes then closed in and nipped the ship fore and aft with terrible force, bending the rudder over to starboard and smashing it off. The solid oak and iron went as though they had been match-wood. The straining and groaning of the timbers were ter-rific. Late in the evening I saw to my horror that the ship was absolutely hogged. Her back was bent upwards in the mid-dle. I was afraid that she would stand very little more and that we should have to abandon her on the following day.

"Next day almost the same thing happened again to the ship. She groaned terribly and seemed about to smash up under the pressure. Things got so bad that I called all hands, gave every man his station for sledging, and made every preparation for abandoning her. That day was one long sus-pense, but at midnight the movements of the floes gradually placed her in a safer position. The pressure continued, how-ever, to be very heavy throughout that night and the fol-lowing day. After that things were quieter for a while.

"The pleasantest thing that happened was our first sight of the sun on August 6th, after months of darkness. I'll read you what I wrote in my diary."

Stenhouse produced his diary and read aloud the following:

"The wind moderated towards 6 A.M. and at about breakfast time, with a clear atmosphere, the land from near Cape Cotter to Cape Adare was visible. What a day of delight! After four days of thick weather we find ourselves in sight of Cape Adare in a position about forty-five miles east of Possession Isles. In these four days we have been set one hundred miles. Good going. Mount Sabine, the first land seen by us when coming south, lies away to the westward, forming the highest peak (10,000 ft.) of a fine range of mountains covered in snow. Due west we can see the Possession Islands lying under the great bluff of Cape Downshire, which shows large patches of black rock. The land slopes down to the north-west of Cape Downshire and rises again into the high peninsula about Cape Adare. We felt excited this morning in anticipation of seeing the sun, which rose about nine-thirty (local time). It was a glorious, joyful time. We drank to something and gave cheers for the sun. We then got hard to work on cutting the iron sheathing plates off the broken rudder. Donnelly, the engineer, was doing splendid work. Several times we got our fingers burned in handling the iron."

(In zero temperatures to touch metal with bare hands produces what might be termed a species of "cold burning." In other words, the skin adheres to the metal, and so is likely to be torn away if it is not very carefully thawed off. The strange thing is that although it is the cold that does the damage, the effect is almost the same as though the metal were red-hot.)

Stenhouse continued to read aloud his diary, turning to August 12th.

"The jury-rudder is nearly completed. This afternoon we

mixed some concrete for the lower part, and had to use boiling water, as the water froze in the mixing. The carpenter has made a good job of the rudder, although he has had to construct it on the quarter-deck in low temperatures and exposed to biting blasts. . . .

"August 24. We lifted the rudder out of the ice and placed it clear of the stern, athwart the fore-and-aft line of the ship. We had quite a job with it (weight: four and a half tons), using treble and double-sheaved blocks' purchase; but with the endless chain tackle from the engine room and plenty of 'beef' and leverage we dragged it clear. All the pintles are gone at the fore part of the rudder; it is a clean break and bears witness to the terrific force exerted on the ship during the nip. I am glad to see the rudder upon the ice and clear of the propeller. The blade itself (which is solid oak and sheathed on two sides and on the after part half way down with three-quarter-inch iron plating) is undamaged save for broken pintles. The twisted portion is in the rudder trunk."

Stenhouse put away his diary and went on: "Three days later I had everything in readiness for the jury-rudder to be put over and used for steering as soon as the pack-ice broke up round the ship.

"In September, I had two sick men to look after, Mugridge and Larkman. Mugridge had a bad rash with large blisters. I don't know what the deuce it was. All I could find in the medical book that seemed at all like it was pemphigus, so pemphigus it was, and I treated him accordingly. As he is alive I suppose it was really pemphigus. Larkman got frostbitten on his big toe and second toe, and through his carelessness in not looking after it gangrene set in before he let me know. The big toe got so bad that it was practically dead, and I whittled away a lot of dead flesh as though it had been a lead pencil. It was a beastly job, and I was very scared, but there was no alternative." Stenhouse paused and added, "He's alive, too, so I am not such a bad doctor, on the whole."

"One day a very beautiful mock-sun formed at five in the morning. The bo'sun was so impressed that he roused me to see it. About that time, in 66° 40′ S. and 154° 45′ E. I took soundings and found bottom at 194 fathoms. We brought up mud and a few small stones from the bottom. I washed out the mud and found several specks of gold.

"By the time that we had drifted out of the pack-ice we were too short of coal for me to attempt to get back to the Antarctic Continent. The floes started to break up on February 12th, 1916, and after the heavy strain the ship was making three and a half feet of water every twenty-four hours, so that we had to keep pumping her. To save our coal I got out of the pack under sail.

"We had a very stormy time, but reached Port Chalmers on April 3rd. There was no news of you, which made me anxious, although I knew, of course, that the *Endurance* might be wintering in the Weddell Sea. We had been here pretty nearly two months before we heard that you were safe."

That concluded Stenhouse's story. It had not relieved Shackleton's mind as regards the men that were stranded, and he was more than ever anxious to get out to them. Stenhouse and I accompanied Shackleton down to Port Chalmers on December 8th, where the *Aurora* was ready to sail.

Shackleton was not fond of writing letters, and therefore I have kept and treasured a note which he wrote to me at that time. We were both feeling acutely the impending separation after our years together in the very closest friendship, and since he could have telephoned if he had wished I think that he wrote for no other reason than that he guessed that I would like to have a letter from him. I have never known him to take a pen in his hand if he could possibly avoid doing so, which is another reason why I cherish this letter.

> *"Dunedin Club*
>
> "My dear old Worsley,
>
> "I am b———y well fed up after losing you. I cannot write about it but you know. Will you post the enclosed letter (to Lady Shackleton) and stamp it yourself? Also send the wire enclosed, not franked. See Tripp about anything you want. God bless you.
>
> "E. H. SHACKLETON."

It was with a heavy heart that I went with Stenhouse to see him off on December 20th.

Shackleton got back on February 9th. I was there awaiting his return. He had become a popular hero in New Zealand, and he and his party received a memorable welcome. As soon as I was alone with him he gave me an account of his adventures: we were sitting in his bedroom in the house of his host, Mr. Leonard Tripp, who had been a very loyal, self-sacrificing and sympathetic friend to him and to all of us. (He and other friends in New Zealand raised five thousand pounds to help Shackleton.)

"We made a fairly quick passage through the pack-ice," he began, "and arrived at Cape Royds in McMurdo Sound on January 10th. I took a party ashore to see if any record had been left in the hut there. That's the hut I set up in 1907. There was a letter saying that the Ross Sea party was at Cape Evans. Just as I was going back to the ship I saw a party of men with a dog-sledge coming from the direction of Cape Evans. Three men were missing. I asked quickly where they were, and the looks I got told me the answer. I knew they were dead before a word was uttered.

"I asked at once how it had happened, and Ernest [Frank Wild's brother] answered. He told me that Spencer-Smith had died of scurvy on the Barrier. I said 'And what about the others?' He then explained that on the morning of May 8th, 1916, Mackintosh, who was at Hut Point, was very anxious to know if the four men at Cape Evans, fifteen miles away, were all right, and decided to cross the sea-ice that lay between them. The others urged him not to take the risk for fear of a blizzard coming on.

"I wish to Heavens that they had kept together. As you know,"—he spoke vehemently—"I have always been against dividing up except in an emergency. I would never allow parties to separate. That has been a guiding principle of mine and I have never deviated from it.

"However, Mackintosh and Hayward started out, promising to return if the weather grew worse. The men left behind watched them from the hill, and the last they saw of them was when they were little more than a mile away, making along parallel with the shore straight to Cape Evans.

"Two hours later a blizzard started, and increased rapidly in violence. Those left behind were naturally anxious about Mackintosh and Hayward. I think we can both imagine what their feelings must have been as the night came on.

"For two days it was impossible for them to go out far enough to examine the sea-ice. Then, with an improvement in the weather, the three men, Joyce, Richards and Ernest Wild, set out to try to find out what had become of them. Their tracks were followed for two miles toward Cape Evans. Then they ended abruptly, where a great stretch of open water was seen as far as the eye could reach. The ice over which they had been travelling had been swept out to sea. As they had no sleeping-bags nor shelter, and very little food, they can't have lived long in that blizzard. And that means that they could not have suffered much."

Shackleton was deeply moved as he spoke. I said, "In that intense cold their nerves would be almost numb and they would hardly feel anything."

He went on. "It was an awful shock. The men that had last seen Mackintosh and Hayward could not even let the other party know what had happened. June was too bad a month to permit them to make the journey that had proved fatal to the other two.

"Joyce, Richards and Wild started out for Cape Evans on July 15th, having chosen that time because of the full moon. It happened that there was an eclipse, so that they had very poor light for their journey. The ice, however, was all right, and they reached Cape Evans without any particular difficulty.

"When they got to the hut they found Stevens, Gaze, Jack and Cope, and I think that they must have cherished some lingering hope that Mackintosh and Hayward had got across because they asked at once whether they had seen anything of them. Of course they hadn't. So the bad news had to be broken to the four in the hut.

"In the summer various searches were made for the bodies of Mackintosh and Hayward. The party examined Inaccessible Island, the shore round Turk's Head and all along the coast between Cape Evans and Hut Point. They went along the glacier-tongue right to Tent Island. But there was nothing ever to indicate what had happened beyond those suddenly ceasing footsteps.

"I am more grieved than words can say at losing a fine,

loyal man like Mackintosh, who was an old friend and had been my shipmate all through my previous expeditions. Hayward and Spencer-Smith going is a great blow, too. It hits me doubly—not only because they were all fine fellows that I liked and respected, but because I have never lost a man of my party before."

It is a matter of history that Shackleton never did lose a man of any party that was under his control. But his caution was a well-thought-out product of an altogether exceptional brain, and unlike some explorers he put the safety of his men far above any achievement that might be possible to him. I have never known anybody so careful. I think that somewhere else in this book I have said that he did the most dangerous things but did them in the safest way, and I repeat it because I think that it describes Shackleton more accurately than a volume of words.

Presently he went on to discuss other aspects of the men's experiences on the Great Barrier.

"Those poor fellows had a hell of a time," he said. "Their job, of course, was to lay depôts to the Beardmore Glacier, and they did it. Their work was really an epic. And if I had succeeded in crossing the Antarctic Continent as I had planned, there would have been ample food for the last stages of my journey. Poor Mackintosh had loyally and faithfully carried out all the duties I had imposed on him, in face of the relentless opposition of the weather and under conditions that would have weakened the resolution of any man less devoted to duty. I don't think that a man could have a finer epitaph than those depôts."

In the summer of 1915 Mackintosh had laid one depôt in 79° S. and another in 80° S. and returned to Hut Point on March 26th. At that time the sea was unfrozen, so that in the absence of ice to walk upon he could not cross it to reach

Hut Point, where, so far as he knew, the *Aurora* was lying moored for the winter. It was midwinter before the ice was safe to cross, and when they got to Cape Evans the *Aurora* was already far away on her northern drift. Unfortunately she was torn away before all the stores and equipment could have been landed, which left the stranded men short.

Mackintosh and his men faced this state of affairs cheerfully enough, and in October they started on the most lengthy sledge journey ever undertaken in Polar work. By so doing he laid depôts in 81° S. and 82° S. and another at the Beardmore Glacier.

Mackintosh was working under a great mental strain at this time, as he had had to leave Spencer-Smith behind in a tent, since the latter was suffering severely from scurvy. When they got back to him they carried him along with them on a sledge. Captain Mackintosh himself was very ill from the same disease. A blizzard held them up for a week on their journey, and then, although much enfeebled, they made a supreme effort to march. Most of the men, however, were too weak to do so, and they were obliged to make camp. It was then decided that Joyce, Richards and Hayward should push on, leaving Mackintosh and Spencer-Smith in the care of Wild. With terrific exertions the three marchers reached the Bluff depot, seventy miles south of Ross Island. They had been pretty close to death, for their food was finished and they were scarcely able to eat when finally they reached the depôt. In my opinion it was nothing less than the determination to save their companions that kept them going. The weather was terrible and it took them till the 29th of February, six days after they had left, to get back to the sick men.

At this stage the lives of the whole party hung in the balance, and they were only saved by the work of the dogs.

Mackintosh, as well as Spencer-Smith, had to be hauled on a sledge, and three days later this was the case also with Hayward.

Mackintosh performed an act of great heroism. Thirty miles away from the base he insisted on being left behind, so that the rest of the party could then drag the other two sick men. He must have realised that he was practically courting death. He was left alone on March 7th in a tent with three weeks' provisions in case of unforeseen delays in returning to him. The feelings of the men that were ordered to leave him can better be imagined than described as they started out with Spencer-Smith and Hayward on the sledge. Two days after this, before the journey was completed, poor Spencer-Smith died, after forty days of sickness borne most bravely. He was buried on the Barrier, and over him they built a cairn of blocks of ice marked by a cross of bamboo. His death was probably accelerated by the cold that night, since the temperature fell to twenty-nine degrees below zero.

Joyce, Richards and Ernest Wild did wonderful work all through, and especially in dragging Hayward into Hut Point. The going was terribly heavy and must have involved great suffering in view of the men's weakened state and the fact that the dogs were enfeebled by lack of food and by overwork.

On March 11th Joyce, Richards and Wild arrived with Hayward at Hut Point. They found the hut invaded by snow, but they soon managed to get a fire going and to get Hayward thoroughly warm. They fed him at once with dried vegetables, and killed two seals so that they could have fresh meat. The whole party was suffering from scurvy, so that it was most important that they should eat fresh meat immediately.

They spent three days in resting and dieting themselves

against the disease, and then set out again on the 14th to fetch Mackintosh. Their condition was so much improved by proper food that they made the return journey in two days, which was exactly half the time they had taken to reach the hut. They had the difficult task of breaking the news of Spencer-Smith's death to the sick man, and they had also to tell him that the ship was not in sight and that they were afraid that she must have gone down with all hands. Two days after this they brought Mackintosh back to the hut, where he improved rapidly.

They had been away laying depôts for a hundred and sixty days and had covered a total distance of one thousand five hundred and sixty-one miles. That is an average of ten miles a day—an historic feat in Polar history.

Joyce, Ernest Wild and Richards accomplished magnificent work. Only those who have fought the difficulties which confront human beings in the world's icy wastes can appreciate the magnitude of the task successfully carried through by them, or even understand the heroism needed to drag along for miles two, and some of the time three, sick men. Undoubtedly by their efforts they saved the lives of Mackintosh and Hayward. The tragedy is that these lives were not afterwards preserved, but that, of course, does not lessen the splendour of the work of those who saved them against almost unbelievably severe odds.

Some little time after his return to New Zealand Shackleton went to Australia, where he had it out with the Relief Committee which had excluded him from the command of his own ship in going to the rescue of his own men. Afterwards he gave me an illuminating account of this interview, and I remember being much amused at the way in which he had got his own back.

He lectured in Australia to collect funds for Captain

Mackintosh's widow, putting his whole heart into this work, which he regarded as an obvious duty—a point of view which I shared. Whilst on the subject of Shackleton's lectures, I might mention that he spoke frequently at public meetings and always for some worth-while cause—the Red Cross or some similar institution. It was part of his temperament to be quixotic—he could not hold on to money, which was one reason perhaps why he was so often short of the means with which to carry on the big undertakings that he was so well fitted to organise.

Before he went to Australia I had taken leave of him; and Stenhouse, who had been staying with me at my home in Christchurch, sailed with me for England and the War.

CHAPTER XII

In Northern Waters

STENHOUSE and I arrived at Liverpool on Saturday, April 9th, 1917, and on Sunday morning we were in London bombarding the Admiralty for a job.

The Admiral commanding Reserves insisted that we wanted leave; we insisted that we wanted a ship. It was arranged that we should have three days in which to get uniforms, and at the end of that time we rushed down to the Naval Barracks at Chatham, to be crammed with a knowledge of the most up-to-date methods of fighting submarines.

A fortnight later I was appointed to the command of His Majesty's ship P.Q.61, fitting out as a Mystery Ship in Belfast. Stenhouse joined as First Lieutenant, and on July 31st the ship was commissioned.

We were disguised to resemble a little coasting steamer. Our semi-automatic four-inch gun aft was hidden by a tarpaulin stretched over what were apparently two cargo derricks above a big case. Camouflage of corners of this were stuck on to the tarpaulin, lifting it up as though it were resting upon the case on what would have been the after-hatch

but was in reality the gun-platform. The idea was that if a
submarine should fire a torpedo at us, a 'panic party,' consisting of what would normally have been the full crew of
such a steamer, would lower the boat, leap into it in a dis-
orderly mob, and abandoning the ship would row away to
some distance. We reckoned that after this the submarine
would inspect the steamer all round with its periscope, and,
finding nothing wrong, would come to the surface. This
would be the signal for 'action stations' to be sounded by us,
the red ensign would be hauled down and the white ensign
hoisted in its place. While this was being done the tarpaulin
would be thrown clear and the four-inch gun trained on the
submarine. The whole operation would take from five to
seven seconds. The submarine would then be sunk by rapid
gunfire.

Practically every ship had a different type of camouflage,
but to add convincement to our ship's 'get-up' we followed
the fairly common practice of having 'the firm's' initials on
the corners of the tarpaulin. On one side were mine, and
on the other those of Stenhouse. I had a pretty free hand in
arranging the camouflage of the P.Q.61. I am afraid, however, that our shape was rather too orthodox and typical of
Admiralty build, for we could never persuade submarines
to attack us, or at all events to do more than fire torpedoes
at us, however much we flirted with them. Therefore we
had to chase them.

We had one glorious day, though. On the 26th September, 1917, forty miles off the south coast of Ireland, a German submarine torpedoed the oiler *San Zeferino*. The
torpedo exploded under the engine room, killing the second engineer and two men. One man, however, had a most
miraculous escape. He was blown through two decks and
landed, practically uninjured, on the upper deck, and when

we ran alongside, the boat opposite the engine room skylight was lying smashed on deck, close to where he must have landed.

Although it was misty we could see about three quarters of a mile, and I thought to myself, "If we hang around here the submarine won't come up, and we shan't get a chance to bag her; then the whole war will be spoiled for me." We therefore sheered off from the oiler, and for once I had an inspiration. I would try a 'sound-camouflage' by gradually reducing the revolutions of the propeller. I guessed that the submarine would be listening on his hydrophone, and with our increased distance and the decreased beat of our propellers he would think that we had cleared off altogether. This actually did happen.

At four miles' distance we turned and came back to the oiler from a different direction. As we swung round her stern Stenhouse spotted a faint blur on the horizon. Evidently the captain of the submarine had not distinguished us against the oiler. I instantly gave the order "Hard a-port and full speed ahead!" and off we went, at twenty-four knots, straight for the submarine.

The crew of the German boat had just emerged on deck, cleared away their gun, and were about to shell the oiler. We were end-on to them, and the first intimation they can have had of our approach through the mist must have been the sight of a great bow-wave travelling towards them.

My aim was to ram the submarine. Had we turned round to bring our four-inch gun aft to bear on her, the few seconds taken in doing this would have given the submarine time to submerge. But ramming seemed certain. So we opened fire with the port twelve-pounder forward. The submarine, of a thousand tons burthen, was now travelling across our bows at a speed of eight knots. We were only six hundred tons, and we were bearing down on her beam at twenty-four knots. We certainly must have looked like the Angel of Death to those unfortunate Germans. I gave the order "Prepare to ram!" and the crew flattened themselves on the deck.

We had the small draught of seven feet forward, but when we were going at high speed our stern settled down and the bows lifted up till her stem was only four feet in the water. I knew that if we struck the submarine in that position, instead of our sinking her she would probably rip the bottom out of us. Accordingly the moment before the impact the engines were stopped, and our bows settled down in the water just as I had timed that they should. Our stern was armed with a small ram which was like a continuation of the keel and was made of solid steel. As the bows fell, the ram caught the submarine amidships, tearing her sides open and rolling her beneath us. We felt a terrific shock, and at the same time heard the unearthly rasp of tearing steel. She sank rapidly beneath us, and immediately afterwards we were shaken by a tremendous explosion. For a moment I thought that another submarine had got us with a torpedo, but it was either the chamber of the rammed vessel bursting open, or her mines exploding (she was a mine-layer). Stenhouse sang out down the tube to the engineer to ask if our engines were all right, and on receiving the reply "Yes" we went full speed ahead again.

The immediate result of our action was that the sea was boiling up in great bubbles and masses of foam, while oil spread over a large area. Amongst the patches of oil we saw the German captain and the steersman or coxswain struggling in the rough water. Coming up to them we threw them life-buoys. The captain secured his smartly and got inside it, calmly awaiting his rescue. The coxswain, however, was in a state of panic. Throwing up his arms he shouted something that sounded like "kamerad," and sank immediately. We were unable to save him.

As soon as we got the captain, Ober-Leutnant Albert Arnold, sole survivor of the U.C. 33, on board, he enquired indignantly why I had not saved his coxswain. I told him that we had done our best and that he himself was lucky to be alive. I then sent him below, taking care of course that he should not see our subsequent operations, and put him in charge of the surgeon and midshipman. Before going below he had volunteered the information "There are three of my pals about," which I judged to mean that he had had enough swimming for one day and wanted to warn me. It also told me just what I wanted to know.

We searched through the mist until we found the oiler again, for we knew that she would be in grave danger should we fail to locate her. When the crew of the *San Zeferino* heard that we had sunk the submarine that had got her they cheered themselves hoarse.

We then prepared for the big operation of taking the disabled oiler in tow. Here Stenhouse's splendid seamanship came into play. He unshackled a length of our chain cable from the anchor, dragged it aft, and connected it to the oiler's heavy steel towing wire. It was a ticklish business in a heavy sea, for we had to make the cable fast in the very confined space between our twenty depth charges. These depth charges each consisted of four hundred pounds of T.N.T. Stenhouse coolly and cleverly carried this work out while I, from the bridge, manœuvred the ship into position. Our job was not simplified by the fact that the oiler was seven thousand tons while we were only six hundred and not fitted for towing. It was not until about twelve hours after we had got the oiler in tow that we finished our journey of eighty miles to Milford Haven, and I was able to go below to see our prisoner again.

Meanwhile the weather had cleared and several ships had come to our assistance in readiness to attack submarines, since, while we were towing the oiler, we could not give chase. Sure enough, in the afternoon, as we approached the shallows near the Smalls at the south-west corner of Wales we saw two enemy submarines. I ordered every ship in the neighborhood to attack them, but to everybody's disappointment the submarines submerged while the going was still good. In the first watch, after sunset, there was bright moonlight, and I was afraid that they might bag both my ship and the oiler with lucky shots as we passed round the islands to get into Milford Haven. I therefore kept the oiler so close in to the coast that, showing no lights, we could not possibly be seen. Her captain afterwards told us that he was much more afraid of being wrecked than torpedoed, as the ship at times was not more than a hundred feet from the cliffs.

After anchoring I still had so much to do that I had very little time to talk to Ober-Leutnant Albert Arnold that night; yet in spite of being dead tired the day had been so packed with thrills and excitement that Stenhouse and I were as jolly as schoolboys. Next morning the German captain, a tall, slender, well-set-up young fellow, of agreeable manners, breakfasted with us in the wardroom. He remarked, "If you'd given me three more seconds to submerge I should have been all right." He knew England well and seemed to have no concern about being a prisoner of war. After we had taken his photograph Stenhouse conducted him ashore with an escort and handed him over to the military guard. Just as he was leaving, I remember, he asked me to come to Germany as his guest when the war was over. He then handed me a little silver whistle, a token, as he put it, of his gratitude to me for saving his life.

All hands undoubtedly wished that they could have such an adventure every day. The destruction of an enemy sub-marine was estimated by the Admiralty to be worth £5,000,000 to England. When Shackleton heard the news he was delighted, and nothing touched me more than his wire, "Well done, Skipper, Tally Ho!" I think he was as pleased as I was when I got the D.S.O. Stenhouse, who got the D.S.C., was appointed to the command of the Q Ship *Ianthe*.

Having been abroad in the early stages of the War I was unfamiliar with the procedure of the Admiralty, and al-though I knew that to bag a submarine brought a thousand pounds I did not understand the disposal of this money. Having an exaggerated idea of the number of submarines that I was going to sink, my estimated wealth was colossal, and when we actually got the *U.C. 33*, Stenhouse and I went to London to spend some of it. We had a really royal time in Town, and returned minus a hundred pounds apiece. Some little time later we received the Admiralty award. My share was £68, and Stenhouse's £48. We therefore found bagging submarines an expensive amusement.

For a time I specialised in dropping depth charges, for which I earned the nickname of "Depth Charge Bill." Later I was appointed to the command of the Q Ship H.M.S. *Pangloss*, operating in the Mediterranean. She had formerly been commanded by Captain (now Admiral) Gordon Campbell, V.C.

On leave in London I met Shackleton, who was preparing to go to Murmansk. He said, "Austria has packed up, and there's not much doing in the Mediterranean for you. Wouldn't you like to come to North Russia with me?" I

said I should love it, and to cut a long story short Stenhouse
and I were lent by the Admiralty to the War Office. We arrived in Murmansk with Shackleton in October 1918.

There was plenty of ice and snow to remind us of old
times, and it was just as though we had never separated at all.
Shackleton had also got hold of Macklin and Hussey. The
old gang was on the war-path!

Shackleton was Director of Arctic Equipment and Transport to the Murmansk Front. I was not to stay long with
him, however. General Ironsides, on the Archangel Front,
wired across to know if one of us could carry out the same
duties for him. Shackleton felt that I ought to go, and so I
said good-bye to him and to my chums, and went to
Archangel.

There was a lot of fighting going on through the vast
forests of North Russia, and over and along the frozen
rivers, and I had a glorious time in the Army. Next summer, when the thaw came, I went down to Archangel and
'pinched' a gunboat from the Naval authorities, and with
her had a few exciting adventures up the Dvina River. For a
short time there I had a flotilla of four gunboats, but we did
not have nearly so much trouble with the enemy as with the
shallowness of the river, and therefore I had few regrets at
handing these over to their rightful commanding officers
when they arrived from England. I then joined General Grogan, V.C., on the Pinega River, a tributary of the Dvina
River, and had a few raids, one of which got me a bar to the
D.S.O.

On one of the many cheery evenings which I spent in the
Hampshires' mess Captain Monty Moore, V.C., whispered
in my ear, "Would you like to join in a bit of fun?" When I
said, "Rather!" he told me of a secret raid that was being
planned, and asked me whether I would like to be in it. Nat-

urally I was delighted at the chance. My friends then advised me not to ask for General Grogan's permission, lest it be withheld. Accordingly, on the appointed afternoon, I had just ferried across the River Pinega with my horse when I beheld the General coming down the opposite bank with an old Ford car that he had requisitioned. The General was a great friend of mine and one of the most delightful men that I have ever met, but he was the last person that I wanted to see at that moment. However, I could not avoid him. The old Ford had done all right on the rough road, but when it came to the soft, deep sand of the river bank it jibbed. The General and all his staff were pushing valiantly at the back of it. I would have liked to sneak away, but common decency demanded that I should go and push as well. The following conversation thereupon ensued:

General Grogan: "Where are you going, Worsley?"

Myself: "For a ride, sir."

General Grogan: "Where are you riding?"

Myself (pushing hard): "Er—along the river bank."

General Grogan: "Where to?"

Myself: "The Hampshires."

General Grogan (suspiciously): "What for?"

Myself (pushing the car with a terrific display of energy): "I beg your pardon, sir? I can't hear you when I am pushing this car."

General Grogan (with sudden fierceness): "Look here, Worsley, you are not going on that raid!"

Myself: "Sir—it's a very fine day for it!"

General Grogan (weakening visibly): "You are not supposed to be mixed up in this raid."

Myself (giving the car the final push that started it): "Goodbye, sir."

General Grogan: "Well, good luck to you."

Two hours later I was off with the Hampshires. We were twenty-five all told—sixteen officers and nine privates. The raid was planned with the intention of getting through the Bolshevik lines and capturing men and getting as much information as possible, as it was believed that the Bolos, as the Bolsheviks were known to us in North Russia, were about to take the offensive. To do this we had to trek through about twenty miles of forest to the Bolo front, and then probably do a slightly shorter distance at the back of their lines. We took two days' provisions, and at the end of the daylight we camped at the edge of the forest close to the River Pocha. Here there were open grasslands about a mile wide, and so we had to wait for darkness to cross these. Then we all went down to the river, and launching logs across, made a very precarious bridge. However, we sat on it and straddled ourselves along and crossed it safely, dragging our three horses with us, which was not too easy a job. Soon we gained the forest within the Bolo lines. We saw several men but they did not notice us.

We then struck across the forest, and about seven or eight miles farther we came upon a road with telegraph wires. Throwing a jack-knife with a wire attached over one of these lines, one of the men who was a telephone operator tapped the line and jotted down a lot of valuable information, some of the messages actually coming from Petrograd. While we were doing this a small convoy of Bolsheviks passed; but we had received news, through tapping the wires, that a larger one was expected. We therefore let the first one go by, and half an hour later the second convoy approached. Just as the head of the convoy was passing us we opened fire, and taken by surprise the drivers and those of the guard who had not been shot down bolted into the forest. We rushed out and secured enough horses to carry us back, and all papers that were left, and then drove the carts into the wood and dismantled them so that they could not be used again. This done, we made off into the depths of the forest, with all the horses. Here we released those we did not need, keeping six of the best, after which we made our way back to the Pocha River. We knew that the countryside would be buzzing like a hive of bees after us, but as they could not know for a time in which direction we had gone they would have some trouble in striking our trail or intercepting us. We made for a different part of the river from that which we had crossed in the night.

It was now broad daylight, and in our haste to get back we cast all caution to the winds and made for a place where we saw two small boats lying. There was a certain amount of danger in embarking owing to the deep mud of the river banks; and when we had got our party into the two boats their gunwales were level with the water. We made the horses swim, leading them by their bridles. The second boat sank just as it reached the bank and the men scrambled out through waist-deep mud. We then smashed up the boats and made across the grasslands at top speed for the forest beyond. Some peasants on the bank that we had left saw us, and we knew that they would carry the news immediately; accordingly we struck off through the forest at right angles to the course that it would naturally be assumed we should take. For a few miles we worked our way through the forest by compass—the same compass that had been used on the crossing of South Georgia—and as we had now been going for two and a half days with three hours' sleep only, we were not sorry to rest. We had no food left, so we gathered handfuls of blueberries and cloudberries, these latter looking something like raspberries on very short stems and of a bright yellow colour.

After an hour we started on again. The forest is intersected with long rides about fifty yards wide that run for hundreds of miles north and south and east and west, chessboard fashion, through the woodlands, and these rides were now lumbered with tree trunks which had not been cleared away for some years, which made our going rather difficult. On the afternoon of the third day, finding that the men's feet were getting into a very bad state from the rough and rapid marching, Captain McFee, who was in charge, said to me, "I think we had better halt and give them a rest." I agreed, so we posted a sentry and slept for an hour, lying down on the edge of one of these rides, in the sun. Presently the sentry, who was scanning the line of our retreat for a possible pursuing party, crawled over to where McFee and I were sleeping and said, "I can see some of the enemy coming along." Taking advantage of good cover we peered cautiously back and saw the heads of a large body of men coming into sight over a rise half a mile away. We at once lined up our party, half on each side of the ride, and awaited the Bolos, McFee taking charge on one side and I on the other. Barely had we done this when the advance guard of the pursuers appeared. They had no idea that they were so close to their quarry, and they were picking berries and eating them as they came along, when suddenly McFee gave the order to fire. Immediately afterwards we fixed bayonets and charged them, but they bolted in all directions into the forest, their retreat being hastened by my blood-curdling yells of "Yoicks! Tally-ho!" which, echoed by our party with great heartiness, seemed to strike terror into them. The main body of the Bolos, which we afterwards learned was composed of over two hundred men, must have been discouraged by our vigour, for after that we had no trouble, although they had plenty of time in which to have cut us off.

We got what information we could from the papers on three of the men that had been killed, and resumed our march with all speed.

Many of our party were suffering from cut heels and bleeding feet, which made marching extremely painful, and soon McFee said, "Worsley, you are much more experienced in tramping this sort of country than I am, so will you take charge of the march?" I then re-arranged the party as well as I could, so that the men who were most acutely affected could ride double-banked on the horses, while others hung on by the stirrups beside them. But this kind of travel with horses was difficult on account of the fallen trees in our path; so we released some of our steeds, leaving ourselves only seven. Before we set out I had guessed what tramping in such a country would be like, so had equipped myself for comfort by wearing an old pair of boots and therefore was not footsore—a fortunate thing, as it enabled me to relieve some of the men of their rifles for a time. I arranged matters so that we should go on for twenty minutes and then have a spell of rest for two minutes; for I remembered our experience in South Georgia, when we had found how valuable had been the two minutes' rest at each halt when crossing the mountains. It also enabled the men to get a meal of berries each hour. Yes, undoubtedly it took me back to old times!

After fording two or three difficult streams we came at dusk to a dangerous-looking marsh. At some period a kind of causeway had been built across this, which we followed until it broke off, and in struggling to another bit of causeway that we could see beyond, our men and horses became very badly bogged. Luckily for us the little Russian ponies that we had with us were tough and game. When they sank into the bog until they were almost submerged, three or four men seized their bridles and hauled as hard as they could without themselves sinking into the swamp, whilst others urged the horses from behind, and the plucky little beggars made a tremendous effort and scrambled forward a few yards till they collapsed exhausted. We let them rest for three or four minutes and then repeated this operation. At the fourth attempt they got clear of the bog. I doubt whether any other horse in the world would have had the spirit to have extricated itself; almost certainly an English animal would have been too highly strung to have done so. When we had got safely through it was dark, misty and piercingly cold. We dared not light a fire, so at my suggestion, we snuggled up together for warmth, just as we had done in the boats when we escaped from the pack-ice and were making for Elephant Island. Next afternoon the whole twenty-five of us were back safely at our starting point. Why General Grogan and Captain McFee should have thought that the small part which I played in this little adventure deserved a bar to my D.S.O. I have never found out. Nevertheless I am deeply grateful to them for obtaining for me an honour which I greatly prize.

The next exciting thing that occurred was the arrival of my chum Stenhouse, who had travelled all the way from the Murmansk front so that we could be together again. After a few more adventures and skirmishes which afforded us plenty of fun with our cheery friends in the Army, with the evacuation of North Russia we returned to England.

I saw a good deal of Shackleton, but knew that he would not be ready for another expedition for some time to come, so in the meantime Stenhouse and I, with some of our Army friends, formed a small company with the intention of trading with the newly-formed Republics of the Baltic. The company itself was rather quaint. It had five directors and among these were five D.S.O.'s. Stenhouse and I, uncertain as to whether the Company should be called Worsley, Stenhouse and Co. or *vice versa*, played a game of billiards to decide that knotty point. He won, so the Company was duly chris-tened.

We bought a little schooner, the *Annie*. She carried about a hundred and fifty tons of cargo, but by the time we had her fitted out the freight market had slumped and we found that it was not worth our while to send her to the Baltic. For a time we traded on the British coast, which did not pay us, and then early in November we sailed with a cargo from Leith to Reykjavik, the capital of Iceland. When we left Leith it blew such a gale from the south that the steamer trading regularly from Leith to Iceland was obliged to put into port for shelter. However, we carried on. Towards the end of the run, as we were nearing the coast of Iceland and reached the edge of the bank of soundings (a hundred fath-oms deep), the swell topped up very dangerously and it be-came a work of extreme difficulty to keep the little vessel dead before it and prevent her from broaching-to. I feared that the strong current would run us far ahead of our reck-oning, in which case we should have made this stormy coast in the dark. Before dawn the sea became steeper still, the waves approaching the roller type, and I was afraid that we were drawing dangerously close inshore. But when day broke we sighted the land and found that our position was correct, so that after all I need not have worried. Next day we beat into Reykjavik against a head wind that had sprung up, and found to our joy that we had arrived before the steamer.

After we had discharged our cargo we spent a long and wearisome time trying to obtain a freight to take back to England. Stenhouse had been offered a chance of crossing

Brazil with Commander Cochrane, R.N., who was connected with our company, and he was very anxious to get back to England as soon as possible. Accordingly he returned to England by steamer. I stayed behind in Iceland and paid off the rest of our crew, as I was getting very short of cash.

While I was at Reykjavik an amusing situation arose concerning the local prison. The jail, a fine big building, was little more than half-full, and as there was a shortage of houses several people approached the Governor for permission to rent and occupy portions of it. This was granted. Shortly after these new tenants had moved in, the Governor considered that good conduct on the part of several of the prisoners entitled them to a remission of their sentences. These remissions were accordingly granted, and the men were told that they were now free. The prisoners, however, objected, saying that they had not completed their sentences.

Said the Governor, "I want these cells for the people who have no houses."

Whereupon one of the prisoners retorted with great indignation, "But we were here first!"

I found the Icelanders most hospitable, and quickly made friends, as nearly all the educated people in Reykjavik spoke English. As a nation they are so honest that in country places it is customary for people to lock their front doors but leave the key hanging outside. Thus strangers who desire food or rest can enter, which they do, take what they need, and—leaving a note to tell the absent owner what they have done—continue their journey.

After months of waiting and chasing elusive cargoes I at last got the promise of one from one of the worst places to which I could possibly have gone—Bildurdal, up a deep Sound, Arnarfjord, that ran into the north-west coast of Iceland. I bought up a quantity of scrap-iron to ballast the little vessel for her three-hundred-and-twenty-mile run to Bildurdal, and I took also a small cargo of provisions for the inhabitants of the fjord.

I then tried to raise a crew. The Icelander is generally a good seaman, but the better-class ones did not take to the idea of sailing in a little vessel without any auxiliary power to the stormy fjords in the depth of winter, and therefore I was obliged to choose from the men hanging about the water-front. Just before we left, one of my friends asked me how long it would take us to reach our destination. I said that with luck I might do it in thirty-two hours. Actually the gales were so bad that it took me as many days.

We started out with a fair wind, but before we had done fifty miles it came on to blow a very heavy gale from the east. This continued almost without intermission for three weeks. As we were going up the west coast this series of easterly gales drove us out into the Denmark Strait and over towards Greenland. I have never been to Greenland, but I very nearly got there that time. However, I stood boldly to the north, across the Arctic Circle, in the hope of getting a change of wind. The gales raged with such intensity that our canvas repeatedly blew away and had to be repaired slowly and painfully in the icy coldness of the ship's hold. We were driven so far that we were almost caught in the Arctic pack-ice. Had that happened probably we should not have returned; for the little vessel was unprotected and we had only a limited amount of provisions with us. The weather grew so cold that the fresh-water tank was frozen into a solid block; the sails were like boards and the schooner was cased with ice. And every day my scratch crew were getting "scratchier and scratchier," if I may misquote Alice.

After three weeks we had a gale from the north which

The author
(*SCOTT POLAR RESEARCH INSTITUTE*)

lasted three days, during which I managed to drive the schooner in again to within forty miles of the north coast of Iceland. Up to this time I had not paid much attention to the attitude of the crew, but I now saw that if opportunity arose they would desert. I was very careful therefore not to bring the vessel to windward of any point of land, since this might have given them a chance to lower the boat and abandon the schooner and me. I also deemed it prudent to sleep with my revolver under my pillow. By now we had got so short of provisions that we were forced to eat some of the cargo that we were carrying—which is permissible according to maritime law. I became very anxious, for I realised that if easterly gales came on again and we failed to meet a trawler which could tow us into harbour, we might get blown off shore once more, and then the provisions would give out. And whether I liked the men or not I was responsible for their lives.

The gale died away, and after twenty-four hours of calms and light airs, during which we made very little progress, it sprang up again, as I had dreaded, from the east. The men were now inclined to panic. By dint of hard driving and continual tacking, however, we managed to work the ship to windward in three days, until she was close up to the land. We were now near the entrance to Arnarfjord, which was only a few miles from our destination. The coast is a series of steep black rock faces, and running into the interior at right angles to the coast are a number of chasm-like rifts in the land—the fjords of the north-west of Iceland. Each time that we tried to enter the fjord in the bay of which Bildurdal lay, the wind would leap up at us with a force and suddenness almost comparable with gunfire. The violence of it was extraordinary. We lost sail after sail and were driven back time after time. After each unsuccessful attempt we repaired our sails and then gradually drew up again close to the shelter of the mountains. There was considerable danger of our being blown bodily out to sea.

For three more days we battled up and down like this. Every time that we opened up the entrance to the fjord we

One of the dangers of Polar navigation
(SCOTT POLAR RESEARCH INSTITUTE)

were hurled away by the wind that funnelled out of it. The men's morale, of course, was getting worse and worse, and the schooner was nearly out of control through loss of sails. On the thirty-first day we were losing ground, and in spite of all our efforts were being driven out to sea. Only two days' food and water were left. Our coal was almost finished. In short, we were in a very precarious state.

At the eleventh hour a battered and rusty old trawler—British—hove in sight. A sailor is naturally reluctant to hoist "N.C." (the international code signal of distress) but I had no alternative. The trawler immediately ran down to us, and after an hour's hard work in the gale we were taken in tow and then brought to Bildurdal. The captain and crew of the trawler were splendid fellows, and we probably owed our lives to them. Two or three days after we were towed in another trawler was wrecked nearby in a snowstorm and a number of the crew were drowned. Accidents of this sort, unfortunately, are not rare in this part of the world, and the coast is dotted with wrecks.

I had come to the conclusion that the crew which I had were not fit to take the vessel to England, and the sooner I got rid of them the better for all concerned. Two of them solved my problem by promptly deserting and skedaddling over the mountains to Reykjavik, evidently as glad to be rid of me as I was to be quit of them. They had not gone empty-handed, however, for later I found that I was short of several shirts and my revolver. I then engaged four fine young seamen, and, as mate, a splendid Viking named Ofegir Gudmundsen. The weather was still so bad that twice we were very nearly wrecked in the harbour. The shipper of the cargo at Bildurdal, when he found that we had no engine, was most bitter against the agents in Reykjavik on our account. He declared that people who would send a little schooner up the northwest fjords of Iceland in the depth of winter ought to be shot.

By this time, since business had been so bad, neither the company nor I had any money. I was so short that I lived for days at a time on a slice of rye bread covered with margarine for breakfast, a small biscuit for lunch, and another slice of the rye bread for dinner. To obtain the full nourishment from it I used to masticate the bread very, very slowly, telling myself meanwhile that I was not really hungry. I bought a ton of coal for ten pounds, which was nearly all I had, and the captain of a Danish steamer in port, who knew how hard up I was, generously gave me another ton. This is typical of the brotherhood of the sea—the finest brotherhood in the world. Even so, in order to eke out the amount

I had aboard, I was obliged to put out the galley fire and live in the forecastle with the crew. The little cooking that was done took place down there. I did the best I could in the way of provisions for the crew, which was not a great deal, but they were very sporting about it. They understood that things were not exactly as I could have wished.

Our cargo was a hundred and twenty tons of salt fish, which we were taking to Kirkwall, Orkney Islands, for orders for the east coast, which meant that on our arrival there we should be given our final port of destination. A week before we sailed the shipper of the cargo, with whom I had become fast friends, came on board in a state of great excitement, with an Icelandic newspaper containing a statement about Sir Ernest Shackleton's forthcoming expedition, which was then planned for the Arctic. It mentioned that he was trying to get in touch with me. But owing to the severe weather, communication was so bad that neither he, my company, nor my sweetheart could get any news of me.

I immediately despatched a cable, which Shackleton received thirty days later, saying that I would be with him before the end of April. The thought of being with him again gave me a new lease of life. Things that had worried me previously now appeared insignificant. I was all eagerness to get back.

We sailed from Bildurdal towards the end of February, 1921, and two days after we had cleared the fjord up came our old enemy the east wind, and twelve hours later we were in the grip of a gale. I headed the schooner south, knowing that eventually I should meet with westerly gales which would carry me towards the Orkney Islands. Three days later, however, the gale headed us by veering to the southeast, and we began the old game of endeavouring to beat to windward and getting driven to leeward. About this time the barometer, which always stands very low in Iceland, fell to an extraordinary degree. Never anywhere in the world have I seen a barometer so low. It was an uncanny sight to watch it falling, as though it would never stop.

Shortly afterwards the hurricane foretold by that drop was upon us. We blew away more sails; all the *Annie's* bulwarks were smashed, so that every sea swept freely across our deck. There followed a truly hellish week, during which we worked incessantly to prevent the schooner from foundering. Our situation took on a still more ominous aspect, when the rigging began to show signs of parting, and the mate, speaking for the crew as well as himself, did his best to persuade me to turn back and make for Reykjavik. I was forced to admit the reasonableness of his argument, and I agreed that if the wind came fair I would do so; but meanwhile I made up my mind that if it were humanly possible I would go on. Accordingly, when three days later a gale sprang up from the west, I placed the ship on the chart sixty miles east of her true position and informed the crew that I was going on. I felt that I was justified in the deception. But another gale sprang up from the south-west. It seemed to me that for over four months now I had been living in a series of wild snowstorms, blizzards, and hurricanes, and I remembered what Stenhouse had said about feeling that it was for all eternity when he was imprisoned in the pack. I experienced something of the same sensation. The seas round Iceland in the winter time are noted for their furious gales, but surely this was an exceptionally stormy winter, even for this fearsome region.

Now, however, the gale had come fair, and I welcomed it. We drove steadily east under a press of canvas; but all the time I kept a wary eye on the rigging. When in port I had not had enough money to effect the repairs I should have liked,

and now I was experiencing the results of my enforced par-
simony.

On the morning of the fourth day after the sou'wester
had sprung up we sighted Suderoe the southernmost of the
Faroe Islands. I brought the ship up to the wind until it was
abeam and we were thundering along three or four miles to
windward of the island, where we could see a heavy sea
breaking on its weather shore. I watched more closely than
ever the weather shrouds of the foremast, and presently decided that these would not hold very much longer. Therefore immediately after breakfast I had all hands out and
unshackled fifteen fathoms of the schooner's heavy chain
cable, to pass it aloft to secure the mast. This was a difficult
job as the ship was driving hard in the gale, most of the ratlines were carried away, and it was complicated by the fact
that my knowledge of Icelandic was as meagre as the crew's
knowledge of English. However, this last difficulty was compensated for somewhat by the fact that I was dealing with
fine seamen. The orders which they did not quite understand their seamanship led them to guess.

We dropped the bight of the chain till it was below the
keel, and then drew both parts—one on each side of the
ship—along till these were abreast of the foremast. Both
ends were then drawn up tight so that the ship was girdled
underneath with the cable, and we made the chain temporarily fast with a long end left over on the one side. This
end was then taken aloft on the starboard side and passed
round the forelowermost head, where it was made fast with
a round turn and well secured to prevent it slipping down.
There was sufficient left over to bring down on the port
side, where it was shackled to the opposite end of the chain.
Wires were made fast on each side to the cable, led through
the hawse pipes forward, and hove taut on the windlass. We

next put a frapping of stout rope round both parts of the cable and across the deck, and bowsed the two parts of the chain together till they were bar-taut.

We were now in a better position. Not only was the mast secured, but the schooner was also bound round with a chain of cable. After all, seamanship has not progressed so very far from the methods used by the shipmates of St. Paul!

This job took us from eight in the morning until two in the afternoon. Immediately we had finished I sent the hands below to lunch and I went aloft with the glasses to look at the land at the same time as I examined the chain cable round the mast. As I was coming down the weather rigging and was just about to spring on to the deck, the last pair of shrouds parted with me. I swung down all right, but I was exceedingly thankful that we had secured the mast in time. If it had not been done we should have had no way of sailing her, for the mast would certainly have been carried away, and inevitably we should have been wrecked on the rocky coast of Suderoe. Now we could laugh at the gale, and we carried on cheerfully for the Orkneys.

I reached Kirkwall four days later and received orders for Grimsby. At Kirkwall I wired to Shackleton "Tally Ho! Just arrived. Sails blown away. Ship frapped and mast held up with cable." He telegraphed back, "Well done, Skipper. Join me as soon as possible."

Even our reception in Chili was outdone by the amazing treatment which was given me in Kirkwall. I told the true state of affairs to my friends there, and I gave one lecture free and one for myself—which meant the ship—which netted me fifteen badly-needed pounds. When the tradespeople realised my difficulties those who could possibly manage to do so refused to present a bill at all. Those who could not afford to do this, with great self-sacrifice, cut their bills by half. I was forced, in the interests of the insurance company, to repair my rigging before proceeding, and the riggers employed on this, whose rate was one-and-tenpence an hour, volunteered to do the work for a shilling, and they worked with a will. The Harbourmaster, Captain Cooper, who had to inspect this work, proved himself a true friend. He went to the trouble of having my breakfast cooked of a morning and sent on board to me. I have never forgotten Mrs. Cooper's curried eggs! To this day it warms my heart to recall the generosity and sincere kindness of all my friends in Kirkwall. I felt then, and feel now, that so long as Great Britain continues to produce such types as these the country has nothing much to worry about. People of such sterling quality are bound to make good, whatever the circumstances.

While I was in Kirkwall I heard that there was an old sea captain lying very ill at Stromness and I was told that he wished to see me. I felt that if it would give the old man any pleasure I ought to go, and I asked a friend to arrange a visit. It had never occurred to me to ask the captain's name. But the moment that I walked into the room where he lay, I cried,

"Why, you are Captain Jock Sutherland, my old Skipper in the ship *Piako!*"

And he replied, "Why, if it isn't little Worsley! To think that it was one of my lads that went south with Shackleton!"

He was tremendously excited and made me spend hours telling him our adventures. Next day I heard that he was feeling much better, having responded well to the stimulation of hearing Shackleton's story from the lips of one whom he remembered as a lad that he had helped to train.

When I left I had paid up everything—which would have

been impossible, of course, had it not been for the whole-hearted kindness of the islanders—but I had only ten shillings in my pocket. The little tug company very generously towed us out free of charge. I felt rather like the man who said that the only thing he had in the shape of money was buttons. We made a rapid run of forty-eight hours to Grimsby, and beat up the Humber River on the flood tide without a chart at night time, with many snow-squalls from the north-west. My indignation may be imagined when, next day, I was presented with a bill for two pounds seventeen-and-six for pilotage, when I had not had any. This was certainly an anti-climax with which to end the eventful journey with the *Annie.*

While the cargo was being discharged I rushed to London to see Shackleton. His first question was, "When can you join me?" I had to explain to him that my company's financial troubles were hindering me from finishing up with the schooner. He asked how much I wanted to pay off the crew and send them back to Iceland and to meet any outstanding debts on the ship. I told him that it would take two hundred pounds. I can see him now as he sat down and dashed off the cheque for that amount, forgetting in his haste to blot it! When I tried to thank him, he cut me short with:

"Forget it. I must have you on the *Quest.*"

Shackleton was full of the fact that he had met his old schoolmate and friend John Quiller Rowett, who had very generously come forward and was helping him to finance the Expedition.

"You must meet him as soon as possible, Skipper," he said; "he's a splendid fellow and it is solely owing to him that I am able to get the Expedition going this year."

"What's the ship like?" I enquired, and he told me that she was a Norwegian sealer, adding:

"She's not very big—only a hundred and eleven feet long, twenty-four feet beam, and less than two hundred tons. She's got a straight stem."

My heart sank. I did not like that description.

"We will go to Southampton together as soon as you have got your schooner fixed up," went on Shackleton, "and we'll see what we can make of her."

"Who is going with us?" I asked.

To my delight I heard that all of the old *Endurance* men that could possibly do so were coming along—Wild, Macklin, McIlroy, Hussey, Kerr, McLeod, and the good old cook, Green.

My financial difficulties still pursued me, owing to a mortgage on the schooner. Shackleton, with his usual generosity, said, "I must have you clear of all financial obligations. How much does this wretched mortgage want?" I replied, "A hundred and fifty pounds, but I don't want you to pay it."

He did not answer. He simply sat down and wrote out another cheque and said, as he handed it to me, "It's worth it to have you free from anxiety and to take that glum look off your old face."

C H A P T E R X I I I

Southwards Again

I WAS now free to work again for Shackleton. Naturally, as soon as possible, I proceeded to inspect the *Quest*. This examination was disquieting to me in view of the demands that I knew must be made on a ship in Polar exploration. She was a small two-masted fore-and-aft vessel, but later, with Shackleton's permission, I mounted two yards aloft on the foremast. The square-sails that they carried later effected an enormous saving of time to the low-powered vessel, as these enabled her to be driven before gales when the fore-and-afters alone would have been almost useless. She looked to me very small, even after the little vessels in which we had previously sailed; in fact she was only a little larger than the schooner that I had just brought back from Iceland. I did not like a straight stem for ice-work, and I thought with regret of the good old *Endurance*. Although the *Quest* seemed quite strong, I thought that she would be a bad boat for heavy seas and weather. It is a curious thing, but without being able to place your finger on the cause you can often tell by intuition whether a ship will be difficult to

The Quest
(*SCOTT POLAR RESEARCH INSTITUTE*)

handle or easy. Two boats might be built to all intents and
purposes alike, and one might turn out to be the kind of
ship that you grow attached to while the other seems always
recalcitrant. This is illustrated by the inexplicable fact that
sister ships built to the same lines and from the same plans
are sometimes entirely different in their behaviour and
speed.

When I first saw her, Shackleton was getting a bridge
built on her. He and I then sketched a plan for the deck-
house that was needed for the accommodation of the staff.
Before this work was finished Shackleton learned that the financial support that he was to have had from Canada would
not materialise. This killed his plan of going north that sum-

mer to the Beaufort Sea, which lies immediately north of the Arctic shores of Canada. He was not altogether sorry, for he felt the lure of the Antarctic. Besides, he was keen on the oceanographical study that could be made of the Pacific. For a long time I had been stirring up his interest in the work to be done in this part of the world, with which I myself was familiar.

Shackleton realised that he could not fight the Antarctic ice so successfully in the *Quest* as in the previous vessels he had used, a factor which helped him to decide that he would devote the Southern winter to oceanography in milder latitudes. With his romantic ideas about treasure he was attracted to the Pacific also by the hope of finding valuable deposits, as had been done by the Challenger Expedition half a century before. My tales of pearl lagoons and coral islands that I had visited in the Pacific helped also, I know, to excite his imagination. At the same time he felt some regret at not seeing the Arctic. He had intended to force his way west from Baffin Bay towards the islands discovered shortly before by Stefansson, and then sledge far out to the northwest to sound the ocean and perhaps discover new lands north of the Beaufort Sea, near Stefansson's "pole of inaccessibility." Apart from the geographical and scientific work that he would have carried out he was amusingly eager to shoot a Polar bear and bring its skin home for the children, and also to get some white fox furs for "Honey"—Lady Shackleton.

Having had experience of both ends of the world, I can say that there are vast and important differences between the Arctic and the Antarctic. Generally speaking, the Antarctic is a continent surrounded by ocean, whereas the Arctic is an ocean almost surrounded by continents, and partly occupied by large and small islands and archipelagos.

Land at the North Pole lies beneath two miles' depth of ocean. At the South there is a great plateau, the extent of which is a million square miles. Its surface rises to eleven thousand feet above sea level, the lower nine thousand feet of which is land. On top of the land spreads a tremendous sheet of ice, two thousand feet thick, with the weight of nearly four hundred tons on every square yard. For thousands of years this massive sheet has been slowly creeping out towards the sea, grinding down the earth and rocks far below. The surface of this ice is the most desolate, storm-swept place on earth. There is no life whatever there—not even a germ lives in that inhospitable climate. Up on this great high frozen sheet, storms rage throughout the five months' winter night. Howling and shrieking, the winds cast the surface snow far aloft in blinding, suffocating clouds—the blizzards of the South—then, gouging and harrowing the fallen snow, they carve it into sastrugi until it resembles long parallel waves of an instantaneously frozen sea.

This lofty continental ice-mass, centred on the South Pole, causes a climate far colder than that of the Arctic. Winter at the South Pole must have a ferocity that no man, beast or bird could survive. Even in summer (as Shackleton found when he got within ninety-seven geographical miles of the Pole in 1908) the temperature had fallen to forty degrees below zero—equal probably to the average winter temperature of the North Pole. In July and August the temperature round the South Pole may drop to a hundred and fifty degrees of frost. The Antarctic average yearly temperature is probably twenty-five or thirty degrees colder than that of the Arctic. This is roughly comparable with the difference of temperature between England and the tropics. The Antarctic refrigerator, as it might be called, has such an effect that in January and February—the Southern summer—the line of average freezing point reaches—towards Africa—to 53½° S. latitude. This is the corresponding latitude of the centre of the British Isles, and is as though all places north of Liverpool had an average temperature, even in summer, of below freezing point. This melting line does not anywhere approach the South Pole within fifteen hundred miles, whereas in the north of Greenland it is only four hundred and twenty miles from the North Pole.

The Arctic climate is less severe because there is much less high land there, and also because the deep ocean circulating in the centre will not freeze save on the surface. The temperature of this reservoir of latent warmth is slightly raised by the Gulf Stream which flows north past Spitsbergen and in summer keeps the sea free of ice to 81° N., which is a hundred and eighty miles nearer than ships can ever approach the South Pole.

(Whilst on the subject of the Gulf Stream, I might add that this current carries valuable driftwood to the Arctic shores. There is no driftwood in the Antarctic, which is a disadvantage to explorers.)

The Arctic summer is so mild that great lakes of fresh water form on many of the ice floes, from which ships can obtain drinking water. The Antarctic is so much colder that pools of fresh water on the pack-ice are practically unknown. Many Arctic floes are stained by sand and dirt blown on to them from the land. In the Antarctic the surfaces of the floes are generally snow-clad and always dazzlingly clean.

On the outskirts of the Arctic Circle I have experienced a shade temperature of 104° F. and have had to wear a protective veil against swarms of large and bloodthirsty mosquitoes that infested the forests.

Roughly speaking, the height of the Antarctic Continent

equals the depth of the Arctic Ocean. This fact once started an illogical theory regarded by most people as far-fetched, to the effect that the North and South Poles were the anode and cathode of the earth considered as a magnet.

In the Arctic the central sea is covered with pack-ice drifting across it. In the Antarctic the pack-ice closely encircles the continent and radiates outward into the Southern Ocean, so that there is generally even more drifting ice outside than inside the Antarctic Circle.

The gulfs that penetrate the Antarctic Continent, as I have already described, are hidden under huge ice barriers a thousand feet thick. The Great Ice Barrier of the Ross Sea, which is two thousand miles south of New Zealand, is one of the wonders of the world. It forms a mighty country, larger than France, of almost level ice, partly afloat. This Barrier is continually calving large and small ice-bergs into the sea, that drift away to the northward, to affect profoundly the meteorology of the Southern Hemisphere.

During the last century, when sailing ships and steamers were continually traversing the Southern Ocean, a keen look-out had to be kept for ice-bergs the whole time. Sometimes, however, a year or more would pass without the report of a single berg being sighted, and then again they would drift north in hundreds and thousands, among them being many of enormous size. My own theory, for what it is worth, is that these tremendous invasions of bergs cannot be accounted for by vagaries of climate alone. I believe that earthquakes and volcanic disturbances must have taken place in the Antarctic Continent, shaking the Barrier until masses of ice were broken off to form processions of northward-drifting bergs.

The Weddell Sea Barrier, the limits of which are unknown, may be as large as that of the Ross Sea. And there

are probably more of these great floating sheets still undis-
covered in the Antarctic. These huge ice-barriers are a dis-
tinguishing feature of the Antarctic and are unknown in the
Arctic.

The great ice-sheet of the Continent is unbroken save
where pierced by lofty peaks and mountain ranges. Here
and there a few bare beaches show. There are no trees, no
real soil nor vegetation, no land animals, land birds, winged
insects nor human beings. There are only herds of seals and
flocks of sea birds along the coast and on the pack-ice,
schools of whales where there is enough open water for
them to blow in, and fish in the sea.

In the Arctic, on the contrary, many of the lands are inhabited by hardy, intelligent races, and permanent habita-
tion reaches, at Spitsbergen, to within seven hundred miles
of the North Pole.

In Arctic lands there flourish in summer, on most of the
low-lying portions, beautiful meadows of grass, dwarf wil-
lows, Arctic poppies—a pale lemon-coloured blossom that
stands about a foot high and grows sometimes amongst
sparse vegetation and sometimes in otherwise barren
ground—ranunculus, saxifrage, of which there are a number
of varieties, and other flowers not very familiar to me. Bees,
singing birds and streams of running water are heard to
within four hundred and twenty miles of the North Pole
during the brief but almost genial summer of the north of
Greenland; but the only sounds heard in the Antarctic are
the strange calls of the penguins, the whistle of the wind, the
sighing blow of a whale, the grinding of the driven ice-pack,
the roar of the avalanche or the heavy boom of a glacier
calving.

Great forests of valuable timber stretch for thousands of
miles in Arctic Asia, Europe and America, in striking con-

trast with the icy desert that is the Antarctic. The Arctic forests are traversed by some of the mightiest rivers in the world—the Ob, the Yenisei, the Lena, the Mackenzie and others, with fertile plains and alluvial gold flats along their courses. At the spring break-up of the ice on these rivers huge ice-jams form, sometimes a hundred feet high. When these give way they sweep downstream with an appalling roar, tearing down the banks of the rivers, sweeping corners off, forming new bends, and, at times, carrying away farms, haystacks, houses, men and cattle.

There is nothing in the Antarctic that can be called a river.

Enormous herds of tens of thousands of reindeer roam the Arctic downs, forests and plains. These provide meat, milk, transport and clothing to the nomadic tribes of the north—Lapps, Finns, Chuckches, Samoyeds and Yakuts— while caribou provide food and clothing for the Esquimaux, who do not domesticate these animals.

Fish abound on the Arctic coasts and salmon swarm in the rivers, forming abundant sources of food. Polar bears wander over the drifting sea-ice, in search of seals. Walruses dig up shell-fish from the sea bottom, prey on fish and seal pups, or lumber about on the floes. Herds of thousands of seals bask on the ice-field or gambol in the sea. White whales and narwhals, with their eight-foot-long spiralled ivory horns, roll and blow in schools along the shores and pack edges. Numerous musk oxen, wolves, foxes, hares and tiny lemmings (rat-like creatures six inches long) in migrating millions, live in the Arctic. Sea and coast swarm with gulls, geese, guillemots, little auks, terns, puffins and eider ducks, breeding in countless thousands. At the report of a rifle fired at the base of the thousand-feet cliffs known as the Alkrange in Spitsbergen I have seen auks and guillemots pour out in such dense clouds that they literally darkened the air. Swans occur to 80° N. All these creatures between them provide the wandering tribes with food, fur, lamp oil, and sinews for sewing-thread, while the eggs and down of the eider duck are shipped south to be used for civilisation.

There is nothing like so much variety of life in the seas of the Antarctic, and the creatures that are found there are peculiar to that region. The seals are of a different species from those of the Arctic and are much larger and more numerous. The Emperor and Adelie penguins are confined to the Antarctic. Their plumage is not of the ordinary type but consists of very closely-packed quill-like feathers, and in place of wings they have paddle-shaped flippers on which the quills grow short and very small. These birds are unable to fly at all, but are magnificent jumpers, divers and swimmers. They are so quick and agile under water that they resemble fish, twisting and turning like lightning. This swiftness of action is the only thing that preserves them from being exterminated by the lithe, active sea-leopard. The sea-elephant of the Southern Ocean at times penetrates the Antarctic Circle, and is often found on the fringes of the pack-ice which has drifted outside it, but chiefly on the beaches of the sub-Antarctic islands.

The fiercest and most dangerous creatures of the Antarctic are the killer-whales *(Orca Gladiator)*. Their high, triangular fins stand five feet or more out of the water. A strange sight is a line-ahead formation of sixty or seventy sinister looking fins cutting the water and rising and falling as the killers blow. The largest of these brutes grow to a length of nearly thirty feet, with a mouth four feet wide and cruel teeth. It is seldom that penguins are caught by killers, as the latter aspire to higher game, and a hundred-foot-long blue whale weighing a hundred and thirty tons is not safe from a pack of these wolves of the sea. Two or three of the killers seize the jaws of the blue whale and force its mouth open, which gives the others an opportunity to dash at it and wrench out the tongue. After tearing the tongue out of their victim they leave it to die, or remain to feast on the carcase. Killers of a different species are found in the North, but in smaller numbers, though large lazy sharks are numerous.

Arctic whaling is now comparatively unimportant, but in the waters of the far South during the last twenty years the whaling industry has yielded a total of sixty million sterling. This fact alone, I think, should answer the many people who cannot see wherein lies the usefulness of Polar exploration.

I myself preferred the Antarctic because there was a tremendous thrill in the knowledge that, when we discovered land there, no mortal eye had ever seen those slopes and ranges before. In the Arctic most discoveries have been anticipated centuries earlier by savages or primitive races.

Antarctic ice-bergs are frequently tabular in shape. These have generally broken off from the great ice-barriers and are of enormous size, though they rarely exceed three hundred feet in height. Arctic bergs, though much smaller, are sometimes loftier and generally more beautiful and varied in shape.

I have pointed out these contrasts between the Arctic and the Antarctic because so few people have the opportunity of becoming acquainted with their essential differences. The similarities that exist should, however, be mentioned. These are the pack-clad seas, the ice-caps on all high lands, the invigorating quality of the pure air, the summer-long day, the winter-long night, mock suns, mock moons (which possess a pale, cold beauty that is most impressive), mirages, wonderful glowing auroras and magically-brilliant stars.

Quaintly enough, the fact that seemed to concern Shackleton a good deal was that he would not see the red snow of the Arctic.

"I know that it seems a small thing to be disappointed about," he said to me, "but I've always wanted to have a look at it."

In the Arctic it is not rare to come across red snow. There one sometimes sees large red areas, a startling contrast to the pure white surroundings. The effect is amazing, and at first one has the feeling that it is an illusion. Red snow is almost peculiar to the Arctic and caused by myriads of minute algæ—microscopic plants—multiplying with astounding rapidity in places where the surface of the snow just reaches melting point. I believe that there are different varieties of the plant, as I have seen the snow in Franz Josef Land stained yellow and also a dull green, as well as red.

When Shackleton decided that after all the Expedition should go south, he and I set to and worked out the routes that we should follow, the places to visit and the work to be done.

While we were discussing the journey and all its possible ramifications I made a remark about the lost island of Tuanaki.

"What was that?" said Shackleton.

"In the South Pacific," I said, "some years ago when I was in command of the New Zealand Government schooner *Countess of Ranfurly* I heard from the natives and missionaries of Rarotonga many tales of a lost island. As far as I could reconstruct events from their stories, about a hundred years ago or more this island, which lay two hundred miles southeast of Rarotonga, was inhabited by Kanakas. It was hilly and well wooded, with plenty of fresh water. It probably had a harbour—at all events it was said to have been visited by whalers. How the island disappeared was never recorded, but apparently a whaler or a native schooner came to Rarotonga after having failed to locate it. Tuanaki had disappeared completely. I was sufficiently interested to look up the chart, and I found that in what appeared to be the neighbourhood where the island had been, the sea bottom shelved from, roughly, two thousand fathoms to about sixty."

"Do you think that it would be possible to trace its history?" Shackleton asked eagerly, "and by dredging on the bank find the explanation of its disappearance?"

"I should think that it might," I answered cautiously.

"Then we will make that part of our programme," he declared promptly.

A little later, having pursued the subject, he obtained from the London Missionary Society some confirmation of the legend of the vanished island.

The tale brought back to his mind the fact that I had once found a pearl lagoon of which I had spoken to him during the boat journey. He now began to question me on the subject and asked me whether I were sure that there really were pearls there. "Certain," I told him. The idea of adventure, especially if it were connected with treasure, always had a glamour of romance in his eyes. This fired his imagination and he was obviously determined to visit the lagoon, although he said, chaffingly, "It will be a pity, Skipper, if it has shared the fate of that island of yours."

Shackleton by now had decided to devote the summer to the Antarctic, exploring as far as possible the area between the Weddell Sea and Enderby Land. He thought that there was the possibility of finding another great barrier and that where there was land we could make sledging journeys to explore it. In the winter he wished to concentrate on oceanography, primarily in the Pacific, and to study the islands of the Southern Ocean.

The idea appealed to me too, since, although I was no scientist, I was interested in all forms of life beneath the waters.

My special job was to be sailing master of the *Quest* and hydrographer to the Expedition. Shackleton insisted on my being given this impressive title. I think he liked the sound of it! My task, apart from my duties as sailing master, was to carry out deep-sea soundings, magnetic work, and to chart or complete the chart of any out-of-the-way places that we visited.

Our sounding appliances were the ordinary Admiralty type of Kelvin sounding machine with three hundred fathoms of thin, fifteen-strand wire and a Lucas sounding machine carrying six thousand fathoms of a single fine steel wire. The Kelvin machine was intended for soundings to a depth of a hundred fathoms while the ship was moving at any speed through the water. For this purpose a thin glass tube was secured above the deep-sea lead. This tube was coated inside with silver chromate. By the pressure of the water forcing itself up inside the tube and discolouring the silver chromate, the fathoms could be measured off on the glass tube as soon as it was brought up again.

Soundings up to a hundred fathoms are constantly used in ordinary navigation, so that in foggy weather any shipmaster approaching the coast can judge his position by the depth of the water and be warned in time of an approach to danger. The deep-sea soundings are taken mainly for scientific purposes. However, commercial use is made of them in the laying of electric cables across the beds of the oceans.

The Lucas machine installed on the *Quest* was lent to Shackleton by the Eastern Extension Telegraph Company. The six-mile long wire was flexible and only as thick as a sewing needle. A fifty pound cast-iron weight was attached to the end of the line, and was automatically released and lost on striking the bottom. Attached to the end of the wire were a pair of powerful nippers that scooped up a section of the bottom and when hove up on board again provided a good sample of the ocean bed. Whilst deep-sea soundings are being taken, it is a work of art to keep the ship perfectly stationary and plumb over the descending weight.

The ship was fitted with a Sperry gyroscope to render us independent of the magnetic compass. This, with the aid of the four feet six inches range-finder on the bridge, was to facilitate rapid running surveys of any coast we might examine.

The magnetic work to be done was to ascertain the variation of the compass, which means the amount of deflection of the compass needle from true north and south in any given part of the world. This is generally done by taking a Kew magnetometer or a good compass on to close pack-ice or any other steady place away from any magnetic rocks or metal. The operation consists of observing the compass bearing of the sun or some other celestial object and comparing it with the true bearing as calculated. The difference is the variation of the compass. The "dip" of the magnetic needle is measured by a Barrow Dip Circle—the dip is the angle made by the magnetic needle with a horizontal line. Over the North and South Magnetic Poles (which are both nearly twelve hundred miles removed from their respective geographical Poles) the dip is ninety degrees, and, roughly, midway between these points, along what is called the magnetic equator, the dip is nil. The dip and variation of the compass are due to the earth's magnetism.

The accurate knowledge of the variation and its steady annual changes is of such importance to the Navy and all those that "go down to the sea in ships" that the Admiralty employs a highly specialised staff for this work alone. Consequently this is almost the most useful work that Polar explorers can carry out; for in the unexplored ends of the earth the variation has to be theoretically assumed, and although this has generally been done with extraordinary nearness to accuracy, there are in some places large discrepancies, which we hoped to correct.

Whilst on the subject of magnetism I might remind my readers that the *geographical* Poles are those two parts of the earth where the sun on their respective midsummer days circles round at the same altitude for the twenty-four hours. After that date each day sees a fall, until the sun gradually sets, sweeping completely round the three hundred and sixty degrees of the horizon as it does so. The *magnetic* Poles have no relation to the sun's track. These are the points at which the magnetic needle loses its directive force and becomes suspended vertically.

In addition to the equipment that I have mentioned, the Admiralty lent us a Naval wireless set. This was very useful in giving us correct Greenwich mean time, which enabled us to check our chronometers at frequent intervals and so ensured that the longitudes that we observed were absolutely accurate. I believe that this was the first time that the exactitude of positions so far south had been precisely recorded.

In June, Shackleton sent me to Cowes for the various papers belonging to his yacht the *Quest*, which was now entitled to fly the white ensign and the burgee of the Royal Yacht Squadron, to which he had just been elected.

The King received him, as he had before his journey in the *Endurance*, and gave him a Union Jack to carry South. Queen Alexandra, who had always been very gracious to him and who showed a great admiration for him, also received him and heard all his plans, taking the same keen and kindly interest as she had in his previous expeditions. On the *Endurance* Shackleton had prized the Bible that Queen Alexandra had presented to him, in which she had inscribed her good wishes in her own handwriting. This time she gave him a talisman that he appreciated equally.

We left London on September 18th, 1921. As we steamed down the river the vessels lined along the banks and coming upstream dipped their ensigns and blew their whistles to us. It was a great send-off, and Shackleton, who took a boyish delight in being made a fuss of, was highly delighted.

In our crew the Empire was well represented. We had men from Canada, New Zealand, Australia and Africa, and were twenty on board, all told. One of the most interesting personalities among us was Hubert Wilkins, who later flew over the Arctic Ocean and the North Pole and also south of Graham Land in the Antarctic. I liked him very much. Deceptively, his outward appearance gave the impression of academic achievement rather than physical prowess, but actually he was lean and tough and had previously done wonderful work in the Arctic with Stefansson. He was in my watch, and was a cheery companion and a willing worker. He was the naturalist of the Expedition, but supplemented this by taking the film records of the journey. I was not surprised when later he distinguished himself so greatly; for I always thought he had it in him.

Almost all the men had had Naval or Military rank as officers during the War, but now everybody was practically on the same level in doing all the work of the ship. Everyone worked hard and did whatever job came to hand, irrespective of rank or title.

Frank Wild was Shackleton's second-in-command. He had changed very little since the days of the old *Endurance* and was as cheery and energetic as ever. Little Hussey, now a full-blown surgeon, was bobbing around as usual and entertaining us all with the old tunes that we had liked so well when he played them on his banjo on the ice and on Elephant Island. The two doctors, Macklin and McIlroy, were again with us, and so was my old friend McLeod, who had kicked me to bring me to consciousness in the boat when we were approaching Elephant Island. Green, the cook, a permanent grin on his face, appeared to me a beautiful sight "for old times' sake." Kerr, who had been second engineer on the *Endurance*, was now chief.

Amongst the new hands were Lieutenant-Commander Jeffrey, D.S.O., navigator; G. V. Douglas, the geologist, a very fine Canadian scientist; and Major Roddy Carr, of New Zealand, an old comrade of mine in North Russia, with a very distinguished flying record. In addition we took two Boy Scouts, one of whom had to be sent back from Madeira owing to serious sea-sickness. Poor chap, I felt sorry for him. The other, James Marr, was a complete success and has now a distinguished record in Polar work. Gerald Lysaght, an old friend of Shackleton's and a case-hardened yachtsman, came with us as far as the Cape Verde Islands. He was a universal favourite and it was with great regret that we saw him leave us.

The voyage appeared ill-starred from the very beginning. Actually we nearly had an accident within a few minutes of the start. We had made arrangements for the bascules of the Tower Bridge to be lifted for us to go through, but as we came up swiftly on the flood tide we could see that some hitch had occurred. The bascules had not moved. It was a critical position, for the little vessel might have swung broadside on to the bridge if we had anchored. But just as our mast seemed about to touch them the bascules rose, and although we had little space to spare we swept through.

At the outset Shackleton did not appear to me to be physically the man he was when he had led the old expedition. Indeed I learned afterwards that he had had a bad spell of pain before leaving London, which, in the light of later knowledge, I realised must have been a heart attack. The one subject that seemed to interest him in these days, and to take his mind off the worries which quickly came upon him, was my pearl lagoon.

All the way from England to Lisbon and from Lisbon to Madeira we had exceptionally bad weather, continually encountering head gales. The ship was exceedingly lively, with a very jerky motion peculiar to herself—so much so that she managed to upset many well-seasoned hands.

Originally we had intended making straight for Madeira, but engine trouble compelled us to put in to Lisbon for repairs. A week later we proceeded to Madeira. From there we went to St. Vincent in the Cape Verde Islands and then on to St. Paul's Rocks, a group of tiny islets situated practically on the Equator.

Just before we sighted these islands we met a beautiful five-masted ship. She was the *France* of Rouen, the largest square-rigged ship in the world at that time. Anything to do with the old sailing ships had for me an irresistible attraction, so I suggested to Shackleton that we should take a photographic record of her. Knowing my weakness he smilingly agreed, and we ran close to the ship with her great towers of canvas completely dwarfing the little *Quest* alongside. Wilkins got out his camera and obtained one of the last records of the days when sails dominated the seven seas.

Next morning at daybreak we reached St. Paul's Rocks, which are specks in the vast Atlantic, white with guano and without vegetation. The highest point is only sixty-four feet above the level of the sea, and the largest rock is less than four hundred feet long. We landed on one of the little islets, and jumped the narrow strip of water that separated it from the next. The sea was alive with sharks. The landing itself was rather difficult on account of the considerable swell that was running there, the rocks being so small that they afforded hardly any lee. Doctor Pirie of the *Scotia*, on the way down to the Weddell Sea, had had, I remembered, a very exciting time when attempting to land here. In the end he had to give up the idea. As far as I know we were the only people who had landed on St. Paul's Rocks since the Challenger Expedition fifty years previously.

The islands were worth visiting, not only on account of the soundings that I got but because Wilkins, assisted by Marr, obtained splendid pictures of the birds, fishes and crabs that crowd about these rocks. Douglas made a geological examination, and completed from a station on the rocks the survey that I was making from the ship. Previous to the Challenger Expedition these islands had been visited by Charles Darwin. Sir James Ross, the Antarctic explorer, also landed.

The animal life there is very interesting. There are two varieties of birds, the brown gannet or "booby" and the "noddy." When we arrived many of these birds were sitting on their eggs, and others had chicks that they were feeding. They are not very pretty, however, and so foolish and spiritless that they can be caught by hand, which is why the sailors have nicknamed them boobies and noddies. Many of these birds were so stuffed with flying fish that if one frightened them they disgorged these before they could fly away.

There were also two varieties of crab, a small greenish one and a large red species. Silvery flying fish with outstretched wings were continually hurling themselves ashore in their attempts to escape the bonita, a large fish which pursues them. These flying fish were immediately seized by the ferocious-looking crabs, which ate them in a manner that was a grotesque parody of a human being's. They would tear the flesh off piece by piece, and stuff these bits into their mouths with their claws. The speed with which these hobgoblin-looking creatures covered the ground was marvellous; and every now and again they would make prodigious leaps forward to secure their prey; otherwise they generally went sideways into action.

The little cove seemed to contain myriads of small fish and of sharks up to eight feet in length. At the bottom of the cove, where the small fish could shelter amongst the rocks they seemed to be utterly fearless of the sharks. But when our men, who were fishing, hauled them to the surface, in almost every case they were snapped off the hook by a shark. In this way several of the lines were broken. Frank Wild then harpooned some of the sharks, killed them, and threw them back. The others tore them to pieces, and while the hungry brutes were eating the food thus supplied, our party secured a good number of fish for our men.

All the time while the shore party was thus variously engaged I worked the ship round the rocks, taking soundings at frequent intervals. At the same time I charted their outline and measured the height of each of the rocks. The hundred-fathoms line was nowhere farther off the rocks than eight hundred yards and in places it came to within a hundred and fifty feet. This chart I eventually handed to the Admiralty, together with one which I made of Gough Island.

Shackleton, although he was interested in this work, was all impatience to get back to the Antarctic Continent. As I was laying off the bearings for the chart, I remember him saying, with an eagerness that he had shown but rarely of late, "I hope that you will be doing this in the Antarctic within a couple of months."

After leaving St. Paul's Rocks we passed Fernando de Noronha, a penal settlement some little way off the coast of

Brazil, and a few days later, as the engines continued to give trouble and the ship leaked, Shackleton decided to put into Rio to have her thoroughly overhauled. On November 21st we arrived at Rio de Janeiro.

The report of Wilson, Sons and Co., the firm that undertook the repairs, perturbed Shackleton. They condemned the previous survey that had been made of the engines. "I wish that you had been in England when I first heard of the vessel," said Shackleton to me, somewhat bitterly, when he received the unpleasant news.

Owing to the vessel's condition we suffered a month's delay. It was a delay which sorely tried Shackleton's nerves and was a source of constant worry to him. The lateness of the season added to his anxieties, for he feared that he would miss part of the brief summer in the Antarctic.

CHAPTER XIV

Shackleton
Looks Back

SHORTLY before we were due to leave Rio a reception had been arranged for Shackleton and our party ashore. However, that evening his manifold worries culminated in a bad heart attack. It was so severe that under Dr. Macklin's advice he remained on board that night. But with his usual consideration for others he insisted that we should all go ashore to enjoy ourselves. This bout of illness made us realise that there was something seriously wrong with Shackleton, although he never complained, and indeed within a few hours was assuring us that he was well again.

It was now too late in the year to carry out his original programme of first visiting Tristan da Cunha and then making Capetown our base. He realised that it had become necessary to utilise the open season in the ice and to take advantage of it to proceed straight to South Georgia. Herein lay our only chance of coaling before we went on to the Antarctic coast that lay over two thousand miles to the southward of Capetown.

We resumed our voyage for South Georgia on December

18th, and for the first few days we had fine weather. Nevertheless Shackleton seemed tired and done up, and spent much of his spare time in his cabin, where he liked me to join him for a smoke and a yarn. It struck me that he was thinking a good deal about the past, which was unusual for him, since he was a man who liked to leap forward mentally and who would generally dismiss memories in favour of speculations as to the future. I was vaguely worried by this strange and new attitude, which seemed to me to have a significance that I could not define. Nevertheless the yarns that he would spin were stirring and made me regret more keenly than ever that I had not met him much earlier in my life.

I will try to string together these memories which he related to me during the many hours that we spent together. Deeply engraved in my memory is every detail of the setting in which we passed the time. I can see now the little white cabin, lighted by one port-hole, which he was so careful should not contain any more comforts than were given to his men; the folding chair that was never quite steady; the blue coverlet on his bunk which was the only splash of colour that relieved the bareness. The door was hooked open, but even in fine weather as she rolled to and fro, the water, which was frequently coming in over the bulwarks, would swish and splash past his doorway—a fitting accompaniment to his conversation, which was nearly always of the sea.

"I wonder how soon we shall be back in the Antarctic," was usually the prelude to his reminiscences. After we had talked this over the first time, he said, thoughtfully:

"I've been at this game a good many years now, Skipper. I wonder whether you will stick to it as I have." He didn't wait for me to answer but went on, "I think you will, probably. If you are once in it, heart and soul, as you are and I am, you can never devote yourself thoroughly to anything else. At the back of your mind there is always the ice—the ice and the hope of finding what lies beyond it.

"I remember how proud I was when I joined Captain Scott in the *Discovery* in 1901. When King Edward and Queen Alexandra came on board to inspect the ship at Cowes and the Queen noticed the fine carnations which my father had sent to decorate the cabin, I was as pleased as a schoolboy.

"When we got to the Ross Sea I had complete charge of the catering, and I had the dickens of a time until I persuaded Captain Scott to give orders to kill seals for food. Even then, although I was pretty young and raw, I had strong ideas on the subject of fresh meat; and you know how particular I have been about food ever since. I had read enough to realise that fresh meat was the only sure preventive of scurvy down there.

"Before we had sailed I had been instructed about balloons by the Army Balloon Department, and so when we landed a balloon on the Great Barrier, after Captain Scott had been up I made an ascent with the camera. I got several good pictures. It was quite a thrill! I shall never forget what I felt as I looked far to the South. Mind you, I couldn't see anything but ice, but that made no difference to me: I still thought it great. I wondered what Scott had felt when he was up.

"It was a wonderful experience for me to be on this expedition with such a fine leader. We made the *Discovery* fast at the south-west corner of Ross Island, landed the observation huts, and built the big hut which we could all have lived in if the ship had been crushed."

It may be of interest to those who have had no experience in these matters to know how these huts are made. A hut of this kind is constructed in sections which can be put up on the spot. Each part is numbered, and diagonal stripes of different colours painted across it, each colour indicating the side to which it belongs; thus no time is lost, nor can any mistake be made when it is finally erected. Before it leaves the makers' hands the numbering and painting is inspected by the leader of the expedition, the hut is then taken to pieces and carefully stowed in the hold of the ship. It is rather a wonderful contrivance altogether, since these huts sometimes have to house and keep warm, in intense cold, as many as thirty or forty men. The upright posts are put into holes in the ice or frozen ground, which are then stamped down with snow on which a little water has been poured, so that it may freeze instantly and cement the "foundations." The usual wood employed is deal. The walls are double and filled in with peat moss, or other insulating substances, in order to conserve the warmth. To assist this further, snow is piled high up against the walls. This also helps to avert the danger of the hut being blown down in a blizzard.

"The hut that we put up is still there," said Shackleton, "or at least it was in 1917, when I went to take off the men that had been stranded.

"I shall never forget my first sledge journey. Scott sent me out to lead a party of three. The other fellows were Doctor Wilson and Ferrar. We each had our own sledging flag. Mine was secured to the bows of the sledge and bore the Shackleton arms and motto, 'Fortitudine vincimus.' We were to reconnoitre for a practical route south across the Barrier between Black Island and White Island. Of course we knew nothing about it, but we went by Nansen's methods which he had worked out so well in the Arctic. We took a light tent with us, a Norwegian pram in case of finding open water, a Nansen cooker and a Primus lamp, and reindeer-skin sleeping-bags.

"The first day out we had a snow blizzard from the south,

and before midnight we were played out and obliged to camp on the sea-ice. This was a very dangerous thing to do, and I wouldn't do it now, however exhausted I felt. We knew so little that we all got frost-bitten. We couldn't eat the pemmican, and we had a pretty rotten time. Frozen boots the next morning seemed the last straw, and I remember how I swore at mine. At last we got to White Island, but we couldn't get our sledge up from the sea-ice. So we roped together and, after a struggle, got to the top of the island, a height of two thousand seven hundred and thirty feet. We were carrying tea in flasks inside our inner clothing, but it had frozen solid. It took us till three in the morning to get back to the tent which we had left on the sea-ice. I remember Bill Wilson laughed when I remarked to him that there was only one thing to be said in favour of White Island and that was that there were no snakes on it.

"Next morning we marched about ten miles to the south and gradually got off the sea-ice on to rough glacier-ice, the broken-up fringes of the Barrier. We had found a possible route, however, which was the important thing. We returned to our little tent that night, dead tired. Just as we were going off to sleep the wind sprang up again from the south and was soon blowing very hard. Ferrar didn't care a hang; he went off to sleep; but Bill and I hung on to the poles of the tent, for if they had gone we should certainly have been in a bad way. It seemed to us as though we had hung on all night, but we must have fallen asleep, for at one in the morning it came as a surprise to us to find that the wind had died down.

"When we started on our return march we discovered that big cracks had opened in the sea-ice, cutting us off from the direction of the ship. So we had to make for the southern part of Ross Island. When we landed we left the pram there, and that's how Pram Point got its name. Scott was pleased with my work, but I realised what a lot I had got to learn. He chose me, however, for the Southern journey that he was planning to explore the Antarctic Continent, and you can imagine how pleased I was, especially as Bill Wilson was also going.

"That was a great journey, Skipper—my first really important one. Scott, Wilson and I started on November 2nd, 1902. Scott adopted the theodolite method of finding our position instead of using the sextant and artificial horizon, so I studied it hard. As you know, I have always considered this a very good innovation. That was why I had light aluminium theodolites especially made for my journeys."

The usual instrument by which seamen obtain their latitude is, of course, the sextant. On a ship the sea horizon is used, but on land it is necessary to have a shining, level surface which is known as an artificial horizon. The usual way is to use mercury in a little trough. By means of the sextant the sun is brought down till it touches its reflection in the mercury. The angle thus measured by the sextant is double that of the true altitude of the sun, and it is consequently halved to give the position. One objection to this method is that mercury freezes at forty degrees below zero and so it often becomes useless in the intense cold of the Polar regions. Scott preferred the theodolite method—the theodolite being an instrument on a tripod stand which is brought to the horizontal by means of screws and spirit levels.

"When we set out," Shackleton continued, "we had three sledges and nineteen dogs. It was very hard work, owing to the terribly broken-up surface, until we got well out on to the Barrier, and even out there we had a fearfully hard struggle. We frequently had to relay, which made our progress one third of what it should have been, and the weather never seemed just right. The sun was too hot in the middle of the day, and the wind was always far too cold. The soft snow was a curse. We hadn't really learnt the best methods of driving the dogs at first, but we gradually improved. We had to keep our rations down to the minimum, so that the three of us were always hungry, and as we went on, the snow seemed to get even softer and deeper than before. The work was so hard that some of the dogs died.

"When we reached 80° 30′ S., on the 14th of December, we made a depôt of everything that it was not absolutely vital that we should have with us. Scott confirmed our fears that it was impossible for us to reach anywhere near the Pole, as we were not making sufficient progress and our food would never have lasted out. For the sake of the exploration, however, we continued southward, parallel to the great range of mountains to the west of us. Peaks were rising to eleven thousand feet, many of which Scott named after various living Admirals. Wise man!" Shackleton winked at me and continued: "In spite of the hardships, it was really a wonderful experience to see those mountains, and the memory of what I felt then has always spurred me on to try to find new land.

"We each got more or less severe touches of snow blindness. One day we had thick mist and we crossed over a tremendously deep crevasse by the only little natural bridge that was there. We never realised that the crevasse was there until we had crossed it.

"On Christmas Day we had a regular feast. For breakfast we had a mugful of seal's liver each, with a piece of bacon and biscuit. On top of that we each had a spoonful of blackberry jam. Then we stood by the sledges with our sledge flags and the Union Jack flying while I fixed up a line to the lever of my camera and took a photograph. It was the finest and warmest day we had. For lunch we had Bovril, chocolate, Plasmon biscuit and a double whack of jam. When we had covered ten miles we camped for the night. I cooked the hoosh. I boiled the pudding and used the water for making cocoa. The pudding was only six ounces, and I had secretly stowed it in my sleeping-bag with a little bit of holly. You ought to have seen their faces when I produced it. Scott got out the emergency brandy to fire it in proper style and when we saw the bottle in his hand we felt like princes. You can imagine our disgust when we found that the spirit was black with corrosion and had to be thrown away.

"Wilson got such bad snow blindness at about this time that he had to tramp along blindfolded. Scott was also suffering from it, and so I had to lead the party for two days. We made what I found by my subsequent experience to be a mistake in keeping too close to the mountains, but this, of course, was not my responsibility. Scott, like the rest of us, had not then acquired the experience to know that the glaciers descending from the mountains disturbed the surface of the Barrier so much in that area that we should have saved time by keeping twice as far off although that meant a slightly longer route. The advance went on until the last day of the year, and then we had to turn back, as Scott and I undoubtedly had scurvy.

"I shall never forget the night when I spilled the hoosh. I was cook, and by some unlucky chance I capsized the pot. Neither Scott nor Bill said a word. I never remember a silence that was so long or so awful. My blood ran cold. In the end we ate it from the tent floor. We had only enough food left to last for a fortnight, and unless we made seven miles a day we could not reach the first depôt in time. It was a back-breaking business, but we did it. I had to have a bandage across my eyes for two days, like Bill, on account of snow-blindness, and at such a critical time this was particularly maddening. When we got to that depôt we were all three suffering from scurvy and Scott laid the course straight for the ship. Thank God, none of my own party has ever had scurvy.

"On the day that we left the depôt I had a very bad fit of coughing which brought on hæmorrhage of the lungs. I am inclined to think that this was due to scurvy. It weakened me a good deal, and Scott would not allow me to pull the sledge any more. But I kept up with them, and was no drag on them. As you know, there have been statements to the effect that I was dragged back on the sledge. That was a lie—or perhaps I ought to say a mis-statement, to give the people who wrote it the benefit of the doubt. But you can imagine how it annoyed me when I saw it. Captain Scott and Bill helped me, like true friends, but you can imagine how it worried me to think that I was unable to help them drag the sledge.

"When we got back to the ship I had a good hot bath, the first for thirteen weeks, and felt much better. On the whole it had been a good time. Everybody has his own idea of fun; hasn't he, Skipper?"

I laughed and said, "My idea is pretty well the same as yours."

Shackleton continued: "When we got back we found that the relief ship *Morning* had arrived, and I needn't tell you, Skipper, what a terrible knock it was to me when Scott decided, on the doctor's report, that I should be invalided home in her. I reckoned that with two or three weeks' rest I should have been completely cured of scurvy, but they wouldn't listen to me. But when I went aboard the *Morning* I gritted my teeth and said to myself, 'Nothing on earth shall prevent me from coming back here at the head of my own expedition!' " He rose to his feet, and exclaimed, "I kept my word, didn't I?"

"After I had been back a little time," he said, "I became Secretary of the Royal Scottish Geographical Society in Edinburgh, and did my first bit of lecturing. Then, three months after my return, I got married. I could never tell you what an enormous help my wife has been to me from that day to this. Still, you and Frank and Micky know what she is. In spite of her hating my going away she helped me in every way possible to keep my promise to myself and get up an independent expedition to reach the South Pole. After tremendous exertions I succeeded, but I was glad that Ray, and Cicely also, were born before I had to leave.

"I had got into McMurdo Sound in my ship *Nimrod* in the January of 1908, after having been towed to the edge of the Ross Sea by the *Koonya*. We had a bad time on that tow. On the fourth day the gale which had blown incessantly after leaving New Zealand increased until the poor old *Nimrod* was rolling to fifty degrees from her perpendicular. You couldn't walk anywhere, and the gale lasted for practically ten days. Two or three times the *Koonya* had to heave-to with us. It was a fearful job keeping the poor ponies alive. All the scientists took watch in looking after them, it was so difficult to keep them on their feet. One poor brute fell and was rolled over on to its back by the ship. We couldn't get it upright again, and as it was suffering considerably it had to be shot. There wasn't a dry spot on the ship, and for a fortnight nobody had dry clothes or a dry bed.

"Your countrymen in New Zealand were always very good to me, and they had generously sent aboard the *Koonya* a large number of sheep to take South with us, so as to provide us with fresh meat for as long as possible. Just before the *Koonya* cast off the tow rope her men slaughtered these animals and we hauled the carcases on board through the sea. The first lot arrived safely. The second was lost through the ship rolling heavily and the rope parting.

"The New Zealand Government had sworn me in as Post-master of the Antarctic,"—he laughed boyishly at the rem-iniscence—"and they gave me a special issue of stamps—the red penny stamps of New Zealand overprinted in green with the words, 'King Edward VII. Land.' It was great fun using them."

"Yes, you gave me half a dozen of them," I remarked.

"It was an amazing thing," he went on, "but we met no pack-ice. Previous expeditions had always lost a lot of time through the delay caused by the pack. You know it has been held against me that I went to McMurdo Sound after promising Scott that I would not, as he was preparing plans to embark on the expedition which started in 1910, two years after mine. I certainly did not intend to go there. But when I got to the Bay of Whales, nearly four hundred miles east of McMurdo Sound, I found that miles of the Barrier had broken away since I had been there with Scott. The place was so altered that I saw that I should be hazarding the lives of the party if I had established my base there. If any-thing had happened to my men there I should have consid-ered myself guilty of murder. All the same, you can imagine my feelings at being forced to do what I had told Scott I would not do."

"A rash promise, but you would have got to the Pole from there," I interjected. He nodded, and said:

"Well, there it was. Mackintosh, who was second officer of the *Nimrod*, was to have been on the land party. But in putting out the stores a cargo hook struck him, and he lost an eye, poor chap. I was very upset, and it meant losing the services, for the time being, of a very fine fellow.[1]

"We found a good site for the hut at Cape Royds on Ross

---

[1] Mackintosh commanded the *Aurora* for Shackleton in 1914.

Island, and the hut, stores and coal, ponies and motor-car were landed. There was still a broad stretch of sea-ice between the ship and the shore. After their terrible journey the ponies were in bad condition and another poor brute had to be shot. As I had taken them to drag the provisions on the journey to the Pole, and to provide fresh meat, this was a serious matter.

"We had terrible difficulty in landing a hundred and eighty tons of stores and sledging these across the ice, which split badly whenever the blizzards swept down on us. Preventing the cases and the ponies from falling into the sea as the ice split and drove out was a fearful job. I don't think that I ever worked harder in my life, but all the men were splendid. When the stores were landed Captain England took the ship back to Lyttleton.

"Professor David,[1] who was then Professor of Geology in Sydney, was persuaded by me to join the shore party. He was older than any of us, but he was a splendid fellow as well as a fine scientist. I was glad that I managed to keep him. Mawson,[2] who also stayed on shore with us, was a lecturer at Adelaide University in those days.

"The heavy sea-ice prevented me getting farther south on Ross Island than Cape Royds. But this same sea-ice promised to afford a good sledging route south to the Barrier. Across this sea-ice I intended to convey stores and through the autumn lay depôts across the Barrier. Unfortunately almost as soon as the *Nimrod* had gone a heavy blizzard from the south broke up all the ice and drove it out to sea. This spoilt our plan to sledge across it, and that was the all-powerful factor against my reaching the South Pole. Had

---

[1] Sir Edgeworth David.
[2] Sir Douglas Mawson.

I been able to lay out depôts that autumn it would have made all the difference.

"We carried out the normal routine of the station, including a good deal of meteorological work. We also studied the animal life on the shores and in the sea. Professor David made a geological examination of Ross Island and was very anxious to climb Mount Erebus.[1] This mountain was the dominating feature of the landscape; steam and smoke blew away from it in a great streamer for miles in the upper atmosphere.

"I sent Mawson and Mackay with David to constitute the summit party, and Adams, with Marshall and Brocklehurst, as a supporting party, with orders to go as far as Adams thought advisable. They set out in early March, with ten days' provisions. It was rather amusing about that supporting party; it simply refused to turn back; the whole lot of them stuck to David and got up to the top with him in four days. That was what Adams thought I meant by 'advisable'! The going was very rough, it appears, and David afterwards described the scenery as magnificent, but so weird as to seem almost unreal, especially where fumaroles (steam escapes) in scores had formed fantastic and wonderful shapes by the freezing of the steam, sometimes into masses as large as a haystack. Some of these they described as looking like lions crouching to spring. When they reached the top they found themselves looking down the walls of a vast crater, half a mile wide and nine hundred feet deep. In spite of the heat from this crater the snow and ice continued right up to the very summit. Clouds of steam and smoke were swirling in the crater below them; nevertheless, they could make out that there was an active cone within the crater.

---

[1]An active volcano, rising to 13,370 feet. It lay directly behind Shackleton's camp at Cape Royds.

"As soon as they had established the height of the mountain they started on their return journey. Almost immediately a blizzard set in, and they were forced to camp on the mountain-side. One of the party was blown down the hillside about four hundred yards, and it took him the best part of an hour to crawl back to the rest. However, on the whole they made a good journey and were back in five days.

"The boys started a book which they called 'Aurora Australis.' Marston set it up and printed it in the hut with lithograph and process illustrations. It was bound in venesta boards from the packing cases, and it was really a beautiful piece of work. No other book has ever been produced so far South.

"All this time I was making every preparation I could for the journey to the Pole. I expected that either the Barrier would lead right up to it or else that I should have to ascend some glacier up the mountains to reach it. Anyway, I had to make 865 statute miles to the Pole—a total of 1,730 there and back—and of course everything depended upon my carrying enough food and fuel to last the party over that distance. My original intention had been to take six ponies and six men; but I had only four ponies left. As we were therefore two ponies short I had to keep the Polar party down to four.

"I started my preliminary sledging trip on the 12th of August—ten days before the return of the sun. It was a beastly job sledging on the Barrier at the end of the winter like that. As soon as we got on to the Barrier, the temperature fell to fifty-six degrees below zero. The paraffin used for cooking was as thick as cream. To sleep in such a temperature was out of the question, and as the weather was getting worse I thought it wiser to return to Hut Point. We were stuck there for several days by the blizzard.

"The big hut that had been put up there by Scott was bit-

terly cold, and so we put up a small one inside it, made of
cases of stores, and we used this with some sort of comfort.
As a matter of fact, in my anxiety to make a beginning I had
started a bit too early. We employed the time from then on
in sledging stores down from Cape Royds to Hut Point. This
made up some of our leeway, while it gave the men a certain
amount of practice with the sledges and also advanced my
base twenty-three miles.

"On the 22nd of September I started laying out the depôts. That part of it went all right. I arranged with Joyce that
he should make a depôt near Minna Bluff on the following
January so that if things went as I expected I should find it
there on my return.

"We made our real start from Hut Point on November
3rd. As soon as I got up on the Barrier I steered well out to
the east-south-east, as I hoped by doing this to avoid the
dangerous crevasses that were found towards the land. You
can judge how careful we had to be when I tell you that the
snow covering of these crevasses was often strong enough to
bear a man while the pony he led would break through. We
were unable to get free of the menace of those accursed
crevasses for ten days. The tension was very wearing. After
that the worst trouble was the soft, deep snow in the hollows
of the long undulations on the Barrier. After three days of
travelling I sent the supporting party back.

"When we got away from the land we steered across that
great sea of ice, and when it was slightly misty the effect was
very weird. There was no horizon anywhere. We were the
only beings in the Universe! We seemed to be marching
through space, and sometimes I had the odd sensation that
we were going through the motions of marching without
moving forward at all.

"We came straight to Depôt 'A,' which had been laid six

weeks before. That's where good navigation comes in, Skipper! The position of that depôt had to be absolutely accurate and so had our navigation, or else there would not have been a chance in the world of our finding it. It was like picking up a buoy in the middle of the Atlantic, and it would of course have meant the certain death of the whole party had we missed any one of these depôts.

"The calmness of the weather at that time was extraordinary. Clouds would appear on one side of the horizon, speed across, and disappear on the other, although we felt no wind whatever. Sometimes it was almost uncanny. I used to feel that we had stepped off our own planet and on to another.

"A hundred miles south of Depôt 'A' we had to kill one of the ponies that was unfit for travel. So we ate all we could that day, took as much as we could drag on the sledges, and left the remainder as a depôt for the return journey. My intention had been to kill the ponies one by one at successive stages of the outward journey; we would then eat well that day, and take on half the meat, making a depôt of the remainder for the return journey. Now, unfortunately, I had to kill a pony earlier than I had intended. This happened just south of the eighty-first parallel of latitude.

"The Barrier surface from about this point became as flat as a billiard table, and, conditions being favourable, I managed to bring up the average of the daily marches to eighteen miles, so that on the 26th November we passed the farthest south that we had reached with Captain Scott—the farthest south that anybody had ever been. It took us thirty-three days less to do it than it had taken Scott, which shows that I had learned something from previous experience anyway.

"The time that followed was extraordinarily interesting. Before us rose huge mountains, never seen before by anybody. Magnificent red cliffs, thousands of feet high, frowned out over the great frozen sea at their base.

"In 82° 40′ S., twenty-five days out, we laid Depôt 'C,' killing a second pony. We then pushed on with two loaded sledges, each weighing six hundred pounds. Two of us helped the ponies by pulling on the sledge. We had lost the flat surface and the Barrier was now marked by long, low undulations. These undulations were so gentle that we did not know they were there until we noticed that the snow pillars that we built at each halt for guides on our return kept disappearing and reappearing. Pulling the sledges was an awful drag, especially as the weather was calm and hot. We stripped to singlet and trousers several times as we dragged the sledges along, in spite of the fact that the snow under foot was unmelted. Of course we were living on such short rations that we were constantly suffering from hunger. The men were awfully good and never complained however much I cut down the grub.

"I found that the mountains were trending across our southward course and knew that I should be compelled to cross them, and I began to wonder what was on the other side. Four days later we came to the foot of the mountains. And there I saw an unforgettable sight—the mightiest glacier in the world. It lay before us, a great river of ice sloping gently and easily upwards, apparently a roadway to the Pole. It flowed between sheer cliffs, thousands of feet high, and where its downthrust struck the Barrier there were tremendous disturbances. On all sides of us were pressure ridges, seracs and deep crevasses. Farther out the disturbances died down into the long undulations which I have told you about. I called our discovery the Beardmore Glacier, and it was up this glacier that I made my way towards the Pole.

"We were on the glacier for twenty-two days, fighting our

way upwards to an altitude of nine thousand five hundred feet above sea level. And every day as we ascended the difficulties increased. The highway to the South was becoming sadly broken up. The one pony that remained had trouble in keeping its feet but Wild continually looked after it with wonderful kindness. The crevasses here were numerous and exceedingly dangerous.

"On the fifth day of our climb it was overcast. Under such conditions, as you know, it is often extraordinarily difficult to see what the surface is like. The light is diffused and reflected back from the snow, and there are no shadows thrown anywhere to warn one of any inequalities. I was going along very cautiously with Adams and Marshall, pulling one sledge. Wild was following, leading the pony and the other sledge, when suddenly I heard a shout for help. Looking round I saw the pony-sledge sticking out of a crevasse. The pony had disappeared but Wild was hanging on to the sledge. We dashed back to his help. His body was in a crevasse that had been snow-covered and into which the pony had fallen, and he was holding on only by his elbows. He did not dare move an inch. It was one of the most nerve-racking sights I have ever seen. I believe that I had a worse fright than poor Frankie.

"We grabbed him and pulled him out. But for the fact that the bridle over Wild's arm had parted he would have lost his life. Fortunately the swingle-tree parting saved the sledge and the stores. Very carefully we hauled the sledge out of the crevasse; this was not so difficult, because it had got caught in a projection of the ice. After this we peered down into the crevasse to try to see where the pony lay, but we saw and heard nothing; all was darkness and silence below.

"Once I saw that Wild was safe I realised that this accident was going to have very grave consequences for us. The pony had represented between five and six hundred pounds of meat, and I knew that this might mean the difference between getting to the Pole and failing to get there. However, I determined to try to make up for this loss by still harder efforts. Two days later, although the surface was improving, I nearly lost another of the party, who fell through a snow bridge into a crevasse. The sledging harness and the sledge saved him. There were no defects in our equipment, otherwise he would have gone down a chasm that I reckoned must have been a thousand feet deep.

"As we were getting near the head of the glacier the slope began to grow steeper; consequently the work of hoisting the sledge over the jagged and slippery ice was back-breaking. We had to relay for the first time. It took us three days to advance fifteen miles—three days of dreadful effort.

"One day we noticed some blackish belts along a high sandstone cliff, and presently found to our amazement that these were seams of coal. This proved that in some bygone age this desolate spot had had a mild, and perhaps tropical, climate, which had produced luxuriant vegetation.

"We made another depôt on the glacier. This was at 85° S., and at last we had come to the great plateau which surrounds the South Pole. Sometimes, for no ascertainable reason, the frozen surface rang hollow beneath our feet. As Wild said, it was like walking on a glass roof. Naturally this was rather alarming, as I was continually fearing that we should crash through. On Christmas Day, on the plateau, we threw caution to the winds, and celebrated. This was our last spree, for after this I was obliged to reduce still further our meagre rations.

"On Boxing Day we lost sight of the mountains, and we were out on the bare, unbroken, gently upsloping plateau.

Then the altitude of eleven thousand feet began to affect us and we felt rotten, suffering from bad headaches. Our temperatures were four degrees sub-normal through under-nourishment and over-exertion.

"On New Year's Day we passed the eighty-seventh parallel, breaking all records towards the Poles, North or South.

"By this time we were in torments from frost-bite and the freezing moisture from our breath and streaming eyes, which caked into solid ice on our faces. Our beards became one solid mass, too, with our clothes, and we had not even a pair of scissors to cut away the matted hair round our mouths. We had to force our way against strong winds in a temperature of forty degrees below zero on half-rations in that terribly rarified atmosphere. I was becoming seriously worried, too, about the slowness of our progress. We were doing all that we could, but I was beginning to realise that we were weakening rapidly, and that owing to the loss of the pony we should not have enough food to take us to the Pole and bring us back even to the nearest depôt.

"In a desperate effort not to abandon the forward march, and with the approval of the other three, I laid a tiny emergency depôt. Three days later, on the 9th January, I saw that to continue was hopeless. Indeed I don't mind admitting to you that I had already gone farther than I was justified in doing with regard to my companions' lives. I am sure that if we had gone on for another ten miles not one of us would ever have got back alive. We were within ninety-seven miles of the South Pole, our position being 88° 23′ South, and 162° East.

"We stuck the staff of Queen Alexandra's Union Jack in the snow, and Marshall took a photograph of us beside the flag. I buried a brass tube in the snow with a sheet of Antarctic stamps and a record of what we had done, and formally annexed the plateau to the British Empire. Then I took up the flag, and although it was perhaps the worst moment that I have ever experienced, gave the order to turn back.

"The whole of that return journey was nothing but a series of races against death. Fortunately, a southerly gale helped to drive us along, with a sail hoisted on the sledge. Two days later we picked up the little emergency depôt that we had left six days before. We were covering the distance at double the rate. The downward slope then increased, and, urging ourselves on, we made still bigger distances. The mountains came in sight again, and our speed increased at the head of the glacier, so that we did twenty-six miles one day and twenty-nine the next—our best day's work. We rushed the sledge down over the precipitous, glass-surfaced ice-falls, and this very nearly smashed her up. But our condition was so desperate by now that we had to take risks.

"In 85° S. we picked up the upper glacier depôt. This meant four days' food, so we felt that we had won another round. The slippery blue ice made us all take some bad jolts and tumbles, and I was so disabled by one that I could do nothing to help the others for the whole of that day. In fact it was as much as I could do to keep up with them. As our food supply became exhausted our efforts grew more and more desperate. For two days we had had nothing to eat as we rushed the sledge down the slopes to the lower glacier depôt. Death very nearly won the round that time!

"The men were simply heroic: there isn't any other word to describe it. They stood up to everything, and they never murmured a complaint. I cannot say how fine Wild was. It is impossible to convey to anybody the mental and physical strain that I, as leader, went through then. Although they were so splendid I felt that every hardship they suffered was a reproach to myself.

"The next complication after we had got off the glacier and on to the Barrier was dysentery. Everybody went down with it and for twenty-four hours we could not move. It was maddening to look out on a sunny calm day and realise that it was ideal marching weather. Our complaint was due to eating the flesh of a horse that had been killed when in an exhausted condition: I did not realise then how this would affect the meat. Wild was the most seriously ill, and I was scared to death about him.

"The three succeeding depôts were picked up with terribly small margins of safety. Then, far away, above the distant horizon, we saw the faint outline of Mount Erebus, with its streamer of steam, and knew that we were in sight of the end of our journey, though we had still a long way to go. Everything now depended upon finding the depôt east of Minna Bluff. There were no tracks to lead to it, and to tell the truth, I could not be perfectly certain that the depôt was there. Again a blizzard sprang up behind us, one in which I would never have dared travel in ordinary times; but it drove us along and we made twenty-one miles in it. The suspense was awful when we were finishing our food and were still uncertain as to whether we should find any or starve.

"On the morning after all our food was done our lives were saved by a miracle. I have often seen you take a great interest in mirages, but to me they will always savour of the miraculous. There were no signs of the depôt, and our spirits were sinking to zero. It looked mighty like the end. Then, suddenly, Wild happened to look to the right. Far away, and just raised into view above the horizon by the mirage, was the depôt flag. Marshall had barely succeeded in taking its bearing when it disappeared. Certainly it was the most mysterious thing that has ever happened to me. I changed our course at once to Marshall's bearing, and after eight hours' marching we reached the depôt.

"At the very end of the journey, after going through all that, I thought that the game was up. Marshall was very ill, and when we got within a reasonable distance of Hut Point I left him, with Adams to look after him, and giving them most of the food, Wild and I, taking only one day's rations and a light sledge, made a forced march. Before we got to Hut Point, however, we found that the ice had blown out, leaving open sea, and we had to march seven miles to get round this. It seemed to me to take a lifetime. At last we got to Hut Point, and there we found the hut empty, and a note saying that the *Nimrod* had returned and would leave on the 26th of February. Wild and I looked at one another in dead silence. It was then the 28th.

"We tried to set fire to one of the small huts, as a signal to the ship in case she was still lying at Glacier Tongue, but failed in our attempt. Then we tried to hoist a flag, but our fingers were too numb to tie a knot. We were too cold and too despondent to sleep that night, but when the darkness had passed we again tried to signal the ship, and luckily succeeded. She soon appeared. Captain Evans of the *Koonya* was in command for that voyage.

"I learned then how narrow had been our escape, for my men had had considerable trouble in delaying her for a few extra days from sailing away. Except by my own party we had been given up for lost. My men had been ordered to leave the base and go on board. Luckily they refused." "Rifles?" I queried. Shackleton smiled, and continued, "I went back and got Marshall and Adams, and on March 4th, 1909, all were on board, safe and sound.

"During my absence from the base, Professor David with Mawson, Murray and Mackay, had made a wonderful journey across the northern slopes of the great plateau, and had reached the Magnetic Pole. They were the first men in the world to get there, and it was a great achievement of Professor David's to lead the Expedition, considering that he was over fifty years of age. He was a most lovable man, and the others worked with him heart and soul. I was mighty proud of the lot of them."

The Death of a Hero

As we drew closer towards South Georgia the weather naturally got worse and on Christmas Day the wind blew at hurricane force, so that we were obliged to heave-to. I then resorted to my favourite device for heavy seas—the using of oil-bags. A canvas bag is filled with oil and in one corner of the bag is a small hole through which a little cotton waste is drawn, partly filling the hole but still allowing a free leakage. The bag is dragged in the sea to windward, and the oil, escaping, spreads a film all over the heavy seas, thereby preventing the crest of the waves from breaking on board the vessel. The swells are just as big as before and the ship's motion as lively as ever, but the tiger leaps of the breaking seas, which do so much damage to a vessel, are completely prevented. The effect is instantaneous and almost magical, and the neglect of this simple precaution has led to the loss of many a vessel and consequently many lives.

One worry after another now seemed to fall upon poor Shackleton. The boiler developed a serious crack, which, if we had tried to drive the vessel at full speed, must have produced an explosion. Our water tank sprang a leak and the fresh water was lost. We had to take water from the exhaust tank where steam from the main engine was condensed. This tasted oily, but it was sufficient to keep us going. In addition the ship herself developed new and disturbing leaks.

This situation, strangely enough, instead of depressing Shackleton roused his fighting spirit, and he became more like the Shackleton of the old days of the *Endurance* than he had been at any time during our journey on the *Quest*. For the first time since we had set sail I saw his shoulders hunched in the old aggressive way, and his jaw thrust forward. To me this was a wonderfully heartening sight; for it brought back a thousand memories of Shackleton's gallantry, his coolness and his power. It even made me think that any forebodings that I might have felt had a touch of the absurd, and that he was as right as rain after all.

After Christmas, gales were of almost daily occurrence, showing what South Georgia could do even in the summer time. Finally the mountains of the island came in sight. Shackleton was excited and happy, and continually pointed out to the newcomers spots which he, Crean and I had crossed six years previously. Several times he called me down from the bridge, saying: "Skipper, show the boys where we slid down," and things like that.

When we arrived at the whaling station of Grytviken, on January 4th, 1922, Shackleton, displaying all his old energy, went ashore to arrange various details of work. Afterwards he came back on board. We dined, and then the others went away fishing, leaving Shackleton and myself together. Although he looked tired he yarned away animatedly enough, and therefore I am unable to offer any explanation of a growing uneasiness which took possession of me. We began to play his favourite game of 'Racing Patience,' but since he seemed to want to talk rather than to play we soon put the cards aside. Our conversation naturally turned to the direction in which our explorations of the Antarctic should take. That talk is unforgettable.

"Would you like to land near Caird Coast and sledge toward Enderby Land?" he asked, and went on, without waiting for me to answer, "I would give you sledges and four or five men, and anything you discovered would be in your own name."

I was greatly moved by this generosity of his. There was nothing he could have proposed that would have touched me or pleased me more. Most men who had endured all that Shackleton had been through would have felt entitled to take the credit of discoveries made by any of their party. Shackleton was of finer calibre. I said, "Thanks, old man," and put my hand on his.

"Now, what about that old lagoon, Skipper?" he said, reverting to the topic that invariably seemed to divert him.

Eagerly we discussed the South Pacific and the fabulous size of pearls that had been found there.

"Do you think we could get anything like the 'Southern Cross'?" he asked, referring to the wonderful cluster that was brought up by a diver off the coast of North-Western Australia.

"It was sold for six thousand pounds, I think," was my reply.

"Yes," commented Shackleton, "but was re-sold for double."

Then a curious thing happened. For upwards of three months he had always spoken of our journey to the lagoon as a certainty and as though there remained only the details to be settled. Now, suddenly, his mood changed. It seemed as if he had forgotten for a moment that I was there, sitting beside him, for he mused aloud, in a tone filled with doubt:

"I wonder whether I *shall* ever see the Skipper's lagoon?"

This sort of thing was unlike Shackleton, and I wondered whether he knew something about himself that was hidden from me. I scanned his face, but could read nothing in his expression, and in less time than it takes to tell he was back on the subject of the size of the pearls.

When it grew late, I said, "We had better turn in now."

"Yes," he agreed, "we'll be out early."

Since his cabin was next to mine, before bidding him good-night, I stood in the doorway talking for a few minutes while he seated himself in the little folding chair. For some reason I did not undress at once, but pottered about the chart-room. Just as I was about to remove my sweater, however, I thought I heard him calling me, but when I popped my head round the door he was sitting exactly as I had left him—to all appearance quite all right.

"Thought you shouted for me," I said, as he motioned me to enter. He smiled and, as he had done often in the past, murmured aloud, "Good old Skipper."

"Well, good-night. Sorry if I disturbed you," I said.

"You didn't disturb me," he said with the hearty kindliness that was one of his most lovable traits. "Have a cigarette, now you're here?"

I had an idea that this suggestion was made only out of good nature, and that in reality he wanted to be quiet and alone. So I shook my head.

"No, thanks. I'll go and get some sleep. Good-night."

I glanced at him as I closed the cabin door, but nothing warned me that this was the last time that I should see him alive.

Less than five hours later he was dead.

His passing was so sudden that Dr. Macklin, summoned

a few minutes before three A.M. on January 5th, by Shackleton blowing his whistle, had no time to call me, and I slept on, all unconscious of the tragedy, as my best friend died.

The fishing party had got back shortly after I had retired to my cabin. I heard them and had recognised Wild's voice as he and Shackleton talked for a bit while I drowsed off.

It appears that Shackleton had been seized with acute pain at about a quarter to three, and Macklin, rushing to him at the sound of his whistle, had seen at once that he was dying. Dr. McIlroy and Wild shared a cabin, and Macklin rushed to fetch his colleague, in the hope that he might be able to help him in easing Shackleton's pain.

Ever since we had left Rio, Macklin had tried to protect Shackleton from over-exertion and strain of any kind. He told me later that, despite his intense pain, Shackleton looked at him with a glint of humour in his eyes, and said:

"I wonder what you'll cut me off from doing after this, Mac?"

Five minutes later Shackleton, a hero in the eyes of the world, as well as in the hearts of his men, lay lifeless.

McIlroy came at once and roused me, asking me to go to Wild. As soon as I got to Wild's cabin he said to me:

"I want you to be prepared for the worst news I could possibly tell you."

"Shackleton?" I questioned.

"Is dead," he replied.

I stared at him, for the shock dazed me, and for a moment or two I was unable to grasp what he meant. Then I said, "Good God, not the Boss?"

"Yes," he said solemnly.

I wanted to go to Shackleton at once, but the Doctor said, "Not yet, old man. Later." Feeling that I must be alone I went back to my cabin with my grief.

DURING the long hours that I sat there, waiting for the dawn to come, a flood of memories surged through my mind. Every incident that I have mentioned in this book came back to me, with a host of others too slight to be recorded, too intimate to be set down. For seven and a half years we had been the closest of friends, and for the greater part of that time we had been in daily contact. We had passed together through many valleys of shadow, and each time that we had won through the bonds which united us had been strengthened. I knew that I should never look upon his like again.

He was not only a great explorer: he was also a great man. Twenty-two years of his life he had devoted to Polar work—work which had brought him fame and had earned him a knighthood. He had forced his way to within ninety-seven miles of the South Pole and had returned with all his men. He had discovered the Beardmore Glacier and had added two hundred miles of Antarctic coastline to the map. He had conquered scurvy—the scourge of all explorers till his time—and had never lost a man who was under his protection. He had been the means of enabling the Magnetic South Pole to be located.

And what of him as a man? I recalled the way in which he had led his party across the ice-floes after the *Endurance* had been lost; how, by his genius for leadership he had kept us all in health; how, by the sheer force of his personality he had kept our spirits up; and how, by his magnificent example, he had enabled us to win through when the dice of the elements were loaded most heavily against us. "Thanks to the strong personality and untiring energy of their leader," a recent writer[1] has remarked, "who encouraged the weaker men, chided the laggards, and looked after the welfare of all

---

[1] Captain H. Taprell Dorling, D.S.O., R.N.

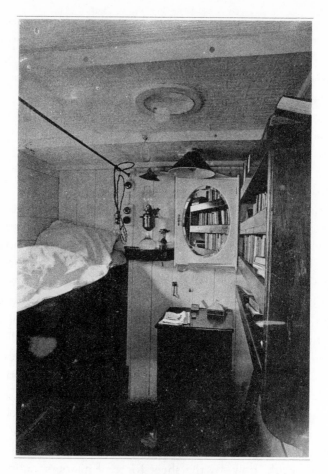

Where Shackleton died
(SCOTT POLAR RESEARCH INSTITUTE)

while maintaining firm discipline, they had won through in safety without the loss of a single man. . . . It was a wonderful achievement."

I thought of the boat journey, that nightmare voyage through 800 miles of storm, through which he had brought us safely. "It is difficult," says the writer whom I have just

The cairn
(*SCOTT POLAR RESEARCH INSTITUTE*)

quoted, "to read of Shackleton's boat journey without feeling a thrill of admiration for those who accomplished it. There have been longer boat voyages . . . but for sheer concentrated discomfort and danger the sixteen days' passage of the little *James Caird* is difficult to beat."

I thought, too, of his wonderful capacity for self-sacrifice.

Wild had told me how, when they were practically at death's door from starvation, and he, Wild, was dangerously ill, Shackleton, on three separate occasions, surreptitiously gave him his biscuit. It is impossible for anybody who has not been so desperately near starvation to understand, perhaps, what such generosity means. I recalled his constant anxiety for his men, his nobleness in always insisting that he himself should be the first to suffer any hardship that had to be undergone.

His was a proud and dauntless spirit, a spirit that made one glad he was an Englishman. Surely there is no end with such a man as Shackleton: something of his spirit must still live on with us; something of his greatness must surely be a legacy to his countrymen. Does he not stand for a symbol of that greatness which is immortal? He was loyal and patriotic. Endurance, courage, determination, imagination, love of adventure and of leading a man's life, self-abnegation, the power to command, presence of mind in facing danger, humour, optimism and kindliness—such were his characteristics. It is by qualities such as these that the mightiest empire in the world has been built up. "We may forget his faults, faults he was aware of and acknowledged, and remember him as a great explorer and a gallant leader, whose subordinates loved him for his firmness of character and unfailing knack of overcoming danger and difficulty when things looked their blackest. 'He had a way of compelling loyalty,' writes one who sailed with him. 'We would have gone anywhere without question just on his order.' What more glowing tribute could any man wish for?"[1]

While this book was being finished, reviews appeared in the Press, of books which have belittled the morale and stamina of the officers and men who fought in the Great War.

---

[1]Captain H. Taprell Dorling, D.S.O., R.N.

Some of these authors have pictured their fellow-countrymen as moral and physical weaklings. Doubtless the opinions of these writers have been coloured by their own personalities; but perhaps it is more charitable to assume that their object in traducing their fellow-men was to attract attention and money to works which otherwise would pass unnoticed. The pioneering spirit, the spirit of sacrifice for the sake of our country, is as manifest to-day as it ever has been, and if this imperfect record of the achievements of a great Englishman shall give the lie to these libels it will not have been penned in vain. Shackleton's body lies buried far from the land of his birth: let us ensure that his spirit continues to be our common heritage.

As the dawn approached I began to think of the crew who would have to be told. All hands were mustered aft at eight o'clock, and Wild broke the news to them. Shackleton and he had been friends and shipmates for twenty years and during that long period had shared their joys and sorrows, disappointments and triumphs. Even while he spoke to the men I thought that he would find it difficult to foresee a life in which Shackleton no longer played a part.

I then went to Shackleton's cabin. Already there was a great change in his appearance. His stillness was startling to me, for stillness was the one thing that I found it impossible to associate with him. And as I stood there I felt that I was looking at a statue of a man, not Shackleton himself.

The vision of his body reposing in the little bunk in the cabin of the *Quest* always brings to my mind the lines:

> 'The rules of the Service are but three:
> When you sail with Admiral Death,
> Steady your hand in time of squalls,

Stand to the last by him who falls,
And answer clear to the voice that calls,
"Aye, aye, Admiral Death!" '

Was it indeed his voice that I thought I heard calling me when I paid that final visit to his cabin the night before? I know not; but I only pray that we may be shipmates again when in my turn the Admiral calls for me.

Wild and I performed our last duty to our leader when we landed the coffin, which was draped with the Union Jack. And as I gazed at the coffin some memory stirred deep within me. For a moment or two I puzzled, then suddenly I remembered that Shackleton had once said to me, as we had stood on that bleak and desolate beach in King Haakon Sound, that he wondered whether he would take his last long sleep among the other sailors whose bones rested in South Georgia.

I do not think he would have wished a different grave. He lies in a spot that for more than a hundred years has been the last home of seamen—whalers, sealers and explorers—a spot swept by the elements among which so much of his life was spent, and facing the great white spaces which for ever called to him.

Our last service to him was to build a cairn to his memory. Every man on the *Quest* took part in this work, which occupied two days. We dragged the stones on sledges from the hillside. And as we raised this rough memorial, which was the best that we could manage, a snowstorm beat down upon us—a ghost, it seemed to me, of the hurricane in which he and I had approached South Georgia after our boat journey from Elephant Island.

During the days that followed it happened sometimes that I would forget for a moment that Shackleton was dead. I found myself waiting for the sound of his voice, listening for the familiar encouraging exclamation of "Good old Skip-per!" that I was never to hear from him again.

On the top of the cairn we erected a solid oak cross, and to the side of the cairn a rough brass plate was fixed bearing these words:

> "SIR ERNEST SHACKLETON,
> EXPLORER,
> DIED HERE JANUARY 5TH, 1922.
> *Erected by his Comrades.*"

Index

Page numbers in *italics* refer to illustrations.

Adams, Jameson Boyce, 278, 283, 288
Adelie penguins, 60, 61, 201, 253
Admiralty:
  and navigation tools, 258, 259
  and rescue attempts, 168, 173–74
  and World War I, 30–32, 79, 217,
    223
Aguirre, Lt. Ramon, 170, 172, 174
Albatross, 36, 134–35
Alexandra, Queen, 259–60, 268, 285
Allardyce mountains, 147, 152
Andes mountains, 195, 197
Annenkov Island, 130
Annie, 231–37, 239, 243
Anson, Lord George, 141
Antarctic Circle, 250, 253
Antarctic Continent:
  vs. Arctic, 247–55
  creatures of, 253–54, 278
  crossing of, as discarded goal,
    13–14, 46, 212
  darkness of, 9
  drifting away from, 47–48
  exploration of, 8, 200, 249, 258
  ice-sheet of, 44, 199–200, 251
  pack-ice surrounding, 36–37, 41
  Ross Barrier on, 199–201, 250–51
  Shackleton as drawn to, 7–8, 35, 46,
    102–3, 247, 264, 267–68, 274,
    295
  sighting of, 40, 64
Archangel, Russia, 224
Arctic, vs. Antarctic, 247–55
Arctic Circle, 249

Arctic expedition plans, 238, 241,
  243–44, 245–47
Army Balloon Department, 268
Arnold, Ober-Lt. Albert, 221, 222
Aurora, 193–94, 199, 202–8, 213, 276n
"Aurora Australis," 279

Baltic republics, trading with, 230–31
Barrier, *see* Ross Barrier
Barrow Dip Circle, 258
Baudin, Nicolas, 31
Bay of Whales, 276
Beagle Channel, 175
Beardmore Glacier, 212, 213, 282–84,
  295
Beaufort Sea, 247
Beveridge, Sir William, 105
Bible, Queen Alexandra's, 259–60
Birds, 35–36, 185, 251
  albatross, 36, 134–35
  at St. Paul's Rocks, 263
  see also Penguins
Blackborow, Percy (stowaway), 6–7,
  96–97, 186–87, *188*, 190
Black Island, 269
Bransfield Straits, 74
Brazil, penal colony of, 264–65
Brocklehurst (*Nimrod* party), 278
Bruce, William Speirs, 41

Caird, Sir James, 41
Caird Coast, 41–43, 45, 292
Campbell, Adm. Gordon, 223
Candlemas Island, 36

Cape Adare, 206
Cape Crozier, 200
Cape Downshire, 206
Cape Evans, 201, 202, 209–10, 211, 213
Cape Horn, 102, 104, 172, 175, 180
Cape Royds, 202, 209, 276–77, 278n, 280
Cape Verde Islands, 262
Carr, Maj. Roddy, 261
Challenger Expedition, 247, 263
Cheetham, Alfred (third mate), 25, 62, 77–78
Cherry-Garrard, A. G., 201
Chile, 170, 174, 175, 191–92, 195–97
Clarence Island, 76
Clark, Robert (biologist), 35, 44, 45, 49, 88, 185
Coats' Land, 41
Cochrane, Commander, 232
Cold burning, 206
Cook, Capt. James, 31
Cooking, see Food
Cooper, Captain, 242
Cope (Ross party), 211
Countess of Ranfurly, 255
Crean, Tom, 25, 50
    and boat journey to South Georgia, 90, 100, 111–12, 120, 124
    crossing South Georgia, 148–61, 164, 291
    and rescue attempts, 168, 171, 190
    on South Georgia, 134, 139, 142
Crew, 6
    clothing of, 94, 97, 151, 183, 184
    on Elephant Island, see Elephant Island
    entertainment of, 5, 6, 7, 8, 49, 52, 53–54, 61, 186
    exercise of, 66
    on James Caird, 105–22, 123–32
    on King Haakon Sound, 132–40
    and loss of Endurance, 14, 20–24
    loyalty to Shackleton of, 90, 190
    morale of, 4–9, 22–23, 29–30, 46, 53–54, 61–62, 65, 95, 99–100, 104, 113, 120, 134, 183–86, 187–88, 236
    receptions for, 165, 191–93, 195, 196
    separation of, 46, 62, 70–71, 77, 83, 89, 202–4, 210, 213, 214

    and Shackleton's death, 299–300
    sleeping-bags of, 108–9, 121, 123–24
    weakness and exhaustion of, 85, 88–89
    work of, 11, 48–49, 53, 88

Darwin, Charles, 263
David, Sir Edgeworth, 277, 278, 288–89
Davis, Capt. J. K., 195, 199
Deception Island, 189
Deep-sea soundings, 257–58
Depôt A, 280–81
Depôt C, 282
Discovery, 43, 173, 174, 202, 268
Dog Derbies, 52
Dogs, 16, 21, 24, 28, 48
    destruction of, 50, 61
    food for, 55
    howling of, 51
    leader selected by, 51–52
    in Ross Sea expedition, 213–14
    in Scott's expedition, 271–72
Donnelly (Ross party), 206
Dorling, Capt. H. Taprell, 295n, 298n
Douglas, G. V., 261, 263
Ducie Fell, 34
Dudley Docker, 55–56, 69, 73–81, 87
Dvina River, 224
Dysentery, 287

Eastern Extension Telegraph Company, 257
Edward, king of England, 268
Elephant Island:
    boat journey from, 101–22
    boat journey to, 73–81
    crew on, 81, 82–91
    departure from, 89, 92, 97–100, 98
    men left behind on, 96, 97–100, 98, 104, 107, 115, 130, 131, 137, 141, 143, 164, 173, 181–90
    preparation for departure from, 91–97, 92, 126
    rescue of crew from, 165–79, 175, 180, 190–92
    sighting of, 76, 79, 80
Emma, 170–71, 174

Index

Emperor penguins, 12–13, 19–20, 39, 41, 45, 60, 200–201, 253
Encyclopaedia Britannica, 62, 183
Enderby Land, 256, 292
Endurance:
  abandoned by crew, 20–24
  caught in pack-ice, 9, 10, 11, 15, 18, 20, 25, 28, 45, 48
  crew and officers of, *see* Crew
  destruction of, 15–22, 17, 18, 26
  and Expedition goals, 7–8
  loss of, 3–6, 11–12, 13–26, 29, 39
  materials retrieved from, 28–29, 54
  "Ritz" in, 5–6
  and Ross Sea party, 194, 208
  sinking of, 29
  at South Georgia, 33–35, 163
England, greatness of people of, 298–99
England, Captain, 277
Evans, Captain, 288

Falkland Islands, 102, 104, 167, 169
Faroe Islands, 240–41
Fernando de Noronha, Brazil, 264–65
Ferrar, Hartley T., 269, 270
Filchner, Wilhelm, 41
Flag, King George's, 29–30, 259
Flag, Queen Alexandra's, 285
Flinders, Matthew, 31
Food:
  albatross, 135
  blubber oil, 95
  Christmas Day feasts, 272–73, 284
  cooking of, 87–88, 111–12, 149–50
  crossing South Georgia, 145–46, 149–50, 157
  for dogs, 55
  on Elephant Island, 87–88, 90, 185–86, 189
  fish, 67, 185
  hoosh, 105, 111, 124, 145, 273
  jettisoned, 71
  on journey to Elephant Island, 75, 76, 77
  on journey to South Georgia, 94, 105–6
  for *Nimrod* expedition, 286–87
  penguins, 45, 60, 61, 66–67, 84, 87, 185, 188

ponies, 277, 281, 284, 285, 287
  scurvy fought by, 55, 214, 268
  sea-elephant, 137–38
  seal meat, 54–55, 57, 60, 66–67, 84, 87, 185, 188
  sheep, 275
  shortages of, 60, 66, 89, 90
  Streimer's Nut Food, 105, 145
  strength from, 61, 285, 286
Fortuna Bay, 159, 160, 161.
France, 262
Frost–bite:
  of Blackborow's toes, 96, 186–87
  on Elephant Island, 182, 186
  on journey to Elephant Island, 77
  on journey to South Georgia, 113, 119
  of *Nimrod* party, 285
  of Ross Sea party, 207–8
Frost-smoke, 48
Fumaroles, 278

Gaze (Ross party), 202, 211
George V, king of England, 29, 167, 259
Glacier Tongue, 288
Glasgow, H.M.S., 169–70
Gough Island, 264
Graham Land, 27, 56, 57
Green, Charles (cook), 87–88, 183, 244, 261
Greenland, 233, 249
Greenstreet, Lionel (first officer):
  on Elephant Island, 91, 95, 180, 185
  and entertainment, 5, 6, 193
  and journey to Elephant Island, 75, 77, 78, 79
  and loss of *Endurance*, 17–18, 20
  on South Georgia, 34
Greenwich mean time, 259
Grogan, General, 224–25, 230
Grytviken Harbour, 33, 34, 40, 291
Gudmundsen, Ofegir, 237
Gulf Stream, 249

Hayward (Ross party), 210, 211, 213–15
Hudson, Hubert (navigating officer), 18, 20, 69

Index

Hurley, Frank, 57
    on Elephant Island, 87, 189
    photos taken by, 28, 44, 180
    on South Georgia, 34, 35
Hussey, Leonard (meteorologist),
        53–54
    on Elephant Island, 182, 186,
        260–61
    in North Russia, 224
    on *Quest* expedition, 244, 260–61
Hut Point, 202, 210, 211, 212–15,
        279–80, 288
Huts, construction of, 268–69

Ianthe, Q ship, 223
Ice, 46
    and boat journey to Elephant
        Island, 73, 75–76, 79
    and boat journey to South Georgia,
        101, 115–22
    for cooking water, 111
    for drinking water, 48, 76, 79, 131
    glacier, *138*, 147, 282–84
    and *Nimrod* party, 277, 282, 285, 286
    pack, *see* Pack-ice
    in Ross Sea, 201–5, 250
    sliding down, 155–57
Ice-bergs, 43, 68, *236*, 250, 254
Ice-blink, 37
Ice-floes, 9–11
    boats launched from, 69, 71, 72–73
    crew separated by, 62, 70–72
    danger of being crushed by, 68–69
    Endurance cutting through, 37,
        38–39
    Endurance destroyed by, 15–22, *18*,
        26
    floating on, 64–67
    making camp on, 69–70, *71*
    see also Pack-ice
Iceland, 231–37
Imperial Trans–Antarctic Expedition,
        3, 34, 65, 180
    formation of, 14–15
    and World War I, 30–32
Inaccessible Island, 211
Instituto de Pesca, 168–69
Ironsides, General, 224

Jack (Ross party), 211
James Caird, 55–56, 165
    cooking on, 111–12
    ice forming on, 115–19
    journey to South Georgia in,
        101–22, 123–32, 297
    journey to Elephant Island in,
        73–77
    landing on King Haakon Sound,
        132–34
    launching from Elephant Island, *92*,
        97–100, *98*, *126*
    preparation of, 90–94, *92*
    pumping out, 110–11, 118, *128*,
        129
    sleeping and living on, 107–8,
        116–17, *125*, *133*
    waves as threat to, 125–26, 127–28
Jeffrey, Lt.-Commander, 261
Joinville Island, 64
Joyce, Ernest E.:
    in *Nimrod* party, 280
    in Ross party, 210, 211, 213–15

Kerr, A. J. (engineer), 183, 244, 261
King Haakon Sound:
    approach to, 127–32
    landing on, 132–34
    leaving, 138–40
    making camp on, 134–38
    men rescued from, 164–65
Koonya, 275, 288

Larkman (Ross party), 207
Larsen, C. A., 36
Lees, Thomas Orde-, 57–58, 104
Leith Harbour, 165
London Missionary Society, 256
Luce, Commodore, 169–70
Luitpold Land, 41
Lysaght, Gerald, 261

McCarthy, Timothy (sailor), 166
    and boat journey to South Georgia,
        90, 97, 108, 109
    rescue of, 164, 165
    on South Georgia, 134, 145
MacDonald, Allan, 170

Index

McFee, Captain, 228–30
McIlroy, James (doctor), 57
  and Blackborow's frost-bite, 96,
    186–87
  on Elephant Island, 96, 183
  and *Quest* expedition, 244, 261, 294
Mackay (*Nimrod* party), 278, 288–89
Mackintosh, Captain:
  and *Nimrod* expedition, 276
  and Ross party, 194, 202, 204,
    210–15
Macklin, Alexander (doctor), 50, 78
  and Blackborow's frost-bite, 96,
    186–87
  on Elephant Island, 95, 96, 183,
    189
  in North Russia, 79, 224
  and *Quest* expedition, 244, 261
  and Shackleton's death, 293–94
  and Shackleton's health, 266, 294
McLeod, Thomas (sailor), 78–79, 97,
  244, 261
McMurdo Sound, 193, 194, 203–4,
  209, 275, 276
McNeish, Harry (carpenter), 50, 54,
  166
  and boat journey to South Georgia,
    90, 91
  rescue of, 164, 165
  on South Georgia, 142, 143, 145
Macquarie Island, 199
Magnetism, 258–59
Marr, James, 261, 263
Marshall, Eric (*Nimrod* party), 278,
  283, 285, 287–88
Marston, George (artist), 93, 189, 279
Mawson, Sir Douglas, 199, 277, 278,
  288–89
Minna Bluff, 280, 287
Moore, Capt. Monty, 224–30
Morning, 274
Mount Erebus, 278–79, 287
Mount Paget, 34, 147
Mount Sabine, 206
Mrs. Chippy (cat), 50, 188
Mugridge (Ross party), 207
Murmansk, Russia, 224, 230
Murray (*Nimrod* party), 288–89

Nansen, Fridtjof, 269
Navigation:
  of Caird Coast, 43
  deep-sea soundings, 257–58
  to depôt positions, 281
  to Elephant Island, 74, 76, 88
  methods of, 67–68, 74, 109–10, 271
  in rescue attempts, 175–76, 179
  to South Georgia, 109–10, 123,
    126–27
  tools for, 110, 146, 227, 257–59, 271
New Zealand:
  Nimrod expedition in, 275–89
  and Ross Sea expedition, 195, 197,
    198, 209, 215
Nimrod expedition, 275–89
Nordenskjold, Nils, 12, 54, 65, 183
North Magnetic Pole, 258, 259
North Pole, geographic, 259
North Pole vs. South Pole, 247–55
North Russia, 79, 223–30

Ocean Camp, 59
Oil-bags, 290
Orde-Lees, Thomas, 57–58, 104
Orita, 170
Orkney Islands, 238–43

Pacific Ocean, study of, 247, 256
Pack-ice:
  of Antarctic Continent, 36–37, 41
  Endurance caught in, 9, 10, 11, 15,
    18, 20, 25, 28, 45, 48
  making camp on, 22–24, 26, 28, 57,
    59
  salt in, 48
  see also Ice-floes
Pangloss, H.M.S., 223
Pardo, Capt. Luis, 174, 196
Parhelia, 46–47
Patience Camp, 57, 59
Paulet Island, 54
Peggotty Camp, 140–44
Penguins:
  Adelie, 60, 61, 201, 253
  Emperor, *see* Emperor penguins
  as food, 45, 60, 61, 66–67, 84, 87,
    185, 188

Piako, 242
Pirie, Doctor, 263
Ponies, on *Nimrod* expedition, 275,
  277, 279, 281–85, 287
Port Chalmers, 208
Port Stanley, 167–69, 173, 190
P.Q.61, H.M.S., 217–23
Pram Point, 271
Providence:
  and crossing South Georgia, 164
  ice-bergs averted by, 69
  and *Nimrod* expedition, 287
  and sea-rudder, 139
Punta Arenas, 170, 173, 174, 190, 191

Quest, 245–47, *246,* 257, 259, 262,
  265, 290–91, 299

Red snow, 254–55
Reykjavik, Iceland, 231–37
Richards (Ross party), 202, 210, 211,
  213–15
Rickenson, Louis (engineer), 35
Rio de Janeiro, 265, 266
Rio Secco, 191
Ross, Sir James, 263
Ross Barrier, 199–201, 212, 214,
  250–51
  Discovery expedition at, 268, 269–74
  Nimrod expedition at, 276, 279–89
Ross Island, 199, 200, 201, 268, 270,
  277–78
Ross Sea expedition, 193–97, 198–216
  Aurora and, 193–94, 199, 202–8,
    213
  crew split in, 202–4, 210, 213, 214
  relief committee and, 194–95, 199
  Shackleton narrative of, 209–15
  Stenhouse narrative of, 199–208
Rowett, John Quiller, 243
Royal Scottish Geographical Society,
  275
Royal Yacht Squadron, 259

Saint (dog), 24
St. Paul's Rocks, 262–64
Samson, 165
San Zeferino, 218–22

Satan (dog), 51–52
Saunders Island, 36
Scott, Capt. Robert F.:
  and food, 268, 273
  hut built by party of, 202–3, 269,
    279–80
  and McMurdo Sound, 276
  party split by, 269, 271–74
  on Ross Island, 201
  Shackleton with *Discovery*
    expedition of, 268–89
  and South Pole, 272
Scurvy, 55, 214, 268, 273–74, 295
Sea-elephants, 137–38, *139,* 140–41,
  253
Sea-leopards, 57–58, 60, 67, 253
Seals, 62, 72, 251, 253
  crab-eating, 43–44
  as food, 54–55, 57, 60, 66–67, 84,
    87, 185, 188
  hunting of, 52–53
  light from oil of, 183
Shackleton, Lady "Honey," 167, 209,
  247, 275
Shackleton, Sir Ernest Henry, *vi, 10*
  achievements of, 197, 295–98
  and Admiralty, 30–32
  aging of, 82–83, 173, 261
  Arctic expedition plans of, 238,
    241, 243–44, 245–47
  Caird Coast discovered by, 41, 42
  cairn and memorial to, *297, 300,*
    301
  caution exercised by, 114, 115, 127,
    131, 176, 212
  crew's loyalty to, 90, 190
  and crossing South Georgia,
    143–44, 148–61, 164
  death of, 293–94, *296,* 299–300
  and departure from Elephant
    Island, 89, 93–96, 99–100
  and *Discovery* expedition, 268–89
  and dreams of treasure, 103, 142,
    247, 256, 262, 292
  and drifting, 64–65, 71, 72
  on Elephant Island, 82–85, 89–90
  family of, 275
  and food, 95, 105–6, 115, 120, 268

Index

and formation of Expedition, 14–15
generosity of, 243, 244, 292, 297–98
health of, 125, 261–62, 266, 267
and journey to Elephant Island,
    73–81
and journey to South Georgia,
    101–8, 114–15, 117–18, 120–22
as leader, 8, 23, 37, 53, 74, 83, 84,
    93–94, 212, 295–98
lectures given by, 193, 215–16, 275
and loss of Endurance, 3–6, 13–15,
    20–23, 29
men's safety and well–being as
    concern of, 13, 63, 68, 70, 82–83,
    89, 106, 107, 113–15, 131, 143,
    173, 190, 212, 276, 286, 295–96,
    297–98
and morale, 7–8, 9, 22–23, 29–30,
    46, 53, 65, 99–100, 113, 120
and navigation, 88, 110, 281
in North Russia, 223–24
as Postmaster of the Antarctic, 276
and Quest expedition, 245–47, 257,
    259–61, 265, 290–93
receptions in honor of, 165, 191–93,
    197, 209, 266
and rescue from Elephant Island,
    165–79, 180, 190–92
responsibility as burden of, 83, 84,
    89, 104, 107, 136, 151, 171, 173,
    180, 190, 286, 290–91
and Ross Sea party, 193–97,
    198–99, 209–15
on splitting the party, 46, 83, 89,
    104, 145, 210
and trek over the ice, 54–57
trust inspired by, 8, 23, 83
and World War I, 31–32, 79, 223
Shackleton boots, 151
Smoke blindness, 183
Sorlle, Captain, 163
Southern Ocean, 250, 253, 256
Southern Sky, 166
South Georgia:
    arrival in, 162, 163–64
    boat journey to, 101–22, 123–32, 297
    crossing of, 131, 137, 141–44,
        145–62, 164, 291

Endurance's visit to to, 33–35, 163
glaciers on, 138, 142–43, 147, 149,
    150, 158
landscape of, 32, 147, 150, 151–52,
    152, 153, 157
preparation for boat journey to,
    90–96
Quest's visit to, 266–67, 290–93
Shackleton's burial on, 297, 299,
    300–301
whaling stations on, 33–34, 35, 40,
    56, 131, 141, 159, 161, 162, 291
South Pole:
    geographic, 259
    magnetic, 258, 259, 289, 295
    vs. North Pole, 247–55
    as Scott's goal, 272
    as Shackleton's goal, 277–79,
        282–85, 295
    turning back from, 286
Spencer-Smith (Ross party), 202, 210,
    213, 214, 215
Spitsbergen, 251, 252
Stancomb Wills, 55, 61, 73–80, 93, 99
Staten Island, 170, 191
Steamer (dog), 51
Stefansson, Vilhjalmur, 247, 260
Stenhouse, Capt., 193–94, 195, 216
    Ross Sea narrative of, 199–208
    and trading company, 230–32
    and World War I, 217–23
Stevens (Ross party), 202, 211
Stromness Bay, 141, 148, 158, 159,
    163, 165
Suderoe Island, 240, 241
Sun:
    in the Antarctic, 55
    and geographic poles, 259
    and mirages, 47
    for navigation, 74
    and parhelia, 46–47
Sutherland, Capt. Jock, 242
Swedish Expedition, 12

Tent Island, 211
Thom, Captain, 166
Tierra del Fuego, 191
Tripp, Leonard, 209

Index

Tristan da Cunha, 266
Tuanaki Island, 255–56
Turk's Head, 211

U.C.33, 221, 223
Uruguay, Government of, 168, 197
Ushuaia, Argentina, 175

Valaparaiso, 187, 195, 196
Vincent, John (boatswain), 166
  and boat journey to South Georgia,
    90, 97, 119
  rescue of, 164, 165
  on South Georgia, 137, 145

Water-sky, 37, 43
Weddell Sea:
  access to Antarctic via, 35, 40
  Endurance caught in, 12, 20, 26, 45
  exploration of, 256
Weddell Sea Barrier, 250–51
Whales, 35, 36, 39, 62–63, 71, 251,
  253–54
White Island, 269, 270
Wild, Ernest, (Ross Sea party),
  210–11, 214, 215
Wild, Frank, 52, 55, 71, 72
  on Elephant Island, 85, 95, 96, 99,
    104, 181–90
  and loss of *Endurance*, 3–6, 20
  and morale, 4–5, 27, 181, 286
  and *Nimrod* party, 283, 284, 286,
    287
  and *Quest* party, 244, 260, 264, 294
  and sea–leopards, 58, 67
  and Shackleton's death, 298, 299,
    300
Wilkins, Sir Hubert, 260, 262, 263

Wilson, Edward A. "Bill," 269, 270,
  271, 273–74
Wilson, Sons and Co., 265
Wilson's Harbour, 131
Winds:
  and boat journey to Elephant
    Island, 74, 76–78
  and boat journey to South Georgia,
    102, 104, 106–7, 108, 112, 115,
    120, 123, 128, 130
  on Elephant Island, 85–86, 182–83,
    184, 188
  on Ross Barrier, 202–3, 213
  on South Georgia, 141–43, 165, 291
Woolaston Island, 175
Wordie, James (geologist), 35
World War I, 217–30, 298
  Admiralty and, 30–32, 79, 217, 223
  crew's participation in, 78, 145, 197
  news of, 164, 168, 191
  submarine warfare in, 217–23
Worsley, Frank, 234
  crossing South Georgia, 148–62,
    164
  diary of, 130
  D.S.O. to, 223, 224, 230
  hiring of, 14–15
  as hydrographer, 257–58
  navigation by, 43, 67–68, 74, 76,
    109–10, 123, 126–27
  as ship's commander, 11–12
  trading company of, 230–44

Yelcho, 170, 174, 176, 177, 191, 195,
  196
Young, Douglas, 169

Zavodovski Island, 36